A MILLION WAYS TO STAY ON THE RUN

For the two brightest stars in my universe who give me reason to celebrate every day
– Donal MacIntyre

To my ever supportive family, forever in my heart
– Karl Howman

A MILLION WAYS TO STAY ON THE RUN

DONAL MACINTYRE
& KARL HOWMAN

MIRROR BOOKS

m
B

MIRROR BOOKS

All of the events in this story are true,
but names and details have been changed to protect
the identities of some individuals where appropriate.

1

Published in Great Britain and Ireland in 2023 by
Mirror Books, a Reach PLC business.

www.mirrorbooks.co.uk
@TheMirrorBooks

Print ISBN 9781915306265
eBook ISBN 9781915306272

Cover design by Rick Cooke
Edited by Chris Brereton
Typeset by Christine Costello

Printed and bound in Great Britain by
CPI Group (UK) Ltd, Croydon, CR0 4YY

CONTENTS

ACKNOWLEDGEMENTS

The authors kindly acknowledge the multiple media sources that have provided a baseline for the research of this book including accounts in print, television, and books from police officers, journalists, commentators and judges among others.

We would note the works of Will Pearson, Marnie Palmer and Tom Morgan, Michael Gillard and Laurie Flynn, Duncan Campbell, Wensley Clarkson, the excellent articles of David Rose, Jeff Edwards, Steven Wright, John Sweeney, Paul Lashmar and the *Sunday Mirror*'s interview with Ann Marie Decabral.

In addition, we would like to thank the staff of the National Archives in Kew for their support in accessing some of the cabinet and Crown Prosecution Service (CPS) papers previously unavailable, and the staff of the British Newspaper Archive. Appreciation is also due to Emma Kelly, Professor James Treadwell, Professor David Wilson, Rtd. Detective Inspector Ian Brown, former Detective Chief Inspector Clive Driscoll, Ian Edmundson, Henry Milner, Graham Johnson, Jon Clarke, The Olive Press, Nick Foster, Amy Rhodes, Steve McQueen, Sean Murray, Dare Films Ireland, Michael Flattery, Nick Kenton and Steve Langridge for their assistance.

Particular thanks also goes to the time given by Nick Biddiss who was cordial and supportive, presenting and protecting the perspective of the Cameron family throughout. The authors acknowledge the assistance given by Kenneth

Noye, who has not benefitted financially from this, for interviews and background information without which this book would not have been possible. The authors accept all errors and omissions as their full responsibility. We are grateful for the work of our book editor Chris Brereton, our literary agent Ben Clark at the Soho Agency and our publisher, Paul Dove at Mirror Books.

AUTHORS' NOTE

Revered in the underworld, Kenny Noye – "Public Enemy No. 1" – is equally reviled in civil society.

The complex equations of life are made simpler by these polarised, and black and white positions. However, within these parameters, there is a grey area where Noye's deeds are likely to find a home in the social and criminal history of the last 50 years. Noye, for example, was a key part of the Brink's-Mat gold bullion robbery, which has already become part of public folklore, captivating audiences and generating thousands of articles, dozens of documentaries, multiple feature films and several televisions dramas. But, for all the mythological status that a heist might generate – long a staple of the true crime genre – the killing of a policeman is taboo and an act that some cannot forgive, despite Noye's acquittal on the grounds of self-defence.

To kill again, in a road rage incident 11 years later, begs the question: is this an unlucky man who was twice in the wrong place at the wrong time, or someone who thinks that events like these are simply part of another day at the office? Is he a 'criminal undertaker'[1] who imagines that to stab a knife into another human being is merely an occupational necessity that shouldn't cause too much soul-searching?

1   Steve Hall & Simon Winlow (2015): *Revitalizing Criminological Theory: Towards a new Ultra Realism*

Or perhaps he really does feel genuine remorse for these moments of terminal tragedy? Noye says that he does, but who would believe him and how could we judge if he is sincere? This book does not seek to answer these questions but with unparalleled access to Noye himself, and many of the key witnesses to the events surrounding his time on the run, we hope to reveal the organised criminal landscape in which he operated, his personal mindset and psychology and leave it to the public to draw their own conclusions.

We believe that our narrative reveals a remarkable demonstration of underworld power, its wealth and influence and, at times, the impotence of the forces of law and order. It also reminds us about the huge struggles that the police have when some of their number are compromised and act against the justice system.

Two men are dead as one man continues to breathe. The futility and tragedy of the loss of these lives watermarks our account, and nothing that we write is intended to cause any further distress or pain to the families of the deceased. However, criminologists know that beyond good and evil, heaven and hell, there is a form of purgatory – a no man's land – where the psychological truth and authenticity of an individual is nuanced and partial, rather than fixed and definitive. The ever-sophisticated true crime audience is au fait with these dynamics and perhaps already accepts that villains like Noye are complex, and their motivations assorted and diverse.

With the warnings of Janet Malcolm in *The Journalist and the Murderer* ever-present, we believe that it is important to understand Noye and the sometimes deadly choices that he made. We are confident that this is a story well worth telling, and we trust the audience to rightfully measure the rights and wrongs of the events that we describe in their own terms.

In writing our account we were also mindful of Truman Capote's *In Cold Blood* – perhaps the greatest work of true crime ever written. However, as many have argued, it pays scant attention to the four members of the Clutter family who were brutally murdered by Perry Smith and Dick Hickock, and that the killers therefore came to dominate Capote's narrative. So we would ask our readers to always be vigilant in the absence of Danielle Cable (in witness protection) and Ken and Toni Cameron (deceased) and to pay close attention to the testimony of Nick Biddiss, the police investigator who carried the torch for Stephen Cameron in the manhunt for Noye, and he does so again throughout this book.

TIMELINE OF EVENTS

May 1947
Kenneth Noye is born in Bexleyheath, Kent.

July 1967
One year sentence to Borstal – 10 charges of theft (car ringing).

February 1977
Fine and two-year suspended sentence for bribing a policeman, receiving stolen parts, handling stolen property and possession of a gun.

November 1983
£26 million in gold bullion and diamonds stolen from Brink's Mat depot near Heathrow Airport.

January 1985
Covert police officer Detective Constable John Fordham, 45, dies after receiving stab wounds in fight with Noye.

December 1985
Noye acquitted of murder of Fordham on grounds of self-defence. His associate Brian Reader is also acquitted.

July 1986

Noye convicted of handling some of the stolen Brink's-Mat gold and conspiracy to evade VAT and is sentenced to 14 years.

May 1994

Noye is released from prison on licence after serving nine years.

May 1996

Stephen Cameron, 21, stabbed in a road rage fight by Noye on a roundabout off the M25 – went on the run.

August 1998

Noye arrested for Stephen Cameron's murder in Barbate, Spain.

April 2000

Noye convicted of the murder of Stephen Cameron and sentenced to serve a minimum of 16 years.

June 2019

Noye is released from prison on life licence after serving 21 years.

The Brink's-Mat Robbery in November 1983 was at the time the biggest heist in UK criminal history and the £26 million in gold bullion was never recovered. Insurance loss adjusters acting independently of the police secured settlements against several people it believed were involved, including Kenneth James Noye, the details of which are confidential to the parties.

1

TAKING FLIGHT

"THE RED MIST DESCENDED AND ONLY ONE MAN WAS LEFT STANDING."

10.30 am, a private helipad, Bristol, England, May 20th, 1996.

A safety check was conducted on the AS355 Twin Squirrel helicopter. The compact utility helicopter was bought at the bargain price of £750,000 from the liquidator of a paint company in Belgium. It was effectively an international courier service for 'Goldfinger' – John Palmer. Sometimes it carried Palmer and sometimes contraband in the shape of gold and diamonds. Today it was both.

At 11am Kenny Noye and John Palmer were in UK airspace heading across the English Channel to Palmer's 200-acre château in Caen in Normandy.

The pilot took off from a large field belonging to Palmer nearby. He was a fastidious professional. Trained by the Royal Navy and a former flight instructor with the Jordanian police, his diary and flight manifest recorded his passenger names correctly. While the two passengers may have been bent, the pilot certainly was not. As soon as he entered French airspace, he radioed in to French immigration asking if officers wanted the helicopter to land at Carpiquet Airport in Caen for a customs check. The French gave Palmer's pilot a pass, as they always did, to land on Palmer's estate. Noye himself had made the journey back and forth nearly 40 times and had never been called in for customs checks on either side of the channel.

With the clearance from air traffic controllers at the nearby regional airline hub, the four-seater helicopter landed close to the main house, Le Château de la Poupelière, a grand country club golf development with manicured grounds which had a membership of zero. And that was its charm – certainly on that Monday. Palmer was developing it as a timeshare opportunity for the Chinese market. As the main house was in disrepair, the pair were holed up in a newly built cottage on the site. They drove into Caen for a late meal.

Noye relished his steak, frites and mushroom sauce downed with a fine bottle of red wine chosen by Palmer, a 1990 Chateau Margaux. It was life on the run but not as we know it.

Just over 24 hours earlier, events had been unravelling – but even with a newly bloodied face, a sore head, and a cut across his nose, nothing would keep Noye from his schedule. He was a creature of habit. He smoothly accelerated away from the Swanley M25-M20 interchange bruised but unbowed. He had plans. An afternoon in the pub with his friends.

In his wake, pandemonium ensued. Startled road users

gawked in shock and awe, ambulances and police cars raced to the scene while he drove away within the 70mph speed limit. His black Nike baseball cap was still on the passenger seat. You never took a hat to a fight. A Dionne Warwick CD[2] blared through the speakers as it had done throughout the incident. It was the soundtrack to a tragedy.

Unaware of the emergency response, Noye pulled himself together and tried to make sense of the unforeseen events. He phoned his son, Kevin[3], to see if he had any history with the red van he had just cut up in a road rage fracas. There was no answer.

Extraordinarily for a man who had killed before, Noye had a reputation in the underworld for avoiding 'direct' physical violence. He always advised his[4] sons to walk away when things threatened to get physical and yet in this instance, a road rage incident had placed Noye at the heart of a gladiatorial battle in the dour and unseemly surrounds of a motorway roundabout on a blue-skied sunny Sunday afternoon in Kent.

"No point fighting, there's no money in it," the business-man in him always said.

The clock was now ticking. And unbeknownst to Noye the countdown had begun towards one of the most high-profile manhunts of a generation.

As Noye made his way from the scene the police were

---

2   Interview with KN.

3   Phone records accepted by both the defence and prosecution noted in Court paperwork.

4   KN evidence in Court – recorded in Court transcripts of March 30th-April 14th 2000.

flooded with reports of the altercation. There were 30 witnesses in all, including a major drug smuggler driving a blue Rolls Royce. For every other witness, this was − you would imagine − a traumatic event but for this colourful character it was later to be alleged that it would be his golden ticket to a sweetheart deal with the police and HM Customs & Excise.

But for now, he was just doing his 'duty' as a good citizen.

***

1.25pm, May 19th 1996
Police: Police Can I help you?
Caller: Hello yeah, I've just seen someone stabbed!
Police: Where?
Caller: Where there's a big roundabout to turn left for the Dartford Tunnel for the M25 and out towards Brighton there were two guys having a fight and I saw a guy in a Range Rover pull a knife out of his right hand pocket and stab the guy in a red van in the chest. And the guy in the Range Rover... jumped right into his car and went off towards the Dartford Tunnel.[5]

As fastidious a timekeeper as he was, Noye didn't rush. There was no retrieving the situation − he would be late. He was always punctual. Usually earlier than punctual. His day was unexpectedly interrupted. He knew there would be fallout but not on the scale that was to unfold.

His immediate thoughts were that he had had an alterca-

---

5   From transcript of Decabral 999 call to Kent Police after incident, as noted in trial paperwork.

tion with a traveller and that the worst he could expect was a barrage of threats and intimidation – but something that he could manage. It wasn't an unreasonable consideration. There was a large traveller community in the area where Noye had cut up the small red utility van in which Stephen Cameron was the passenger.

STEPHEN CAMERON (21) DIED AT THE HANDS OF KENNETH NOYE ON THE 19TH OF MAY 1996

With the bloodied scene receding into his rear-view mirror, Noye rightly conjectured that if it was a fight with a traveller, his assailant would be unlikely to contact the police and would much more likely exact their own retribution. He was right on that front but wrong crucially on two others – his ethnicity and the extent of Cameron's injuries. He was not a traveller; and he was not going to live.

Police: Have you got the index of the Range Rover?

Caller: It was L964 or something, I didn't catch the last… to be honest with you I'm not 100% sure because it was such a shock you know… but it was definitely an L Reg.[6]

No sirens followed Noye. No police cars passed him towards the crime scene on the motorway contraflow but the Rolls Royce driver who witnessed the attack also claimed to have followed the 'suspect' car and saw it "bobbing and weaving in and out of traffic lanes". The 30-year-old blue

---

6   Extracted from excerpts of the Decabral 999 call.

Rolls Royce was a bit beyond shabby chic, as was its driver. But it served two purposes for Alan Decabral (37) – it easily accommodated his 27-stone frame and had several secret compartments for storing illicit drugs and firearms.

The motorway cameras which could have captured the getaway vehicle were not working that day and could not confirm Noye's apparent erratic driving. The caller's other confident but indisputably erroneous assertion about the registration and model of the car Noye was driving, would later buy the future fugitive a valuable buffer from the police.

The distinctive Decabral, who wore his thinning brown hair swept back, resting on his shoulders, was very keen to help the police. Understandably, though he got some key details wrong. In the first instance, he told police he saw a Range Rover, rather than a Land Rover, which Kenny Noye was driving. And while he got the first letter of the registration correct – he got the digits wrong, expanding the police search for the suspect vehicle from potentially thousands to over 17,000 possible 'L' indexed[7] Land Rovers and Range Rovers registered between August 1993 and July 1994. In a statement the next day to the police he gave more details and recollections. However, the Police would not rely upon his recollections and would hunt down all the vehicles and focus on those local to the scene initially.

Kenneth Noye had spent nine years and four months[8] of a 14-year prison sentence in relation to the infamous 1983

---

7   Source: Nick Biddiss, Kent Police.

8   Notes from conversation with KN & DM, 2021.

twenty-six million Brink's-Mat gold bullion robbery and knew better than to draw attention to himself when leaving the scene of a crime. He was cooler and smarter than that. He drove as if he was driving to meet his mates in the pub, which is exactly what he was doing.

Noye had an appointment with his friends at an old haunt about five miles away, which he intended to keep. It was a weekly lunchtime date. His £2,000 leather jacket was torn at the collar and his blue dress shirt stained in sweat and spit – some of it his own. The scuffs and scrapes, a result of his wild and frenzied fight with a man less than half his age, had left him smudged in blood and had left his adversary – unbeknownst to Noye – in a battle for his life. He was also frustrated and bemused at the escalation of an innocuous incident into a fully-fledged brawl. Noye had "cut up people a thousand times and been cut up likewise plenty", [9] but none had ended up in a fight, least of all in an explosive frenzy like this.

Some witnesses reported that this was a fight that Kenny Noye was decidedly losing[10] to the self-employed electrician and kickboxer, Cameron – until he wasn't. Danielle Cable, Cameron's girlfriend, kept beckoning her fiancé[11] to stop and return to the van, but he refused. Then he was stabbed. And the fight was over.

Danielle Cable had phoned Ken Cameron, Stephen's father. He lived just five minutes from the roundabout and arrived to see Stephen ghostly pale and unresponsive. The

9   KN interview transcripts with Karl Howman.
10   Evidence (Appeal judgement 2011).
11   Cable testimony, Old Bailey 30th March, 2000.

paramedics never stopped but Ken Cameron knew his son was dead. He and his wife, Toni comforted Danielle who was in a 'delirious state'.

At 1.27pm an emergency radio call was transmitted to ambulances in the area. As luck would have it, a private ambulance happened upon the scene by accident. The driver manoeuvred closer, and the crew got out to assist Stephen Cameron. "He was lying on his back on the off side of a grassy bank, with his head closer to it and his feet in the carriage way", the police statements would record. He was wearing a white jacket, and blue t-shirt, blue Adidas bottoms and white Adidas trainers. One had slipped off in the fight.

The paramedics met with a desperate scene. Blood covered the top half of Stephen's clothing, his white jacket was now crimson and his t-shirt soaked through. Instantly, the first responders could see a stab wound – a point of entry. There were no signs of breathing and no pulse. The private crew commenced ventilation and compression and 10 minutes after the emergency call, the first of two Kent Ambulances pulled up at 1.37pm.

The two crews assisted in resuscitation and loaded the lifeless Stephen into the Kent County Ambulance.

***

As Noye pondered his own injuries and had driven a mile or so from the interchange – he reached into his jacket pocket and felt what he identified as a Swiss Army knife; the police would later describe it as the murder weapon. He had regularly carried one for protection and fear of kidnapping because he was a target, he thought, as long as the missing bullion was never found. He considered tossing it out of the window but decided there was no need for it. The police would have the same thought later as they scoured nearly every inch of the dual carriage way for miles to retrieve it. They never did.

As planned, Kenny Noye then called by his long-time pal, Tommy Lee, in nearby Bexley, two miles away from the motorway interchange to bring him to the pub. Every Sunday he would pick Tommy up and then drop him off on the way home after a couple. Today would be no different. There was no need to change tack. The apparent small matter of the altercation might have delayed him – it might have ruffled him, but it would not alter the diary.

The doors in Tommy's 3000 sq ft mansion were French polished. All of them. It cost £50,000 at 1990 prices. The bathroom where Noye went to clean up was resplendent with luxurious Farrow and Ball paint, polished gold taps, with a large silver ornate mirror taking centre stage in the spotlessly clean house.

In the near clinical conditions, he gave his face a wash down and as he did so, looked intensely into the mirror. His prison gym physique was battered. It was a little less scuffed and war weary than it had been after he battled and stabbed covert police operator, DC John Fordham on the grounds of his own home 11 years previously. A jury found that the death of Fordham was self-defence. That was the last time Noye engaged in physical violence. The last time he wielded a knife – the last time he killed a man.

The adrenaline flush was ebbing from the fight. He took

a moment to breathe and ponder his predicament. In the same moment, paramedics continued CPR and resuscitation procedures on Stephen as the ambulance made its way on blue lights at 80 miles an hour, to the West Hill Hospital in Dartford, situated on the historic site of an old

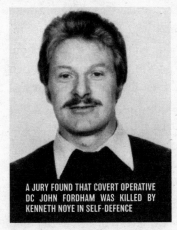

workhouse for the poor and destitute. The ambulance arrived at 1.42pm.

The hospital resuscitation team had been alerted to the chronic case coming to the unit and were ready to exhaust all efforts to revive Stephen although they were told

A JURY FOUND THAT COVERT OPERATIVE DC JOHN FORDHAM WAS KILLED BY KENNETH NOYE IN SELF-DEFENCE

that the situation was grave. The ER unit confirmed that there was no pulse or blood

pressure and continued resuscitation with no response. For 28 minutes they would persevere even when all hope had really disappeared before he was even lifted into the ambulance from the motorway gutter.

As Noye made his getaway, the second Kent ambulances arrived to oversee the emergency response. Police cars raced to the location to try and capture and catch all the witnesses and maybe even the perpetrator. Ken and Toni Cameron had already left with Danielle in the back of their car, inconsolable with distress.

By 2.05pm, Noye had made it to the pub half an hour late. Oblivious to the unfolding storm around him, he parked the hottest vehicle on the PNC (Police National Computer), on the busy road outside the pub. The knife was still in his pocket and Stephen Cameron's DNA inevitably shrouded most of the clothes he was still wearing. Back then, pubs were required by law to close at 2.00pm but Noye and his friends enjoyed an afternoon lock-in, as normal.

It was here where the 'Brink's-Mat boys' often congregated. Glamorous women would call to the pub to seek out the men who had played their part in the UK's biggest theft of gold bullion in the hope of literally gold digging or just to feed off the notoriety and whiff of outlaw attraction that major criminals sometimes carry, particularly, when, as in this case, the three tons of gold and stash of diamonds were never recovered.

At today's (December 2022) prices, the missing three tons of gold alone is worth close to £140 million.

The landlord knew the crew and served drinks to the men standing at the bar in the back recesses of the pub and drew cash from a kitty jar that the group of six to eight would fill upon arrival and then regularly top up with a fresh whip-round. As the song from the latest Levi advert (Babylon Zoo's Spaceman) played on the jukebox, Noye was given his usual – a Bacardi and lemonade.

It went down fast. He wasn't a drinker. He didn't have his first drink until he was 29 and then it was a lager shandy.

"I hated the loss of control. I didn't like it in me, and I didn't like it in others," he said.

The heat on him since the death of the Metropolitan police officer; DC Fordham, the acquittal that followed, together with the infamy that came with the folklore surrounding the Brink's-Mat heist had taken its toll on Noye. It meant that he would be a marked man forever and this was more reason why his instantaneous combustion with Stephen Cameron annoyed and irritated him in these post-fight fallow moments amid the dim surrounds of an English country pub.

He knew trouble was coming his way. But he just had no idea how much and from whom? By the time he brought his second drink, another Bacardi and lemonade, to his lips savouring every sup, Stephen Cameron had been pronounced dead. His liver had been cut and his heart nicked by what Danielle described as a silver three-inch blade[12]. Despite near immediate medical assistance involving three ambulance crews, Cameron never recovered consciousness and his death certificate marks his passing officially as 2.10pm on Sunday May 19th 1996[13].

It was just over 40 minutes after he'd received a knife wound from Noye. In due course, the prosecution would claim that Noye was the aggressor without mitigation. Noye would say he used the knife as a deterrent, in self-defence. The jury would have the ultimate say.

But that battle between briefs would play out on another day.

For now, Noye was enjoying the convivial company of his lifelong pals – many also lifelong Charlton Athletic fans. He

---

12   Cable drew a triangular design for police and marked, signed and noted it as three inches May 20th, 1996. Source: Indictment files.

13   Source: Paragraph 'C', admitted facts in Central Criminal Court, R v Kenneth James Noye – Indictment, 1999.

had been taken there by his father as a boy but ironically, kept his own children away because of the football violence. Today the chat surrounded Charlton's defeat by Crystal Palace during the week, and although Noye was distracted and disengaged, it was not enough to alert his comrades in crime.

His lumps and bumps were slowly emerging, but he had cleaned himself up sufficiently to thwart any questions from his associates. Perhaps, it was the smoke or the poor backroom lighting, but no one asked, and Noye was not volunteering any details. It wasn't his style. In any case, it is far from certain that any of his party would have enquired about why he looked like he had just emerged from a fight to the death with a stranger six miles away. It wasn't their style either.

* * *

When he emerged from the pub at around 3.30pm into the bright but cold May day, he had already done some preliminary housekeeping. His priority was to disguise his association with the Land Rover he was driving. Half the work was already done. His car was registered in another name and at another address. It was an occupational requirement to obscure and deflect his links to addresses, cars and associates by such means. None of this was by any means foolproof but just might be sufficient to buy some valuable time, when necessary. And necessity was certainly on the agenda. While at the pub he phoned an old friend, who owned the property where the car was registered.

The DVLA recorded the vehicle in the name of Anthony

Francis, an alias long associated with Noye. A further call was made to another friend, Terry Hole, who sold him the 1994 built Land Rover, the year before. The motivation behind these calls is not hard to decipher but for the moment Noye was operating on strategic instinct and little else in the information vacuum.

The mobile phone tracking conducted later by Kent Police[14] was able to monitor the calls and movements of Noye and those linked to him. The cell site analysis available at the time could only place him within six kilometres of any signal tower[15], in this instance, the nearby Brands Hatch mobile mast for some brief time. Crisscrossing masts in Swanley and Sevenoaks also registered hits[16]. Despite its limitations, it showed Noye within six miles of the M20–M25 interchange at the time of the fight. It also revealed a frenzy of calls between Noye's wife, Brenda, and himself, back and forth as Noye tried to distance himself between the car, the fight and himself.

He had never met or seen Cameron before, contrary to rumours that the fight was over a drug deal gone wrong or some other underworld beef. It was none of the above. The resulting loss though was the same, but the 'origin story' was sadly as ordinary as it was tragic.

By 4.00pm. he had made it home, to his detached, mock Georgian house, Bridge Cottage, in Sevenoaks. The property spoke in part to Noye's considerable wealth and his role over the years as a wide boy entrepreneur.

---

14   Sourced from agreed facts – Appeal 2011, p24 list of calls made/received by KN compiled by Kent Police.

15   Admitted and agreed facts – Appeal 2011, R v KN.

16   Agreed and admitted facts – Appeal 2011, R v KN.

Upon arrival, he immediately greeted his wife, Brenda. By now, the lumps and bumps were beginning to reveal themselves. There was no hiding them in the bright open light of the kitchen.

"What the hell, happened to you?" his son Kevin said, the first to notice the injuries. "What did you do that for?" Kevin challenged.

"The geezer was a nutcase," Noye exclaimed. He then told his two sons and his wife what happened. It was agreed by everyone, as one judge would later remark, that the dispute which led to the death of Mr Cameron "blew up over nothing".

What a waste of a life.

A despondent Brenda raised her eyebrows. She had sadly been in this space before.

Still in the clothes from the fight, and with the knife still in the car, the Noye family sat down to their familiar and standard Sunday roast. The same scene was repeated in thousands of homes across the country. After ice cream and strawberries were served, they sat down in the living room to watch television and chat.

It soon became clear that in one other household, a very different family scene was unfolding.

Sky News had a crime desk that was always among the fastest with breaking news and at 5.00pm they were already on the hunt for Noye. The presenter reported that Kent Police were asking for witnesses in relation to the death of a 21-year-old man at the Swanley M25–M20 Interchange near the Dartford Tunnel in Kent at lunchtime today 'in what the Force are describing as a road rage incident'. Police said that it was a 'busy intersection with likely a large number of witnesses and have asked in particular for the driver of a dark coloured Range Rover like vehicle to contact them to assist with their enquiries'. The deceased was not named.

The Noye 'kitchen cabinet' was stunned by the turn of events[17]. A man was dead. Their loved one, a father and husband, was clearly in the firing line and all the ramifications were poured over. There was time in hand but not much. The family collectively braced themselves for the fallout from the sins of the father. Since Brink's-Mat and the death of DC Fordham, Kenny Noye was a staple of the red-tops with his every movement and sighting reported and published. Now the white-hot tentacles of the press and the police would envelope them in a way beyond their worst imagination.

"We discussed it," Noye said. "Brenda told me that there was no chance I would get a fair trial. I was fucked! I thought my only chance at getting a fair crack at the whip was to let the police get their first round of statements and then to come back and deal with them before the police tainted them and twisted them for their own agenda."

The police he was sure were going to be out to get him. It was only human nature. He had killed one of their own and despite an acquittal in Court Number 1 at the Old Bailey, officers were convinced that he had gotten away with murder. They would not let him get away with another – he was certain of that – no matter how innocent he felt he was of this crime.

---

17   KN testimony, transcripts in R v KN, 2000.

To kill one man with a knife may be misfortune but to kill a second by the same means surely cannot be a coincidence. Every right-minded police officer would believe this to be the deliberate act of a reckless and violent man.

Only those officers in Noye's pay would believe otherwise.

Noye had only one option in his mind: "I had to get the hell out of here and lay low for a couple of weeks." The family agreed. At this stage, he was not under arrest, charged or under suspicion, therefore any assistance to him could be considered within the rule of law. His mind raced at 100 miles an hour. Even if the police got a trace on the registration of the car, it would be 24 hours at least before it would be likely connected to him, his friends, or fixers[18]. If it was a partial number plate, then he had more time. Noye wasn't taking any chances.

On a golf course in Norfolk, the beeping of a pager disrupted one poor golfer's swing. Hand to pocket to eye line. Det. Superintendent Nick Biddiss read a message from the *Daily Mail*'s crime correspondent. *'Could you give me a call about the road rage incident, Nick – urgent Rosey.'*[19] It was the first the senior murder detective had heard of it. Biddiss was enjoying a day off and had already had a few 'swifties'. He was next on the rota on Tuesday, but he made his way to the 19th hole (clubhouse) to phone.

As he did so, he saw the report of the death on the rolling news ticker on *Sky News*.

He phoned headquarters at Maidstone and asked if he was needed. 'No need to worry, Governor, it's all in hand'. Biddiss,

18   It was three days before KN came on the police radar. Source: Nick Biddiss, Kent Police.

19   Interview with Nick Biddiss, November 2022.

then, was confident that the case would be cleared up quickly. What could possibly go wrong?'

***

DS NICK BIDDISS LED THE MANHUNT FOR FUGITIVE KENNETH NOYE

Time for a shower. Noye stripped naked. His clothes and Chelsea boots were sprawled over the bathroom floor. They would have to disappear.

As he was being drenched in soothing droplets, he navigated the road map ahead – one replete with jeopardy and peril. He would have to go on the run. Not for the first time he would have to rely on decades old relationships, good deeds and favours to get through the next chapter of his tumultuous life.

There would be incentives, rewards and any number of inducements offered for information on his future whereabouts and someone at some stage would grass him up. That was a certainty. Gangland was a whispering city. Information was a cherished currency which you could trade to your advantage. Who could he trust to get him out of this hole? There was only one man he could bank on. John Palmer, aka Goldfinger.

Noye and the timeshare king, who were both inextricably linked to the Brink's-Mat robbery, were close. Noye trusted John implicitly. Both men had extensive business and criminal contacts from Russia to Brazil and Palmer had access to helicopters and a personal jet. If you were a friend in need – Palmer was just the right kind of friend to have.

While Noye showered, about 10 miles away, forensic officers attended the mortuary at West Hill Hospital to photograph Stephen Cameron's corpse. Blood remained caked on his forehead. Scratches and scrapes on either side of both cheeks and scuffs on his knuckles. His clothes had been stripped off him and put in sequentially numbered plastic bags, before being placed in heavier evidence sacks for future examination.

The body would not be fully cleansed until before his funeral which would be held just a month or so later. The state autopsy and the necessary forensics would forbid any early ablutions.

Noye scrubbed his hands and nails deeply. He then dried himself off, shaved and dressed for life on the run. Despite the ticking clock, he splashed his usual Guerlain 'Habit Rouge' on his now puffy face. It wasn't a particular preference. He got it free, in volume, from a mate. That was the way he rolled. Noye was never one to pass up a good deal. Perfume aside, the planning would now go into overdrive. He packed everything he had worn in the fight into a carrier bag. His ankle boots, jacket, shirt, trousers, boxers and socks. It would all be burned.

"Everything had to go – to be disposed of – including the car," Noye said.

Although DNA and forensics were in their relative infancy in 1996 (the first UK conviction based on DNA was 1988) Noye kept up with these technological advances.

The clothing would simply be placed into a furnace. This key evidence would soon be turned into a heap of ash. There were quicker ways to dispose of it but none more certain –

none more secure. The issue of the car was more complex. The police who regularly surveilled Noye knew he drove an 'L' reg Land Rover Discovery, but this information was not widely shared within the service. The constant fear among those following him was that other officers in the Metropolitan Police were too close to Noye and had been compromised.

It surely was inevitable, Noye thought, that the car would eventually be linked to him.

To buy more time, he arranged for a replica 'L' Reg Discovery with a different legal registration to be purchased the next day and to replace the one on his driveway. At 9.30am, on the morning of May 20th, a man with the false name of John Grittins attended a garage in Swiss Cottage, London where he bought the replacement car for £12,000 cash which it was noted was produced from a plastic bag[20]. Within hours, it was at the Noye family home.

The dummy car wasn't going to fool anyone for very long, but it might buy a day or two for him on the run.

Short telephone calls were made by Noye and those in the know. In essence he 'phoned a friend'. The 'suspect' car would disappear. Noye had a hundred contacts who could crush a car with 200 tons of force into a small mixed metal cube.

"Leave it with me, I know exactly what to do," his pal said. "That's what friends are for in this world in these times – the worst of times."[21]

Before the police could connect Kenny Noye to the car, it would be on a shipping container on the way to China to

---

20   Admitted facts, R v KN Appeal 2011.

21   Interview with KN, December 2021.

be recycled into washing machines or any variety of white goods – take your pick. Critically, though, buried within its metal heart, was the weapon which cost Stephen Cameron's life.

As Noye prepared to go walkabout, the team of Kent detectives were confronted with what at first appeared to be a 'self-solver' of a crime. The crime took place in broad daylight, with tens of witnesses, blood on site, potential DNA and multiple road traffic and CCTV cameras on one of the busiest interchanges on one of the busiest motorways in the country.

"It was one of those that on the face of it, twenty past one on a Sunday, busiest roundabout in the world – M25 – quite a few witnesses, that would be fairly straight forward to trace the driver of the vehicle," Det Supt. John Grace, the then lead officer, surmised at the scene. But the driver, Kenny Noye, had other ideas. Initial police optimism would soon vanish as quickly as the killer himself.

All his preparations were in train and more besides. It was akin to a military operation. In truth, this operation had access to more resources and independent international operatives and contacts than most legitimate military covert manoeuvres.

In those terms it was an 'IA' – an 'immediate action' plan. A very precise and detailed strategy was unfolding at a pace; the resilience of Noye's contacts and his support structure would soon reveal themselves. By 6.00pm, Noye had left his home, never to return.

He hugged his two sons, Brett (21) a share trader and

Kevin (23), a builder. His boys were more or less the same age as the young man he'd just killed. They had their lives ahead of them and Cameron did not. There was a meaningful and deep embrace for the mother of his two boys and the woman who would hold steadfast as his protector and defender through thick and thin. No tears were shed. It was business 'unusual'. It was an occupational hazard.

***

In parallel, Home Office Pathologist Dr Michael Heath, who would carry out 20,000 autopsies in his career, set about doing a forensic examination of Stephen to discover how he died, the force used and the manner in which he was stabbed. That day it appeared nearly irrelevant – it was an obvious fact that Stephen had been stabbed – but evidence from this experienced pathologist might prove significant in the long run. That was the principle upon which all pathologists worked. He recorded the 5ft 10in height of Stephen, a couple of tattoos, some injection wounds from the attempts at resuscitation and the critical injuries. Basic toxicology would confirm that there were no drugs or any alcohol of note in his system. There were two stab wounds recorded.

Noye arranged his departure from Sevenoaks, in Kent to Somerset, in the south west of England, where he would stay overnight. Phone records show that he was phoned by a helicopter pilot, about his proposed journey exiting Blighty the next day. Noye and John Palmer would fly out together. Palmer was worth over £300 million and was named in *The Sunday Times* rich list that same year (1996) and shared 105th place with the Queen.

He owned a Lear jet, two helicopters and a superyacht (worth £7 million) and he had put his entire transport fleet at his good friend's disposal to help him disappear. Noye trusted Palmer implicitly but was decidedly uncomfortable with the people Palmer had around him. He could rely upon Goldfinger, but he struggled to trust his lieutenants. A man on the run has limited choices though and needs must.

What a difference a day makes! The previous night Noye and his wife, Brenda shared a night out at the cinema in Bromley with close friends. He slept through most of the movie 'Copycat Killers' – a film about a serial killer drawing inspiration from a selection of notorious murderers – starring Sigourney Weaver. He was in good spirits. The group then went to a nearby Chinese restaurant before heading for a nightcap in Chislehurst.

Some of the conversation focused on a business proposition that Noye developed in prison with a fellow inmate. They had designed a set of greeting cards and Noye's friend was offering to introduce them to a buyer at Woolworths the following week. It was arranged that Noye would bring the designs to the pub the next day. This benign hustle was in sharp contrast to claims that Noye was directing and funding serious criminal activities while serving at Her Majesty's pleasure. Hallmark or Clinton Cards were hardly shaking in their boots by the prospect of this 'greeting cards' competitor but it did demonstrate Noye's addiction to entrepreneurial activities and sideways deals, even honest ones. He had already visited

Harrods and met with a purchasing manager there who had expressed interest.

The Woolworths' meeting never happened because Noye was delayed by the fight and the high street store never got to consider the potential of Noye's artwork and greeting card enterprise.

Noye drove the two couples from venue to venue in his second car, a metallic 300D Mercedes with 500 miles on the clock. It was black, fully loaded with leather seats and all the trimmings. His cars always were.

This rare slice of modest domesticity would prove to be short lived. Looking at the two middle-aged couples out and about that night, nobody could imagine that amongst their number was one of the most infamous criminals of modern times. And surely no one could have predicted the events that were to consume the next 24 hours or so.

Noye made a two-and-a-half-hour dash on the M25 and M4 to John Palmer's estate, at the Battlefields in North Lansdown, near Bath. This was where Palmer smelted gold and silver in his backyard, and where it was alleged he smelted the Brink's-Mat gold, although he was acquitted of the crime at the Old Bailey.

"How the fuck had it come to this?"

Even the judge who was to adjudicate on the case later, described the incident as "banal"[22]. Considering Noye's underworld heritage, Judge Sir David Latham was right,

---

22   Source: https://www.mirror.co.uk/news/uk-news/judge-who-jailed-kenneth-noye-16496187

if a little insensitive. It wasn't a shootout between mobsters carrying AK47s or a sniper's bullet from 1000m – it was a hot-headed road rage incident.

Noye had abandoned his old mobile phone. He replaced it with a burner. Driven by a friend, he didn't speak the entire journey. He was thinking. Not reflecting. There would be another day for that. This evening all his tradecraft and guile would be called upon to weigh up his options. That evening, elsewhere, Danielle Cable was helping police with a description of the perpetrator.

Danielle reported that the other protagonist was around forty, slim, white haired, about 5ft 10in with strong facial features. If you knew Noye was involved, you might recognise the photofit that she later helped produce. After the fight she was inconsolable and was screaming uncontrollably over Stephen's motionless body[23]. Extreme distress inhibits forensic recall but the 17-year-old triumphed over her trauma.

She spent three hours with detectives in the hours after Stephen's death writing her first statement. What an ordeal for her! She returned home to spend a sleepless night crying and being consoled by Ken and Toni Cameron who were also beyond grief at the loss of Stephen.

John Palmer and Kenny Noye spent the night together mapping out the tactics for the days and possible weeks ahead. They were in effect preparing a counter insurgency operation against multiple border agencies, national justice departments, Interpol, GCHQ, and the UK deep state. In

---

23   Transcript from R v KN March 30th-April 14th, 2000.

MI6 terminology it was a 'black bag' operation. Neither of the men had military training – and John Palmer could barely read or write – but it was green for go and there was no telling when or if Noye's race would be run.

Noye slept badly because Cameron slept in a mortuary. He had never been on the run before. He had been hunted, targeted by rivals, hitmen and the police but he had never been forced out of his Kent stomping ground. He was now lost to his own family potentially for decades. He had taken Cameron away from his family for evermore. Noye was devastated for both families.

***

While the two grandees of the criminal world crashed out at Palmer's mansion, a private jet based in St Petersburg, Russia was being fuelled and readied to intersect the fugitive in Paris and to fly him as directed. His bogus passports were being couriered to him for his travels. He would carry a fake passport and a couple of others spare. Most were legitimate passports issued by Her Majesty's Government with Noye's own photograph but in different names.

Contact was made on Noye's behalf to Customs staff and senior police officers across Europe to call in favours to ease the path, open doors and turn a blind eye if, and when, necessary. He knew he could rely upon an information trail about police inquiries from his well-paid contacts in Scotland Yard, a product of years of cultivation, cash payments and a long list of contacts in the craft or Freemasons, as we would recognise it. On the way to the makeshift helicopter pad, he took a lingering look around the 'green and pleasant land'.

How long would it be before he'd set foot here again? Would he come back on his terms, in handcuffs or a coffin?

Every mile away from Kent was an inch closer to safety.

The next day he inched his way to Paris. He took the train and then a taxi to a private airport frequented by the rich and famous – Le Bourget, about 25km from the city centre. There, he was met by the private jet. It was white with two distinctive red track lines on the side and was the jet of choice for high-end international travellers and the US military. Noye told a Customs Officer on site that he was expecting a plane in from Russia and asked if he could leave his suitcase down in the corner.

Noye explained: "It could have contained a bomb instead of 10k, a toothbrush and travelling clothes, but he said no problem. As long as you like."

The jet took the pair to Madrid Airport. They were alone in the cabin which seated six. There were no bodyguards this time. Palmer regularly travelled with a team of them. Kenny Noye thought them an unnecessary fashion accessory, and believed they were a magnet for trouble: "I didn't need to be flash. The last thing I needed was everyone knowing I was in a bar or restaurant doing business. Of course, for all the times John had a needless security entourage – the moment he actually needed one – he never had one."

Palmer would be executed by a likely contract killer in June 2015 while under covert surveillance by M15, the UK domestic secret-service. The murder remains unsolved. His family, in cooperation with Crimestoppers, have offered a £100,000 reward for information.

Both these men travelled very dangerous terrain. Palmer would get out his bodyguards when he and Noye were together in Tenerife, but for now the fashion accessories would stay locked away.

Upon arrival at the Adolfo Suárez Madrid-Barajas, the city's main airport, the £5 million pound plane taxied away from the main terminal building. The passengers walked out to a nearby perimeter fence and were escorted by security personnel through a gate into a taxi waiting outside. This was a covert concierge service that diplomats and VIPs could only dream of.

They would spend the night in a five-star hotel. At the bar, Palmer, with his dark hair and boyish good looks was treating his party to the finest of wines, generously tipping the waiters. The two pilots studiously made their excuses and left for an early night, as Noye and Palmer considered their options.

One call to the concierge, and their other necessities were sorted. They spent the night enjoying the company of two women they met at the bar. Noye had eyed up a blonde but when Palmer expressed a preference for her, Noye said, "I don't give a fuck I'll take the dark haired one."

Callous as it may seem, so shortly after Stephen Cameron's death, old habits die hard. He was always a 'ladies man' and his reputation in the press rarely sent partners packing. Indeed, it may have been part of the attraction. Kenny Noye was not looking for a relationship at this arduous time, just a distraction. It was much more lust than love obviously. This was part of his character. He liked women and the attraction it seemed was mutual

The next day they flew to Tenerife.

Over the course of two weeks, Noye would leave the UK, and enter and exit France, Spain, Morocco, and the Ivory Coast, without ever having to show his passport – legitimate or otherwise.

That's how it is when you take the routes that only money and influence can buy.

2

THEY HUNT HIM HERE...

The make-up artists in the green room in *BBC* Television Centre worked on the guests about to appear on *BBC's* *Crimewatch* programme. Det. Supt. John Grace looked into the mirror as the work was being done and was more than a little anxious about a rare appearance in front of the cameras.

"We start with the murder of Stephen Cameron. It's been called the road rage murder. Stephen was killed on a roundabout off the M25. Interestingly tonight, Det. Supt. John Grace in charge of the investigation doesn't like to call it road rage. The man who did it is extremely dangerous," so kicked off Nick Ross on the *Crimewatch* update. "And you've got the response you didn't want – it turned out to be massive."

Grace nearly appeared disappointed by the public response to the case launched earlier in the evening with the primetime show. Facing up to a thousand calls from the public he told viewers that it was too much work to process and work through: "What we really want is information that hits me right between the eyes," at which point he pointed to his bald forehead with the sweep of dark hair drifting from the right-hand side. The producers in the gallery called up on screen the photofit of the suspect which bore a distant resemblance to Noye – perhaps a second cousin first removed. It was a sight to behold, an officer at this stage in an investigation on *Crimewatch* requesting only quality information. Grace said: "There are a number of people giving us good information but what we need is just that little bit more which makes us sit up and be excited about this information. So that we know this is the right person we're looking for."

Operation Quern[24] as it was named by Kent Police, had commenced. Some in the force, however, were not impressed with the *Crimewatch* appeal.

The Dartford incident room was filled with cigarette smoke. It was the way it was back then. On the Tuesday morning Nick Biddiss came into the office to meet Grace who was on duty on the day and was assigned the job.

"Immediately I was concerned," Biddiss said. "John was already talking to *Crimewatch* and very early in the week, the *BBC* team were doing reconstructions. We usually only go to *Crimewatch* after a while when we are struggling with an investigation, but it had just started. The *Crimewatch* appeal asking for the public to be discriminating with their information was a little blunt because you can never know what is good and what is not."

Within the week, Biddiss was assigned the case after Grace went on holiday, as was standard for a high profile case in its infancy

Biddiss entered the fray at top speed. His task was to I.T.E

---

24   Interview with Nick Biddiss, August 2022.

suspects – that is Identify, Trace and Eliminate – people on his radar and one of those was Kenneth James Noye.

Within days of Noye going on the lam, the investigation into him was well and truly up and running. By the time he was recovering from his night of high jinks in his five-star hotel in the heart of Madrid, he was already being considered a leading person of interest among 17,000 Land Rover Discovery drivers. It would take 834 cars and drivers to be eliminated at record speed before the police settled upon Noye and Noye alone. Sixty-nine men named 'Anthony Francis' – in whose name the Land Rover Noye was driving was registered – were traced and eliminated before the police came to one certain conclusion. They had their man in their sights but not in custody. By May 22nd Noye had made a long suspect list.

A week later he was the only one on it.

***

Of all the drivers under suspicion, Noye knew that he alone was operating in a world where knowledge of his movements was valuable currency. Four thousand nine hundred and thirty-six calls were made to Dartford Police Station with information. It was inevitable that someone would trade the news of Kenneth Noye's unexpected departure on the day after the murder. As he lived relatively close to the scene of the fight, questions were asked precipitating the indisputable link between Noye and the events of May 19th at 1.15pm on the M25-M20 Swanley Interchange.

The news channels and newspapers were driving the emotional vortex around the crime that was shocking a nation. "It had everything that made crime stories attractive. It was one of those that just took off and led the newspapers nearly the entire week after it happened," Nick Biddiss said.

He knew the equation. He knew the crime had all the ingredients to ingrain itself into the consciousness of the nation. It had a young handsome victim, an equally attractive and loving fiancée, Danielle Cable and two families advocating for justice around this seemingly inexplicable crime. It also had a perpetrator who had already killed a policeman – a final ingredient that would help the crime sear itself into the memory of generations to follow.

"The tabloids couldn't have a better story to get their talons into. Danielle was very pretty and that made for a great photograph. She was engaged to the victim, and it was the country's first road rage killing – we all drive – it could happen to any of us, that's what made it fertile ground for the tabloids," explained Biddiss.

The police were pulling everything together but were hampered by missing CCTV at the Dartford Tunnel and at the Swanley Interchange junction. This could have confirmed the direction of travel and timings of the alleged driver of the Land Rover Discovery involved in the incident and it would also have corroborated or otherwise the testimony of key witnesses who had already given preliminary statements.

"It was devastating to us that with CCTV on the roundabout and in the Dartford Tunnel that none were working," Biddis said. "Immediately we were facing an uphill battle. Even if we did identify a lead suspect, how could we link him to the scene when no one could identify the vehicle registration. On top of that, Biddiss explained how the investigation had also been dealt another serious blow: "Not a shred of DNA was recovered from Stephen's clothing to link with any third party outside of Danielle Cable. Suddenly, all our initial optimism was looking deeply misplaced. We had nothing of evidential consequence and the pressure was on. There was hysteria in the newspapers and there were orders from on high."

Biddiss was known as a strict no-nonsense disciplinarian. An old school copper. One detective working on the case with him said, "He demands all his officers go the extra mile and while he was not everyone's cup of tea his hand-picked team on the case would do anything for him. The first time I met him he threw me 20p and told me to get him a newspaper. But he is a perfectionist and inspires loyalty in everyone who works for him."[25] Biddiss was greatly offended. "I'd never have given him any money," he said.

The basics would get done under Biddiss − that was a certainty − and the killer piece of evidence was an innocuous Automobile Association card in Noye's name found in the offices of a scrap yard near to where Noye lived.

Despite buying a replica car with a different number plate to place on his drive to distract the police − and arranging the destruction of the actual car he drove on the day − his best laid plans were only drawing attention to him.

Noye was honest about the machinations around the car: "I was just trying to buy time. Every little hindrance and interruption or visit the coppers would have to make would

---

25   *How I Caught The Killer*, Sky 2020.

give me an extra day, hour or maybe even minute to make good my escape until things settled down."

His associates worked their magic while he travelled across Europe. That's what friends do. But there would always be mistakes when things are done in a hurry.

Unfortunately, a car matching its description was spied entering his friend Tommy Lee's scrap yard the day after the incident. Noye had gone to Lee's home to wash and tidy up immediately after the stabbing of Stephen Cameron, but Lee was unaware of the details of the incident.

A witness reported a distinctive black Land Rover travelling in convoy sandwiched between two other Land Rover Discoveries the morning after the road rage incident. The scene was likely to draw attention. It did. The car Noye drove or any evidence of it was not found there. There were plenty of legitimate reasons why his AA card was there and equally plenty of circumstantial evidence to substantiate the link between the apparent disposal of the car after the stabbing and Noye, as potential owner of the car driven by the killer.

Kenny Noye bought the suspect car from old friend Terry Hole in 1995.

"It had 600 miles on the clock," Noye said. "I told him I wanted a twin car with the same registration and number plate L794 JFT – a ringer – to send to Northern Cyprus to use there. He kept that in a garage in his home until I was getting it shipped out there. But I asked him to assure me that the car I was buying, the car I drove on the 19th of May, the day of the incident, was Kosher. I paid £20k but got rolled over. It was a ringer too."

The mysterious colour of the car which so confused witnesses was 'Avalon Blue'. Noye was told that the raid on his pal Tommy Lee's scrap yard was imminent and knew that his mobile phone calls to friends after the attack would bring another constellation of witnesses into the police loop. Still, Noye knew that without the actual car that he could still lie low and allow things to settle down until he could negotiate a manslaughter charge.

He explained: "As long as I could get the coppers to get the preliminary statements down and get the notebooks and their accounts in the system then I figured the witnesses couldn't change their stories and then I would know the weight of evidence against me. That was the plan. Find out what they had and then act accordingly. I could sit and wait it out or I could come home and front it up. It was a waiting game!"

And of course, there were the snitches, grasses and turncoats that are in every criminal community professing Judas-like loyalty only to betray their brethren for 30 pieces of silver, a lighter sentence, or the occasional blind eye to their own activities. It is the human condition. Noye was alive to this matrix. He has operated out of his small clique of close friends and associates growing up and was always mindful of touts. In every conversation he carefully delivered his words and enunciated his directions with clarity to his fellow villains. Occasionally, he would throw in a bogus fact or 'MacGuffin' to a singular individual and if it came back to him by another route, he would then isolate and manage that person as a suspected 'informer'.

"I never let anyone know that I knew they were operating against me," Noye said. "I kept them close. I often gave them dummy scenarios and sent them up the wrong path. But I tried to never fall out with them. I'd slowly manage them out of my business life."

Meanwhile, to law enforcement, Noye was uniquely the enemy within and the enemy without.

***

High ranking officers in the Metropolitan Police and other forces in the UK, notwithstanding contacts with US and European Law enforcement, were at Noye's beck and call. It was a matter of economics. Noye understood that above all else, information is power. If he knew what the police were up to, then he could act accordingly. He could even feed information into the mix which would disrupt legitimate investigations. This would become apparent later during his escapade on the run. In his own words he, "Had them in his pocket".

Nick Biddiss was aware that outside the standard 'cops'n'robbers' pugilistic relationship there was another battleground behind the scenes. There was an invisible front against dark forces within the police. Biddiss was an incorruptible officer fighting for justice for Stephen Cameron, while police forces around him and in particular the Metropolitan Police were riddled with corruption; where officers struggled to trust one another and where loyalties could quickly run dry.

Biddiss said: "I kept my own counsel. I tried to appoint my own officers, those who I trusted. It wasn't a terror case.

There was no special branch at this stage so information inevitably came into the office and it was soon common knowledge. I tried to keep it as watertight as possible."

Biddiss hoped that the underworld was equally porous and vulnerable: "The Noye connection was simply incredible," he said. "What was he doing carrying a knife? Of all people – you could not have made it up. No one could have imagined in the first days of the inquiry that such a high-profile offender could be involved. But he was and it changed everything."

The pressure was on – and it was rising exponentially. As Noye rose quickly through the ranks of potential suspects, this crime would escalate from a tragic violent death to a political matter of public order and confidence and failure to catch such a high-profile figure could signal the hasty end of a career.

Biddiss was fully alive to the likelihood that there were brethren among his own ranks, perhaps his own station, willing to take 30 pieces of silver from Noye. He knew anecdotally that some had done so already, and it was already public knowledge within the force and beyond.

But corruption wasn't Noye's only weapon to stay several steps ahead of the law. Noye's not inconsiderable guile and imagination were working at their optimum. Every option was considered. From plastic surgery to playing possum – it was all on the table.

For now, a basic baseball hat, sunglasses and a goatee would suffice. "I hated the beard. Still hate them. I would have chosen surgery over growing a beard any day," he said.

He left everything behind. His wedding ring stayed in the family bedroom in Sevenoaks. His modest – by his standards – Rolex Submariner watch worth about £15k was also abandoned. He had his wits and friends in high places and those luxury items that would prove to be invaluable.

Associates, forgers, blaggers and bagmen[26] were all engaged in the battle to keep Noye in the shadows. It was clear though, that the Land Rover that he was driving in the road rage incident was hot. Grand Theft Auto-hot. There was one knocked off car, a dead body – and a major gangster on the run – soon people would start talking. The underworld was twitching, and the police had their snouts (informers) working overtime.

It was time to lay low. Maybe it was time to die? "You can't charge a dead man," was the way Noye put it.

Would it be drowning? Suicide? Or he could send out the story that he was the victim of a gangland execution with his body buried at an undisclosed location. All these scenarios were on the agenda. They would be called upon in due course. For the moment it was all about keeping his head down. Only he knew that he was on the run. It was only a matter of time before the rest of the world would know too.

The Financial Times was a rare sight in Tenerife. Even rarer was the combination of the *FT* and *The Sun* newspaper. Sipping his coffee at a beach bar just a walk from a timeshare complex owned by John Palmer, the fugitive caught up on the latest gold prices and currency exchange rates. One mobile phone sat on the table. Another two were in a travel bag in

---

26   Interview with KN by Karl Howman, 2021.

his grace and favour villa. The bags were always packed for instant departure – fake passports on the ready and a bundle of cash in multiple denominations stuffed in the suitcase linings. His eyes, hidden behind his Ray-Ban Wayfarers, scanned the location and drifted to the red top with the latest news on the road rage death of Stephen Cameron. Noye's secret was still safe. He was on the Interpol wanted list, but the British Police were not sharing it with the voraciously news hungry crime reporters – yet. Of course, Noye had been told the game was up. He was in the know.

He had a man on the inside.

Several. It was time to move.

3

BREAKING NEWS

Bad news travels quickly.

As fast as the News International printing presses spat out paper at its 15-acre Wapping headquarters. Editor Phil Hall, a legendary newsman, knew his front page was sorted from Thursday night. Crime really pays for newsmen if no one else. However, sex sells more, and the veteran newsman was determined to follow up the last week's splash about a MP and sex in the Commons with more lurid details. He was an old-fashioned hands-off delegator and hugely respected among his print brethren. His mind was made up and only a huge story would displace it.

Any story that would supersede the 'sex in Parliament' tale would have to be earth-shatteringly significant to win over the 10x8in frontpage and Phil Hall's steadfast mind. Every Tuesday morning the paper was a blank page and there was a Darwinian battle among the reporters across all the departments in the prime editorial conference of the week to take ownership of this precious real estate. This week was no different. In the news was a bubbling prospect of fresh IRA ceasefire talks; the carnival around Euro 96' and the use of a virtual Ouija board to promote 150 years of proud spirit produced by Dewar's Whisky[27].

News of the World journalists Ian Edmondson and Gary Jones had contacts in the Met and other police forces. It was part of every reporter's brief to wine and dine detectives and curry favour with them. Expense accounts with anonymised contacts were the standard and senior police officers were often encouraged to mix work with journalists in a benign fashion, and often to the benefit of a police investigation. The newspaper ruled the world back in 1996 but its later demise, in July 2011, would be celebrated by some in the Kent police force.

Nick Biddiss had been fastidious in creating strict information circles – Chinese walls – around the list of potential suspects. There was a small team in his office who knew about Noye's increasing prominence in the investigation, but it was such a combustible piece of information that keeping a lid on it was going to prove very difficult. Nonetheless, he had imposed a strict embargo on sharing any information with the Met out of a legitimate fear that he could not trust the force to keep its counsel. As a straight shooter, he had never felt the need to cultivate media contacts but that was the job; and reporters had an open invitation to call without going through the press office. The key national crime journalists had his pager and contact numbers, but this was one story he was not discussing – on or off the record.

Biddiss said: "This was my one priority. I got up in the morning and I knew every day that there was a possibility

27   Source: *The Guardian* June 8th, 1996.

the investigation into Kenny Noye would be derailed by a damaging leak and a headline."

He was desperately concerned in the early days of June that the story would break and with it any chance of rounding on the well-connected suspect and arresting him before he became aware that he was being hunted.

"I just needed to try and claw back some advantage. He had a head start and the last thing he needed was another key bit of information that he would use to stay away or even to help prepare his defence."

It was on Thursday afternoon when reporter Ian Edmondson got a call from a nervous tipster. It was a timely opportunity for a Sunday newspaper. Back then he was an ambitious reporter seeking to make his name every week. The contact was cagey. Edmondson told his editor that his contact wouldn't say over the phone what the story was. It was pondered and then he was given permission to meet his 'deep throat' with the apparently dangerous story.

"He told me that he didn't want to speak on the telephone," Edmondson said. "And we arranged to meet in a pub near Greenwich and over a few drinks he said you'll never guess who killed Stephen Cameron. I just remember my jaw hitting the ground, it was incredible. When he told me Noye it was just staggering. It nearly was unbelievable – too true to be true!"

Meanwhile, earlier that day, on June 6th, Noye had reached out to his lawyer, Henry Milner, through family contacts to try and get a lie of the land. Milner had worked magic with high grade underworld defendants and if there was a deal to be done with the prosecution or the police, then Milner was your man.

The deal was as it was when Noye first contemplated it within moments of hearing the news that Stephen Cameron had died. The plan was for a manslaughter charge which Noye would then take his chances with in front of the '12 Angry Men' (and women) of the jury.

Noye had acted as nonchalantly as one could do after a hugely physical row where you had drawn blood with a short knife and after a quick wash had attended the pub with your mates before meandering home to your wife for the Sunday dinner. He never knew Stephen Cameron had passed away until the news broke on *Sky*. That would surely be sufficient grounds for a manslaughter charge – at least it would be for most offenders if their name was not Kenneth James Noye.

The deal was compelling for all parties. The police would get their man without much delay or embarrassment and Noye would limit his legal jeopardy and likely run the self-defence case he had run so successfully previously in the murder trial over the death of John Fordham. There were plenty of obstacles however, to any potential deal, chief among them the way the case and his role in it, was portrayed in the media.

Ian Edmondson phoned the news editor immediately after his meeting with the 'confidential source'. He had news of an extraordinary scoop. Always keen to keep his reporters in their place, Alex Marunchak, told him that they had a hint of that story already and they also had tips that Noye was currently hiding in Northern Cyprus.

He was to immediately fly to Turkey and then to Cyprus on the trail of the 'lead suspect' in the 'M25 road rage case' as it became known. By Friday evening, Edmondson was writing his copy on the plane en route to Cyprus with a photographer in tow. He wrote it straight with some background and he figured other reporters would be dispatched to write supporting colour pieces.

As Edmondson put his pen to paper, his colleague, Gary Jones, was in conference with the media lawyers and senior editors at the *News of the World* which was the testing ground for legally sensitive copy[28]. There was no copy yet, but the narrative was simple. The team were considering if there were any legal or libel issues. Edmundson would phone the copy through the next morning.

Newsroom reporters kept their scoops close to their chest like cold war spies. There was a toxic rivalry between reporters which meant that no one other than the senior editors and the lawyers could be trusted with the news that Kent Police had rounded on Noye, the 'notorious killer' of DC John Fordham and one of the key men in the Brink's-Mat robbery. For the reporters, it was as if all their Christmases had come at once.

Although Noye was a key person of interest he had not yet been charged and consequently it was potentially open season on the story. The legal team had adjudicated that there were no reporting restrictions as no charges were pending, and as such there was no technical risk of the publication being held in contempt for prejudicing any future

---

28   Interview with Ian Edmondson, November 2022.

proceedings. Effectively, until he was charged, the papers could and would say what they wanted. And they did. Noye knew that he had no reputation to defend and any inaccuracy or lie would never be challenged. Thus, the die was cast but the police would have to be contacted for confirmation and comment.

It was left to Gary Jones, a future editor of the *Daily Express*, to contact Kent Police and ask them if the force was seeking to interview Noye about the death of Stephen Cameron.

An irate and very concerned Biddiss was on the other end of the phone. "The guys from the *News of the World* were ringing me up asking me to confirm whether or not we were seeking Noye in relation to the M25," Biddiss said. "I said quite clearly it was not my policy to discuss any individual we may seek in relation to this or any other murder."

The response came as no surprise to the seasoned *News of the World* reporter, Gary Jones.

"You could see he was shocked and surprised that we had this information," Jones said. "You could hear his brain whirring with the sound of, 'Oh my God this throws my investigation completely out of sync, what are we going to do now'."

Biddiss pleaded with the paper not to publish the story to protect the investigation. "You can't possibly print now, can you?" he said.

The *News of the World* told him in no uncertain terms that it could print and that they would print.

On Wednesday afternoon, Biddiss had already been phoned by Jeff Edwards, the *Daily Mirror*'s chief crime correspondent. Edwards, a master of his trade, asked Biddiss to confirm the story. Nick, building upon his long-term relationship with Jeff, pleaded with him for a favour.

"Could I ask you to hold onto that for a while," Biddiss asked. "We are really trying to get a break on the case Jeff, and this could damage that?"

Edwards, a man with an eye for the long road and a man of his word, respectfully agreed to defer the story to allow the investigation to take priority. Crime journalists often did this, but this was a scoop of the year and it hurt. However, it was decisions like these that have kept Edwards trusted by his contacts over those nearly four decades of crime reporting.

The *News of the World* reporters were proceeding at a pace, racing towards their anticipated front page Sunday splash. Other efforts were made at a more senior level in the Kent force to have the story pulled but to no avail. The *News of the World* reporters were naturally nervous, as they always were, that their sensational expose would turn up in another newspaper or on television and thus robbing them of their hard-earned exclusive. They had every reason to be concerned because the news was out there – but who would get there first?

There was a strict timetable to the Saturday newsroom protocol on the eve of a latent bombshell story.

The paper trusted their reporters and the credentials of the source were exemplary and the senior editors sat back waiting to bask in the glory of their scoop. Both reporters had earned their stripes before and would make headlines again, but this was a massive breakthrough and a genuine 'water-cooler' moment of a story.

On Saturday morning from Nicosia, in Cyprus, Ian Edmondson[29] read out his handwritten copy to a typist – a 'copy girl' on the news desk – a practice that continued until the turn of the century. That was Edmondson's job done and now he was on the trail for next week's story which meant on the trail of Noye. When Edmondson asked the news editor why he had to go then and there to Cyprus – he was told, 'If you don't go now by Tuesday the place will be swarming with reporters after the story breaks, so, enjoy your head start'.

Kent Police continued to make no official comment. Gary Jones knew that official confirmation would never be forthcoming.

Nick Biddiss at the Maidstone headquarters-based incident room knew from the moment he received the call from the paper that 36 hours later word that Kent Police were looking for Noye would be national news. The paper was robust but there was always the hope that some potential legal action or late-night injunctions might come to haunt the story. It wasn't likely.

Biddiss was devastated. "It was not very helpful," he said. "I was livid. It was so arrogant. Normally, you can talk a paper down in the interests of the investigation but not the *News of the World*."

His first task was to phone the Camerons and Danielle Cable to advise them of the breaking story.

Both were shocked at the development. Cable already had an inkling. She was briefed about a range of suspects about a week earlier. In fact, she had been given, "a very good photo-

---

29   Interview with Ian Edmondson, November 2022.

graph of Noye to look at in respect of possible suspects. But she didn't identify him even though it was a good likeness".[30]

Biddiss had told her Noye was a suspect but said she wasn't aware that he was the 'prime suspect'[31].

She was living with the Camerons as she had done when Stephen was alive. Collectively, they were furious that the story could impede the investigation. Biddiss continued his rounds and then phoned Jeff Edwards who was none too happy but took it on the chin.

His time would come again. This was a story that had plenty more to give and plenty more scoops at its heart.

The first editions made it to Kings Cross by 11.30pm and by then all the other editors had the story. The edition was then dispatched to Spain along with the other national papers utilising News International's hyper-efficient distribution operation. Expats would soon revel in the salacious detail and the re-running of the Brink's-Mat and Fordham stories by Sunday afternoon. 'Cop Killer to be Quizzed Over Road Rage Murder,' shouted the inside pages. The police investigation would now mutate into uncontrollable and unchartered waters.

The journalists at the paper, however, were disappointed. Phil Hall, the editor, kept the sex story on the front page and consigned the Noye story to the second and third pages. He would later apologise to the team at the Tuesday conference. Despite the secondary placement of the story, there was hardly a paper to be found on the newsstands. Most of

---

30   Interview with Nick Biddiss, November 2022.

31   Interview with Nick Biddiss, November 2022

the other television and radio stations ran with the story as headline news.

"It sent the story into the stratosphere… It was an incredible, sensational story, which everybody wanted a piece of. The police became incredibly excited at the prospect of hunting this man down," Gary Jones said.

As much as it propelled the news agenda there was a more important consideration percolating in the background. The story begged the question, who leaked it? The question carried even more resonance because of the widespread concern over Noye's moles in the Met and other forces.

Biddiss wasn't naive and knew that there were officers prepared to divulge information about Noye. He was shocked that some of his fellow officers would give the information to a national newspaper and disrupt the investigation at a critical stage. He knew only too well that Noye had the wealth and power that could corrupt. And from then on, he would restrict all information about the case to a chosen and trusted few. "Need to know. If they don't need to know, don't tell them".

Biddiss faced the threat of his own officers either telling the press or Noye himself about the progress of the investigation. "This Sunday counted as a bad day in the investigation. When the paper closed down 16 years later, I raised a glass I can tell you," Biddiss said[32].

On the Monday after the *News of the World* story, Mark Pugach, chief press officer at the Kent Police called all local and national journalists covering the story to the Maidstone Headquarters for a briefing. Reporters thought it would be to

---

32   Source: Granada TV, 2005.

officially confirm Kenny Noye as a person of interest but in fact it was the opposite.

Nick Biddiss solemnly told the assembled cast of Fleet Street's finest that contrary to 'recent media reports', the force were confirming that Noye was NOT a suspect in the Stephen Cameron murder investigation.

A murmur settled over the assembled throng which was broken by one eagle-eyed local reporter who raised his hand. Nick nodded permission to pose a question: "Nick, if Noye is not a suspect then why is there an aerial photograph of Noye's house 'Bridge Cottage' on the operational board behind you?"

With much kerfuffle and embarrassment, the meeting was hastily adjourned and reconvened 30 minutes later where Biddiss went on the record to unequivocally confirm that Noye was the prime suspect in the case.

Biddiss was certain that officers within his force or other security agencies leaked the intelligence on Noye.

"There were leaks, and definitely there were people who were telling the media, making phone calls to the media, and giving them information," he said.

"I had no doubt that those responsible were receiving something in return, if not money. I don't know what they were receiving because [we] never got to the bottom of it."[33]

Shortly after the closure of the *News of the World*, Biddiss was walking into Waterloo station up the steps when by chance coming down was Ian Edmondson. "Biddiss, Nick Biddiss," came the salutation. "Edmondson," came the

---

33   Interview with Nick Biddiss, October 2022

reply. The two men then did what old adversaries often do with the passage of time and chatted through events over a coffee. Edmondson offered polite contrition and said that pressure from the news desk meant that he had to publish[34]. Peace broke out over cappuccinos.

Nonetheless, the damage was done. Before the print run was dry, Noye had left his bolthole at Palmer's luxury sanctuary and was on his toes. He now found himself the "most wanted man in Europe if not the world".[35]

---

34   Interview with Ian Edmondson, November 2022.

35   Wensley Clarkson: *Crime Stories*; Kenneth Noye *Road Rage Killer*, ITV 2017.

4

THE GRAND TOUR BEGINS

Tenerife was safe for most villains on the run from the law – but not those on the front page. Africa came calling.

"There is a time to move and there's no time like the present," Kenny Noye said.

It was strange fleeing Tenerife because it was always in his mind to move there permanently to swerve the attention that followed him in England even prior to the current trouble stalking him.

Noye explained: "I had made my money. I needed for nothing, and all I got back home was trouble. Trouble for stuff I may have done and certainly gigs I was 100% never involved in."

Although there were push factors driving him to move to Tenerife – there were also plenty of pull factors to make it a base for his family. It was a home from home for him despite the circumstances. Tenerife was the wild west, where criminals of every nationality walked about and did business with nigh on complete impunity. The sun was decidedly Spanish, but the atmosphere and accent were decidedly Ramsgate. There were so many East End villains out and about, that one wag called it "a virtual extension of the District Line".[36]

To hijack Somerset Maughan's note about Monaco, "Tenerife, was certainly a sunny place for shady people". This was home to the empire that John Palmer built and a perfect bolthole for Noye and those he loved. It was his family that was preoccupying him now. He was a family man. It was also beyond doubt that he was an unfaithful rogue who had lovers and women in nearly every city he visited and he loved women and female company. He had a list of his long-term lovers and by 50 he had notched one for every year. This is not a boast just an honest figure from a man past his prime. If you count his 30 years without sex while in prison, you

NOYE WITH WIFE BRENDA AND SONS BRETT AND KEVIN

might think it is quite a number. Perhaps, his time in lock-up is the reason why his number of conquests was so high. That though, in a very modern sense did not damage the affection he had for his wife Brenda and the adoration he had for his children.

Although long separated, he remains close to his wife Brenda, and he says she was, "About the best choice I ever made in my life. I've made plenty of bad decisions but certainly luck was shining on me the day I married her".

---

36   John Sweeney, 'Blood Money', *Observer*, 25th February 2001.

Now though, as before, the police would turn the spotlight on those Noye left behind.

***

During the Brink's-Mat money laundering trial, detectives arrested Brenda in a tried and trusted tactic of putting pressure on the key suspect by pulling in those close to him.

As their lawyer Henry Milner put it, "To my mind the case against Mrs Noye was non-existent but that didn't prevent her from being kept in Holloway Prison for two months before being granted bail."[37]

But if you are a villain, you don't make the rules. Noye's activities has caused his wife to be arrested for murder in respect of DC John Fordham and conspiracy to launder illicit funds. Both charges were dropped by the Crown Prosecution Service (CPS) on grounds of lack of evidence. For all the wealth and lifestyle that marriage to Noye afforded her, this was surely a bridge too far and prison must have been a horrifying experience for her. And yet more than a decade later, the long-suffering Brenda once again was under the umbrella of press intrusion and, more importantly, police raids.

Noye said: "There is no getting away from the devastation I caused my family over the years but it nearly is unforgivable that Brenda was placed on remand for the murder charge and the Brink's-Mat gold. It was only ever to pressurise me, and, in the end, they never offered any evidence against her. It is of course on me all that. I brought it all down on the family because that's what happens if you are a villain – the consequences are shared."

37   Interview with Henry Milner, October 2022.

Just before the *News of the World* revelations, Kent Police raided the family home in West Kingsdown, Sevenoaks. Noye had long felt that his house had been bugged by the 14th Field Security and Intelligence Company known as the 'DET' which, although part of the elite British Army Intelligence Corps, were occasionally drafted in from their base in Northern Ireland to provide high grade support to the special branch.

The unit's specialism had been infiltration of the Republican and Loyalist paramilitary operations in the province and it has been the subject of considerable controversy in respect of collusion with loyalist paramilitaries regarding the killing of prominent republicans. Noye was well informed of the DET's activities by IRA members who shared the numerous high security prisons with him over the years.

Permission had to be given by the Home Secretary for their involvement in civilian policing operations. In 2001, the then Home Secretary Jack Straw imposed a gagging order to protect the role of the intelligence agencies in hunting down the fugitive. Sometimes when you think they are all out to get you – you are right. History may have proved Noye's suspicions correct as the banning order was the first official confirmation of MI5's involvement in tracking him down. One could also read that MI6, the state agency dealing with international intelligence, were also engaged in the hunt for Noye yet reports of the involvement of the security services in the hunt for Noye have been widely exaggerated according to Nick Biddiss. He should know.

"All the successes and failures in the case were the responsibility of Kent Police. I can assure you that there was no MI5, MI6 or James Bond in this investigation and if they were then they never gave me any information," Biddiss said, with a very wide smile. "It is a seductive thought for reporters and most of the suggestions came from them."

Of course, if the agencies were involved, we would not be told and Biddiss would not be telling us.

In any case it was nearly taken as a given that the homes and phones of his family and associates were bugged. It also may have been the case that Kent Police were not aware themselves of the exact nature of the covert operatives. Certainly, after DC Fordham's death, no covert operatives from within the police ranks would ever be tasked to risk repeating the ruse.

Kent Constabulary were apparently given intelligence that Noye was at the house from those monitoring the hidden devices or by other covert surveillance techniques. Brenda Noye was terrified. Given the history that a serving police officer had died on the grounds of their home previously, a platoon of armed police storming her house left her terrified that Kevin and Brett, her sons, could be caught up in the raid and even shot. It was Kevin's voice that precipitated the raid. He sounded uncannily like his father. For one short moment, the police thought that they had their man. It wasn't to be. Even close family friends could not distinguish between father and son and the raid was to prove fruitless. Though police did discover his current passport. The fact it was left behind came as no surprise.

Brenda and all the children could now guarantee that they would be under constant surveillance by the police and by the press. News of this dragged Noye to the floor.

He said: "The day would start black. Depression I suppose. I'd struggle to get up and out. And then I think that's exactly how the old bill would want me to feel, So, I'd pick myself up and attack the day. Being chased for a crime that didn't fit the bill – it was manslaughter if it was anything and not murder – is always going to drag you down especially when I had everything. I had money, family and we all had our health and now this."

Timing is everything. As disappointed as the police were after the raid at the Noye family home, they were very optimistic about their tip-off from French aircraft controllers. A flight had been booked for John Palmer's Lear Jet to Paris. British police thought that Noye was onboard. The passenger manifest had five on board including two crew.

Nick Biddiss got the call in the morning that the plane was leaving St Petersburg, and he was under pressure to act because the information was that Kenny Noye was on board. His officers could not get to Paris in time and so Biddiss had to rely upon his long-established contacts with the French Border Police, which were standard for any senior officer in Kent well used to sharing operations on ferry and cross channel matters.

"There was a limit to what I could do this end, but the information was emphatic," Biddiss said. "A definite passenger of interest. We were told that if we pulled the plane, we would not be disappointed. We were tracking everyone close to

Noye, and Palmer was obviously his key contact and we, at this stage, believed that he was spirited out of England by Palmer. It was a good call to tug the plane."[38]

As the flight came to land at Le Bourget's Airport on the outskirts of the city, the French detectives supporting their Kent Police colleagues, were frothing with anticipation.

Biddiss was at the end of the phone waiting for news and ready to act if the news was good.

The officers were salivating. Noye was all over the newspapers. Glory was to descend upon the investigators if they got their man and every officer would celebrate the capture. The takedown was on and their informant had said that Noye would be found on board. As the plane landed, a 'platoon' of police cars and army jeeps made their way to the landing slot.

"It was overkill to say the least. I had said low key and they did the exact opposite. Clearly something was lost in translation," a frustrated Biddiss exhaled.

No-nonsense gendarmes rushed on board and slammed everyone including the pilots onto the floor and conducted a full search of personnel and the plane.

But the 'most wanted' cargo was not on board. The crew outwardly took the imposition in their stride, but Palmer was informed immediately about the raid. And so was Noye. It was clear to the crew who their target was because Noye was on previous flights. In fact Noye had taken pilot lessons in

---

38   W. Clarkson '*Killer on the Run*' and interview with Nick Biddiss, November 2022.

the past and had even been given the controls and flown it (under supervision), but on this occasion he was nowhere to be seen.

"I couldn't believe how rough the police were to the crew. And I found out about it nearly immediately from Palmer. They were late – about 21 days late," Noye recalled.

It is not clear on what grounds they could have taken Noye into custody given that he wasn't charged and there was no warrant for his arrest sanctioned but Biddiss believes that if Noye was on board he would have been arrested: "They could have held him on passport offences until we got our identification and extradition warrants sorted but it wasn't to be. We would have to wait another day."

While police were trying to take Noye down in Paris, the press were trying to take him down in Northern Cyprus. The *News of the World* journalist Ian Edmondson was on the ground knocking on the doors of the British based gangsters there including Brian Reader, Noye's old friend.

Back in Tenerife, Noye's exit from the island was being planned meticulously. Palmer had dispatched the so-called head of his security team to look after Noye's every need and to organise the next chapter in his life as a fugitive. Mohamad Derbah is a colourful character, who spectacularly decorates the Palmer and Noye narratives – a circle of storylines that is not lacking the eccentric, bizarre and exotic.

Derbah is now a successful businessman in Tenerife but had been investigated for nearly 20 years by Spanish authorities for money laundering over £7 million of timeshare profits in part with Palmer and other assorted individuals and criminal groups. He was first arrested in 2001 and remained under investigation on and off for nearly 15 years.

Previously, an investigative judge in Spain, Baltasar Garzon, impounded two 747 jetliners parked at Madrid's international airport belonging to a company run by Mohamed Derbah and an unidentified Russian. He was ultimately released without charge and then looked to have escaped all charges. He is no longer under investigation by the Spanish authorities at the time of publication. Make no mistake, though, Mohamad Derbah is a serious player, and he plays his hands at the top table of international intrigue.

He described Noye and Palmer as his family in a recent authorised biography. The Lebanese-born businessman, alone among Palmer and Noye, would stay out of jail and in the company he kept he could also count his lucky stars that he remained alive.[39]

In 1996 he was described as a 'Don Corleone' character, according to one investor who met him. Quietly spoken and ice cool – he was formidable, powerful and efficient with a particular eye for detail. He was the beating heart of Palmer's fraudulent timeshare operation and he helped orchestrate the timely departure of Noye out of harm's way. He met Palmer in Sierra Leone and Liberia in 1989, moved to Tenerife and never left. He and Palmer also forged murky connections in respect of trade, and all that glitters – gold and diamonds – were never too far from the conversation. He soon became the 'infamous' CEO of Palmer's hotel operations. Noye enjoyed his company.

---

39   Interview with Mohamed Derbah, December 2022.

"He was very quiet. He really liked me. Ken was just a man for business," Derbah said, recalling their bromance.

"Every time I went out there, Mo (as he calls him) always had a present for me. He was ever the gentleman," Noye explained.

The security executive as he styled himself, had swarthy good looks and surrounded himself by five or six immaculately dressed security operatives. He was a class apart from the sometimes petty and vindictive Palmer. So were Derbah's men.

While Palmer's personal enforcers, "would love nothing more than getting coked out of their heads and smashing some heads in before they went out for a night on the town, Derbah's men were impeccably polite and cooperative," Noye said.

Palmer's crew, led by Dennis New, were part of his escape plan but Noye had fallen out with New so badly during his time in Tenerife that New became a huge concern for him.

Noye said: "On a night out, I was told that Dennis New randomly smashed a straight punter in the face with a bottle. His crew joined in, and no one could believe it as the poor man was pulverised. I went to Derbah, and he had to hold me back from taking on New then and there. He took me onto John's [Palmer's] boat, the Brave Goose in the harbour and I said untie those ropes else I'll do something stupid. I knew then that Palmer's assistance, welcome as it was – like all good things could not last because the people around him could not be trusted."

Palmer also had a nasty and mean streak. He was cruel

sometimes but never to Noye: "In a deal he was straight up. I always thought if something passed me by, John would always catch it. He was shrewd but petty and vindictive. I was one of the few to be able to hold him to account."

One night, during his sojourn on the run at the four-star El Duque Hotel, Palmer was holding court. He and Ken were staying there in penthouse suites even though Palmer had two hotels of his own nearby. It was the height of elegance in 1996 – even if it's a little tired and worn today – but then as now, the pool lighting and open veranda dining experience made for an opulent evening.

Before entering, Derbah's men would go into the lift and scan the corridors and check the rooms for bugs and covert surveillance. In the dining room Palmer was chastising an architect for overcharging him on the refurb of some apartments. The architect was irate and in a fit of pique threw a 'Breitling' watch that Palmer had sold to him some months previously, screaming at him, "You're a fraud and this watch is a fucking knock-off, a fucking fake just like you" and stormed off.

Palmer had swindled him out of about £35k. Noye said: "I said to him, 'Why did you do that John?' He said, 'I just thought that he would never find out.' Then I realised that I was safe for now with John but if he is very comfortable cheating his friends then better watch out!"

Kenny Noye told Palmer face-to-face that he was abusing his power and it would catch up with him sooner or later.

The same night John's then 19-year-old German girl-friend, Ruby, who had been without a car while with Palmer in Tenerife, was promised transport in grand style by 'Gold-finger' – then worth hundreds of millions. With grand fanfare, the party came outside to see him present a gift to Ruby. It was a second-hand scooter. Humiliation was part of Palmer's currency and Noye was increasingly concerned[40] about Palmer's behaviour.

Derbah shared Noye's worries and was keen to get Noye off the island as quickly as possible. Derbah and his brother were later to fall out spectacularly with John Palmer who ordered a hit on their lives over the management of their timeshare investments. The local newspapers reported **'Timeshare barons fight it out on the streets'** as pistol shots rang out in Los Cristianos on November 10th 1998.

Two men on a motorbike bore down on a car driven by Derbah's brother Hussein Jamil, otherwise known as Sam, took aim and let off one shot. The assailants then doubled back and shot at Derbah again without leaving a mark. But gangland warfare had erupted in Tenerife and Dennis New and John Palmer were at the heart of it.

In July 1999, both brothers were attacked by six men in what Spanish police called a murder attempt. They survived. And ultimately, Derbah would succeed in triumphing over Palmer, his former boss and later rival.

But in 1996 while Noye laid low, Derbah and Palmer were in a different head space. Palmer was the boss and Derbah the loyal lieutenant. As ever Noye still sought out female company. He loved women and women loved him. When his blue eyes twinkled, he would turn on the charm. The

---

40   Interview with KN, November 2022.

night before he left the island, Noye was troubled, stressed and concerned. Returning from a last supper with Derbah and Palmer, he entered his plush bolthole. He heard some rustling in his bedroom. Was this the moment the authorities would nab their man? He nervously skirted the flat. He tentatively opened the door to the double bedroom. He was stunned at the sight. Naked on the mattress was a French Brigitte Bardot lookalike inviting him to bed. Normally, the highly sexed Noye would be more than happy to oblige but on this occasion he declined. The parting gift from Derbah was appreciated but declined.

Nothing like an Interpol alert to dampen your libido. Palmer had informed him that Interpol had issued an international 'blue warrant' for all law enforcement to pass on any sightings of Noye to British police and specifically "to collect additional information about a person's identity, location or activities in relation to a criminal investigation". Palmer naturally had heard the information from his contacts in the Spanish Policia Nacional. Across the planet wherever he ran, eyes would be on Noye. His photograph would now be at every border post and passport check. Although he had not been charged and was not technically on the run, he nonetheless had the unenviable glory of being on the World's Most Wanted list.

"Interpol was my friend until I realised that the moment I asked them to do anything I saw it in the newspapers the next day. It was a blunt instrument," Nick Biddiss said. "I learned to use it with extreme reluctance but at least there was a chance he might be spotted, and I would hear about it before he did."

Noye had options. Where would they expect him to go? And that was his guide on where to avoid. Many commentators still believe Noye headed to the Turkish Republic of Northern Cyprus where he was investing heavily in property and had strong connections with, among others, another fugitive from British justice called Azil Nadir. Some newspapers claimed he even played a couple of rounds of golf with Nadir.

"Apart from the occasional hit, I played little golf and in any case, never played with Azil and that's apart from the fact I never went to Northern Cyprus while on the run," Noye said.

The former chief executive of Polly Peck was facing 70 charges of fraud and false accounting related to the collapse of the group and lived there from 1993 until 2010 when he returned voluntarily to the UK to face charges which ultimately saw him receive a 10-year sentence.

Noye and Nadir were pals. Noye and his family were guests of Nadir, and they went diving on his boat off the coast after Noye and his sons completed PADI courses there. Such was their relationship that Noye trained in the gym with Nadir's bodyguards who were exclusively from the Turkish equivalent of the US Navy Seals.

***

Nadir, like Noye, had escaped by plane from the UK in a hastily arranged flight to France and then to Cyprus to avoid his 1993 trial for the collapse of his company. At the time it had £2 billion of debts of which close to £500 million, the *FT* reported, was siphoned off to companies and accounts in Northern Cyprus prior to the collapse.

The pair shared dinner together regularly at the 'Rita on

the Rocks' a renowned restaurant set in a private bay and a magnet for diplomats and military figures – including British military on weekend leave from across the border. This was a 'Checkpoint Charlie' rendezvous for spies and scoundrels and Noye had factored this in when deciding to swerve this inviting opportunity.

There was no extradition agreement between the UK and Northern Cyprus – but in truth while no one was ever extradited, the country often just declared them undesirable and required them to leave of their own accord. Nadir was a citizen and would be afforded the non-extradition courtesy but the same was unlikely for Noye. He would not take that chance. He refused to be that predictable. But he was thinking on his feet and every decision he made had consequences. Sliding Door moments confronted him at every turn.

Derbah was his guiding path on his next step into oblivion or as close to it as he could get. Building on their mutual contacts in Africa, Noye began to make plans to get to Morocco in the first instance. Derbah dropped Noye off at the Santa Cruz de Tenerife port and where he boarded as a walk-on passenger. Noye travelled incognito on another false passport on the ferry and while sad at leaving all of his past behind, he desperately hoped little of it would catch up with him anytime soon.

The destination was the so-called 'continent in miniature' – Gran Canaria. A cogent plan was unfolding carefully. His immediate destination was Gando Airport on the eastern part of the island and a crucial hub for travellers to West

Africa. He carried a small suitcase and about $5000 cash in multiple denominations. Alternative passports were en route by post to his next bolthole and more cash would be available upon arrival there too.

Wearing khaki trousers and a blue polo shirt he quietly boarded a flight to Casablanca which would be a transit point for his ultimate destination and next safe haven – the Ivory Coast.

5

THE FUNERAL

On July 29th, the funeral cortege had left the Cameron family home about an hour before the service. Stephen's father Ken and his elder son Michael led the mourners. In the close-knit community people lined the streets and paused for thought as the cortege passed by.

This was a community and for a moment, the country offered its shoulder to those suffering and the palpable grief was especially graphic and raw when Danielle Cable, Stephen's girlfriend of four years, spoke from the pulpit. It was hard to imagine the trauma of such a devastating event being foisted on the innocent face of such a young woman.

"I will miss Steve. We were going to get married – we were going to have children. We thought we were going to grow old together, but life has proved us wrong," the 17-year-old said after her dreams of a life together with the deceased, ebbed away in the gutter of an M25 slip road. "I wish he had stabbed me as well so we could be together," Danielle said.[41]

Hundreds joined close family and friends for the sad day. "God only takes the special ones and that's what Steve was... I close my eyes and picture his face, the sound, the

41   *The Herald*, 30th July 1996.

smell, the love. I will never forget him," Danielle went on to tell the congregation.

For Stephen's parents, it was simply unbearable. They sat silently throughout the service. A family friend sent their son off with some heartfelt words on their behalf.

"He was kind, generous, friendly, always ready with a smile. He had an appetite for life which was an inspiration to all those who met him, young and old. The memories will live on in our hearts and in all those who loved him."

The Church of England vicar spoke of purging evil from society. There was no mistaking who he had in mind. Not for him the Matthew's (18:10-14) parable of the lost sheep. Today, there would be no welcome back to the fold for Noye. He was to all and sundry present, the personification of iniquity and immorality. Two hundred well-wishers paid their respects as the *'Love is All Around'* track from the film *'Four Weddings and a Funeral'*, was played at Danielle's request.

The body was laid to rest at nearby St Paul's graveyard and the service was attended by the team pursuing Stephen's killer. Any murder detective will tell you that it is poignant days like these that propel them and keep them on track in the darkest and most hopeless of days. This was a desperate day.

At the scene of the stabbing, a short drive away, Danielle had left a floral tribute in homage to the memories that they could no longer make together. In the midst of heartfelt and immeasurable grief for one so young, her memorial note was one of gravity and everlasting torment: *"You're not here with me to give you a birthday kiss. But I send these roses as a token of my love for you. You will forever be in my heart, and I will love you always."*

It was an inconsolable loss that Ken Cameron said the family would take to their graves.

The funeral was delayed in case Noye's legal team wanted to challenge the state's autopsy. Because he was not in custody he could not do that but that would eventually come, further down the track as Nick Biddiss explained: "Normally, the defence has the option to get another autopsy done. At that stage there was no official defendant, so I asked the coroner to appoint an independent pathologist to fulfil that role so the funeral could go ahead." While Noye was in Tenerife with John Palmer, on July 4th, Dr Peter Jerreat conducted a fresh autopsy in Dartford Mortuary with Biddiss in attendance. Biddiss had attended many as a senior investigator. Jerreat disagreed with the original autopsy in respect of whether the knife went into the body up to the hilt – which is the handle of the knife. Dr Michael Heath, the original pathologist, said it had and Jerreat[42] said it had not. This was a precursor to a debate about the extent of the force applied. Heath had said 'severe' and Jerreat could not say that with certainty. These differences would be played out in a courtroom – if the offender was ever caught.

After the emotional service, Nick Biddiss said that he wished to speak to Noye to "eliminate him from their inquiries". It was in police speak as much as saying 'he is our man'. Previously, Kent Police had also asked for one 'Anthony Francis' to come forward to assist the police in the investigation. Noye

---

42   Trial transcript R v KN, March 30th-April 14th 2000.

and Mr. Francis were one and the same. It was the name the suspect Land Rover was registered in and a pseudonym that Noye regularly used to deflect attention from the authorities.

While Biddiss gave his press conference, other officers chaperoned Danielle Cable away from the press. She was at the centre of the media storm as the only reliable eyewitness to the perpetrator of the attack on her fiancé.

Aside from the witness testimony of Danielle, 12 weeks into the investigation and there was still only weak circumstantial evidence linking Noye to the crime. This was an investigation facing an uphill battle. Crucially, because Noye was not charged – and therefore not technically a fugitive – anyone assisting him could not be charged with aiding and abetting an offender. Anyone had free rein to assist Noye in any legal way and the police could not apply pressure in any respect. Normally, the police could impose moral and legal pressure on those close to the offender and underline the very real threat of jail in the event of someone being convicted.

From afar, Noye treated himself to a swim in the Gulf of Guinea and sucked in the cooling sea air, amidst the everlasting blue skies and palm trees. He lived as if he did not have a care in the world. Tomorrow, Noye would read a small sidebar snippet in an English daily available in the Ivory Coast. French speaking papers would likewise cover the story in brief with only the names of the victim and his own, comprehensible to Noye. He knew the script.

He had been here before, except that for DC John Fordham's funeral he was held at Her Majesty's pleasure. The soundtrack then was *Amazing Grace*' sung by the Metropolitan Police choir. On the public green in West Kingsdown a dignified memorial stone declares: *'Near here fell DC John Fordham 26th of January 1985'*. It was every bit as poignant as the bunch of roses left at the scene of Stephen Cameron's death by Danielle.

More than five thousand kilometres away, all Kenny Noye heard was the crashing of the waves and the rustle of wind through the beach umbrellas as he basked in the kiss of the African sun.

6

AFRICA CALLING

Before take-off, Kenny Noye breezed through Spanish passport control where officers took his passport without comment – stamped it and returned it. No one blinked an eye.

Casablanca then called – as it often does to those escaping from the jaws of justice. But he wasn't stopping there for more than a couple of hours. It was merely a pitstop.

On the plane Noye was breathing easy but not for long. As the Iberia Air flight was taking off there was a blaze of blue lights and sirens. The plane taxied to a halt on the runway. There was no facial recognition, but eyes were eyes and eagle-eyed detectives may have clocked the 'blue warranted' man on the Interpol watch list. Noye squeezed the arm rests in his seat. The steps were opened, and police officers boarded in a hurry. Determined and aggressive they headed towards Noye and then raced past him to take another passenger off the flight. There would be more close calls in the years to come. But for now, it was time for a drink and a little contemplation. Two hours later he entered the transit lounge in Casablanca Airport.

His itinerary was closely guarded. There's no TripAdvisor or AA hotel guide for those on the run. But near as dammit, he had access to its mid 90's equivalent. His ticket read Casablanca (CMN) to Brazzaville (BZV) Economy. He was stopping in the Ivory Coast.

On the flight he made small talk with a beautiful African woman beside him who tried to persuade him to continue to the Congo with her, but he declined. He had more pressing priorities. With high-powered friends in the Ivory Coast who could provide secure protection for him, the decision was made for him to stop at Abidjan, the capital of the Ivory Coast, the midway point of the plane's route and facing onto the North Atlantic Ocean. It was known as the 'Paris of Africa' and was an epicentre for fashion, music and culture but in 1996, its glory days were on the wane amid political and ethnic tensions, armed militias and a scramble for vast reserves of natural resources, which ultimately spawned two bloody civil wars.

Europe's 'most wanted' bypassed customs upon arrival but then nearly fell foul of a minor technicality. He didn't have a Yellow Fever vaccination certificate and refused to get the vaccine on site for a paltry $20. Why would someone in his position want to attract this attention? But Noye is a contrarian and wouldn't budge. Anyone else on the run would be happy to slip through unnoticed but it was a point of principle for Noye. He then took out a crisp $100 note. Without delay, a bogus vaccine cert was produced by the airport doctor. And another border was crossed effortlessly (nearly).

Other than swerving the vaccine, his arrival was uneventful. A driver was there with his fake name on a board waiting to pick him up. He was brought to a city centre hotel, the one arranged by Palmer's team.

There was no mistaking the building. It was the Hotel Ivoire, 100m high and for decades a magnet for the international business community in the region and a proud symbol of the country's independence in 1960. The 24-storey building was home to several swimming pools and even an ice rink, plenty of attractions that previously hosted luminaries such as Michael Jackson and Barry White, among others. But Noye went to his bed. Life on the run is not always a bed of roses, even when it comes with a five-star rating.

Noye slept straight through until the next evening. He came down for dinner. In the restaurant he caught the eye of a woman sitting alone at another table. He joined her. She was Egyptian. Straight to the point Noye invited her up to his room. "She warned me that I would never forget our encounter," he recalled. "I didn't. She was beautiful and charming. She wasn't on the game but at the end she asked me to pay her electricity bill. I said 'I don't pay for mine at home, but I'd be more than happy to sort out yours.'" It was a poignant reminder of the many people he would meet whose circumstances were significantly worse than his own – very privileged – life on the run, a point that completely bypassed him in the moment.

It was a strange introduction to the country for the former printer's apprentice. He had never been here before but he had connections and within days he would have to call those in quickly. He became very concerned that Palmer's inner circle might be about to betray him. Noye had brokered multi-million gold and diamond deals in the country and the trust was well earned over years of shared and lucrative profits plus, in his own words: "Here no one gave a fuck who I was or what I was up to." There was no pressure on him locally. His only concern was for those who helped get him there.

Noye took time out to phone Palmer in Tenerife and after the call he grew alarmed. It appeared that Dennis New had followed him on his journey to Morocco.

Their falling out did not result in a direct contretemps but there was a serious dispute bubbling. Would it shadow him on the run? Palmer suggested that Dennis New had some business in Casablanca. Noye wasn't so sure but didn't say. He kept his fears to himself, but he knew that he was vulnerable. It was time to cut the umbilical cord.

It was time to move. For now, he would simply transverse the city which meant it was time to call in a favour.

In his parlance, he was "owed a drink". It must have been a big one because Noye was then given secret sanctuary in a consular mission. He had travelled across Europe as if on a diplomatic passport and now he was living effectively as a consular attaché. While detectives had received information that he was in Casablanca and were searching expat gin joints, no one could have anticipated that of all the gin joints he was to be found in – the actual one – was under the protection of the Vienna Convention. Noye had made his new home in West Africa, beyond the Sahara, and beyond capture.

It would have simply seemed fantastical to the detectives

hunting him down if they were told that a little over five weeks after flying out of England on the day after Stephen Cameron died, this killer on the run was enjoying luxurious refuge in the Embassy quarter of Abidjan and on the grounds of a 'friendly' European embassy. Interpol's watch list held no sway there. Those UK police forces who thought that Noye would take the road 'most travelled on' would be decidedly disappointed.

Noye was addicted to sex and a good deal. In all else, he was unpredictable. There was no telling where he would turn up next.

7

THE SECRETS OF...

Shortly before Stephen Cameron's funeral, Detective John Donald, a serving policeman, was convicted and jailed for corruption in the Old Bailey for giving and offering to give information to protect the underworld in return for cash.

Judge Heather Steel in sentencing named Noye as one of the potential beneficiaries of this corrupt officer. The court knew that Noye was on the run, and a lead suspect in the Cameron murder inquiry. It was a bold statement from the bench and if it was intended to shock – it succeeded.

Donald admitted agreeing to take bribes to provide criminals with critical information about sensitive police undercover operations. On June 28th 1996, he was sentenced to 11 years in prison and tellingly pleaded guilty and avoided giving evidence. The court was told: "Noye is a dishonest, professional criminal. Dishonest and unscrupulous… he exercises a malevolent and baleful influence both from inside and outside of prison."[43]

No reporting restrictions were placed upon these specific comments which were devastating to Noye's reputation – if he

---

43   *The Independent,* 28th June 1996.

had any left worth protecting. The judge was entirely within her rights to say what she said of Noye as he had not been arrested or charged. Considering though, that he could have been days or hours away from arrest it was a seismic intervention.

It was a perfect storm for Noye. His life was being played out in the glare of the national papers and every day, story after story multiplied his legal jeopardy. His world was like a black hole which sucked in scandal after scandal and touched on nearly every major crime over the last 50 years, but which at its heart was apparently the rotten spectre of bent coppers in the Metropolitan Police.

He had greased the palms of plenty of coppers, but had he paid the scruffy and disorganised John Donald to get access to the secrets of the Metropolitan Police?

It was in September 1993 when *BBC*'s *Panorama*[44] broadcast a report on Detective Donald who had been secretly filmed demanding money from a London drug dealer who was facing trial and who had been arrested by him. It was a naked extortion attempt by Donald and even more brazen of the arrested man – the 'collar' – to contact the *BBC* and try and hold the detective to account.

Donald was reckless in his actions. Brazen. Other officers were corrupt, but few were as outrageous as the 5ft 9in, 14st scruffy Surbiton officer – which is why he was caught and convicted, while so many of his like-minded officers got away with it.

It is hard to imagine the impact of the allegations regarding

---

44   Gillard and Flynn (2004): Page 71, *The Untouchables*

Donald's corruption on Noye at this very time. Scotland Yard was passed the Panorama files and it suggested an explicit corrupt relationship between Donald and a drug dealer he had arrested and then apparently turned as a registered informant.

In their classic bible on police corruption, *'The Untouchables'* 2004, Mike Gillard and Laurie Flynn write that, *'Under the cover of the informant-handler relationship (Kevin) Cressey corruptly paid Donald for bail and for information to be passed to Noye,'* who was in prison at the time.

Donald had asked for £30,000 to arrange for the charges against Cressey for possession of 50kg of cannabis, to go away.[45] Undoubtedly, Donald was guilty of corruption, but Noye, who does not deny he corrupted some officers, was at pains to say that the claims that he was in receipt of files from Detective John Donald were fictional.

"Cressey was clearly using me as some kind of collateral to get a reduced sentence and curry favour," Noye said. "He was gilding the lily and trying to implicate me. It was a set-up, pure and simple."

Kenny Noye was in Latchmere House open prison in Ham, near Richmond upon Thames, finishing the end of his 14-year sentence for handling and laundering the Brink's-Mat gold in early 1993.

The 200-man prison allowed inmates out for local employment and training Monday to Friday. The prison, now closed, was used as a MI5 interrogation centre during World War Two for Nazis outside of the glare of the Red Cross

---

45   Page 532, ibid

and the Geneva Convention. When Noye was there it was a cherished category 'D' prison and the prison officers ran a loose regime affording chancers like Noye every opportunity to take advantage of the system.

Noye was out on day release and had bogus arrangements for apparent work experience but spent most of his days in Dartford attending the local Temple Hill gym and then attending his wife's nearby racquet and social club. It was there where an associate of Cressey passed on a message of apparent critical importance.

Kenny Noye recalls: "I was sitting in the middle of a squash court at my wife's squash club. I'd just come from the gym and a contact of Kevin Cressey's said that Donald had some information that would be of real value to me, and it would cost five thousand pounds I told him to fuck right off. I could smell a stitch up when I see one. I know the way it works. I'd been dealing with coppers since the 70s. I wasn't going to let Cressey hang me out to dry to get a lesser sentence. I wouldn't be his sacrificial lamb."

Shortly after, in advance of Detective Donald's trial and Stephen Cameron's death, Noye was out with his family at a Chinese restaurant in West Malling, Kent when Cressey walked in with his then girlfriend and sat down. Noye caught his eye. Cressey spotted Noye. Cressey was rooted to his seat with few face-saving options available.

Noye said: "I went over to him and said: 'You fuck off right now and never come back. I know exactly what you were up to,' I told him. He just nodded and left. I haven't seen him since."

Perhaps, sometimes even a story about corruption is just too good to be true. Maybe Noye – who regularly paid coppers – did not pay off Donald. In any event it is indisputable that Donald was corrupt and that Noye paid off police officers. But it is also of note that Noye was never interviewed by officers who went on to charge and convict Donald.

One might think that they would have done so if there was real merit to it. However you interpret this maelstrom, it is undoubtedly a window into the malevolent world of distrust within the police. Who can you believe? The officer who has asked for a £30k bribe? The confidential police informer with 50kg of cannabis or Noye; a man who has not disowned his connections to several corrupt police officers (without directly incriminating himself).

The crux of the Donald trial, however, was clear. If the police had any doubt about the enormity of the task they faced bringing Noye to justice – they knew now.

Noye was under no illusions either about his prospects – certainly not after Judge Heather Steel's words…

"I was fucked," Noye said. "What chance did I have when this was being said at the most important criminal court in the land? Any villain just wants a fair trial a chance to make his point, but the starting point here was that the press and the police decided I was guilty of murder – what happened to presumed innocent? – that is not the way the justice system is supposed to work."

Ironically, the very public and devastating claims from the Old Bailey that Noye paid Donald through intermediaries for access to sensitive Scotland Yard files could, in the fullness of time, have been his one-way ticket to freedom. It was a latent legal opportunity to allege that this publicity made a fair trial impossible, if it came to that. But Noye knew that with the Donald trial still reverberating in the UK his chance of a deal with the authorities for a manslaughter charge was diminishing. He had to let the story run out of steam before he could contemplate returning home.

His current liberty could be curtailed at any time and so he set about extending it for now. He would enjoy life for as long as he could. It was time for another night out in the Ivory Coast.

8

OUR MAN ABROAD

Consular Life for the fugitive abroad was more 'French than French', as was often said of the life of diplomats in the former French colonies. Noye enjoyed the epitome of the colonial experience with a French twist in an embassy where the lingua Franca was not French.

The life was to his liking but not always the food. Although well-travelled, his appetites were never too far from home. His 'first world' troubles multiplied as bacon — which he loved — was off the menu as swine flu swept the country. Despite this, Noye would undoubtedly manage.

Silver service at mealtimes was standard and the food, while excellent, was often too 'French' for Noye who eschewed such cuisine unless it was his favourite steak and frites. Noye was living in a compound with a small contingent of embassy staff in an apartment on site. All domestic duties, laundry and food was catered for. Security guards manned the gates and it was never recommended to leave unless accompanied by an embassy driver with diplomatic plates.

Under the protective umbrella of one of the senior diplomats, Noye had access to all the consular privileges and travelled the city and its environs with diplomatic protection for the most part. His access could only have derived from his established heritage in the gold and diamond markets, both of which had stakeholders in the Ivory Coast. Noye had heritage here and his contacts ran deep enough to luck into the most unlikely bolthole.

He said: "I hated anyone knowing where I was going. Palmer and his crew knew my route and so I had to break that connection. For all they would know I had disappeared. I left the hotel he and Derbah had arranged for me without notice. John (Palmer) knew I had friends across the continent and would make my own way without him. The embassy would be the last place anyone would go looking for me."

Indisputably he was correct. Back in the UK, the police were fielding hundreds of sightings from well-meaning callers prompting an extraordinary deployment of resources to no effect. A frustrated Nick Biddiss found the situation nearly impossible. Every tip had to be investigated because you never knew – it just might be the one.

As local embassy staff served six course meals as standard to Noye and the other diplomats he dined with, none could have imagined that he was a man on the run let alone one of the most wanted men on the planet.

"I fitted right in," Noye remembers. "Only one person knew who I was and of course he wasn't saying. Everyone else just thought that I was a 'connected' person being looked after. Maybe they thought I was a spy or some rogue operator lying low but what was remarkable was they asked so few questions. So, I gave very few answers."

After the evening meal Noye often skirted the company at consular events. When asked what he did at these gatherings he usually claimed to be a South African businessman.

"Occasionally, I would say that I worked in the plastic mouldings' industry," Noye said. "That would usually stop this line of conversation and they'd move on. It is important to be invisible, even boring in these times. Of course, if they worked in that industry I was fucked."

It was a claustrophobic existence as the tiny circle of diplomats entertained each other at their own events and particularly on their respective national holidays, and despite an invite to the US embassy for their July 4th celebrations, Noye remained where he was in the compound, protected by armed guards.

Bored and antsy, he persuaded the security staff to arrange a local driver to go to the glorious and renowned Grand Bassam beach about 35 miles away. He was delighted to escape the confines of the secure enclave that would eventually be his home for nearly two months.

His chauffeur wasn't a designated driver. He was a brother of one of the security guards and the inside of the maroon Peugeot 405 was drowned in a fog of smoke from the driver's Dunhill cigarettes. It was in the middle of the hot and dry season and today it scorched and rained in equal measure. Noye sat in the back of the car and watched the cosmopolitan city recede into the rear-view mirror as the verdant tropical landscape flew by. He had been cautioned against the unauthorised departure, but Noye disregarded the advice. The driver spoke only French and Noye could only understand just a few words. As they headed to the coast, the driver pointed to various scenic pitstops and roadside restaurants, but his passenger was more determined to make it to the beach to top up his Tenerife tan and the bleach blond hair on his forearms.

Noye sipped on his can of Coke and as his eyes wandered across the terrain, he caught some billows of smoke. His car turned the corner and across the road was a roadblock of smouldering tyres and a burnt-out car. As his driver tried to comprehend the situation, a platoon of 15 heavily armed men in a mix of civilian and khaki dress came out of the roadside ditches and verges. The unmistakable message was, 'Stop or you'll be shot'.

"Très dangereux," the driver whispered as the brakes came.

Of all the ends that were likely to meet Noye; death in a remote checkpoint in the sub-Sahara at the hands of an armed militia in one of the poorest countries in Africa was not one of them. Not a man to normally lose his nerve under pressure, this was considerably out of his comfort zone. The driver was dragged-out of the car. He took a slap on the head with the butt of a gun. The boss demanded to see his chauffeur credentials and driving licence. It was a standard ruse. The driver was buckling under the fear.

Noye said: "I could see this could get out of hand, so I stepped out of the car with my hands up. In broken French I explained that he wasn't a chauffeur, but a friend and we were in a hurry. The leader asked why I sat in the back? and I said that we dropped off a friend back up the road. I was losing the argument until I took a thick roll of dollars wrapped by elastic band. On the outside was a hundred dollar note and inside that, all the notes were all ten-dollar bills, but it looked like it was about $5000. It wasn't. When he let us back into the car and on our way, I said to the driver: 'Best not come back this way, there may be some very disappointed gunmen looking for us.'"

Meanwhile, Kent Police were receiving up to 30 sightings a day of Noye around the UK and abroad into their Maidstone headquarters. One captured their attention that was reported in one of the red tops. A credible source apparently said that Noye had flown into the UK on one occasion to go to one of his favourite restaurants 'China Gardens' in West Kingsdown, Kent.[46]

Biddiss said: "What was I to do? I sent two officers down there and it was frankly a load of rubbish. But we really had no choice but to follow up particularly on those leads that turned up in the papers. Sometimes you can have simply too many leads."

Consternation unfolded as it appeared Noye was putting two fingers up to the UK police. It was audacious and bold and just the kind of thing people thought Noye was capable of.

The quick dash to England for a take-out was, however, untrue. Was this a legitimate tip delivered in all good faith or was it an orchestrated decoy to keep the police off the scent? "We were pouring loads of resources into this," Biddiss

---

46   Steven Wright, *Daily Mail* podcast – interview Henry Milner
https://www.listennotes.com/top-podcasts/kenneth-noye/

explained. "But some of the news agencies and news desks were spending thousands and thousands of pounds. They had access to millions of readers and so when tips filtered through from the news desks, we were under pressure to follow up. There was always the chance that a newspaper could find him before us which would have been embarrassing but I wouldn't have cared less."

Typically, the papers would have a huge splash on the manhunt and ask those with information to call the police incident room number but not before – in much bigger font – they gave their own contact details. The message was, 'Please call the police – BUT CALL US FIRST!'

In the Ivory Coast, Noye was now a familiar figure around the embassy grounds. He had nearly taken a lease in the consular living quarters. There were occasional random threats to his freedom and when the international papers arrived in the late afternoon, a day late, he would scan them just grateful that diplomatic missions did not purchase the red tops. It was strictly international papers of record, *The New York Times, The Washington Post, The Times* and the like.

There were early morning swims, a game or two of tennis and a bit of chess which he learned while in prison on the Brink's-Mat job. He obviously had built an incredible amount of goodwill with his diplomatic benefactor. Noye's gold trading – his commodity of choice – was the bedrock of the extraordinary goodwill and good living he was enjoying at some taxpayers' expense. One day, Noye was travelling outside of Abidjan with his protector. The car carried the distinctive diplomatic plates affording the passenger clear passage around the country with complete immunity from prosecution or arrest. It was a universe away from the transport awaiting him in the UK. The plates are black numbers on orange plates with a two-letter designation of the status of the passengers. In this case the letters were CD, for 'Corps Diplomatique'.

He effectively had the freedom of the country, and he was relishing it because he had free food and free board and transport. On their drive to the outskirts of the city, the pair called by a small market square and stopped to have a coffee outside. By invitation, they entered a warehouse with rolls and rolls of silk.

"I remember thinking who could pay for this stock," Noye remembers. "It was completely out of place – just like me I suppose. It was worth hundreds of thousands of dollars. The traders were Lebanese. How could they afford this? Then a couple of long silk rolls were moved revealing a garage door which then opened. I was utterly shocked by what I saw. It was an Aladdin's cave of rocket launchers, sub machine guns, shoulder launched missiles and every array of pistols, RPGs, anti-tank weapons and handguns. No one passed any remarks."

Noye wasn't there for guns, but it was an insight into the instability of the region and the games and maybe dangerous ones that his powerful friend was playing, as if protecting Public Enemy No.1 was not reckless enough.

On the way back to the city, they drove past a wonderful seaside village. The houses were postcard perfect. Thatched roofs, palm trees, stunning houses – a whole village which was deserted. His first thought was, 'I could do a deal here' before, Noye said, "I asked around and then I saw the bullet holes. It was attacked with grenades the previous week. What a tragedy? What a waste? It would be worth a fortune anywhere else."

As much as he was contemplating the human cost of the attack, a little part of him was grieving at the loss of a great development opportunity. Despite the police hunt, the lure of the deal could always draw him in. It may be his undoing.

Noye knew this was as close to paradise as you could get while being on the run but he also understood that it couldn't last.

The sounds of bullets on successive nights were encroaching on Noye's sleeping quarters in the embassy. A bubbling civil war is a good place to seek refuge, but it has its risks. Despite his gold trading connections in the turbulent African country and the diplomatic plates outside the consular grounds, he knew that life was more important than liberty. He could have both but maybe not if he stayed. His freedom depended upon being fast on his feet. Standing still was not an option. Besides, history moves very fast in this part of the world and Noye didn't want to get caught up in it.

He had gotten a head start on the police but every effort, the latest technology, the security agencies, and the best human intelligence was being used to track him down. He had his own counter-manoeuvres, but it was now time to find his next international bolthole.

He raced down to the local Air France office and booked a direct flight. The city was tense. Noye was wasting no time.

On the way back with ticket in hand he met some expat oil rig workers who were also making tracks out of the country. Their pockets were packed with uncut diamonds. The three men – an Australian, an Irishman and a German – were dressed for shore leave and keen to have some fun, splash the cash, get some girls and make some money with likely 'blood' diamonds on the side. Noye thought about going back into business but decided against it. "I considered it," he said. "But there was gunfire nearby. You could be easily robbed and be taken out, it was just too volatile for me. Besides, I couldn't check their quality." Another time perhaps, outside the earshot of small arms fire.

He packed his bags and arranged transport to the airport for a night-time flight. Paris was the stated destination. It made sense. The ex-colony was a favourite destination for the French and there were daily flights to Paris. The original thought was to geographically keep moving away from the UK. He had considered South Africa, but while in the embassy he made a connection. A visiting French business-man who was completely unaware of his background had by chance an apartment in Paris and would not be returning for two months. He was a 'Pied-Noir'. A person of French extraction but born in Algeria and forced into 'exile' back to France after independence in 1962. The man in his early sixties had lived a colourful life and was euphemistically in the 'import/export' game. Clearly, he and Noye had a meeting of minds and undoubtedly, he figured that they could be of mutual assistance to each other in the future. This was how Noye operated, whether fleeing from justice or not. He would carefully cultivate contacts and call-in favours as and when. Now someone else was working him in the same manner.

He didn't know how long he would need the apartment. Needs must and needs change but he was very grateful, nonetheless. Noye no longer would call upon Palmer and his contacts. Now he was on his own. He was living on his wits. This is where he prospered. Thinking on his feet. It was an opportunity too good to pass up. Noye offered to pay rent, but the affable businessman refused. Sometimes a deal can be too good to be wrong.

But waiting in Paris was a pressing problem. Europe's most wanted man was fleeing bullets in the Ivory Coast and walking into one of the most heavily policed airports in the world. Interpol had a satellite office at Charles de Gaulle Airport and Noye's photo occupied the offices of customs and passport staff at all international borders. It was close to home. The risks would multiply. Could Noye, armed with only a goatee and glasses to distract, enter France unhindered and make Paris his new home?

9

PARIS

'Goldfinger'– John Palmer – was as flash as you might expect. Travelling on Concorde[47] from Barbados to Heathrow was hardly the low-key return to England for someone who had recently helped spirit Noye out of the country and was instrumental in keeping him out of reach of the law.

He was a showman and most memorably taunted the UK authorities when he gave news interviews to the BBC's Kate Adie while a wanted man, living in Spain, which did not have an extradition arrangement with Britain. Then, the clean-shaven, dark-haired Palmer, with his wife, Marnie by his side – and while their baby bounced on his knee, brazenly fielded questions like the professional conman that he was. It was a performance of extraordinary bravado.

"I am completely innocent of this so-called Mat Brinks [*sic*] bullion raid. I know nothing of it," he told the reporter.

With equal bravado in front of a jury, and not a little jury tampering, Palmer was ultimately acquitted of the Brink's-Mat charge much to the chagrin of the authorities. This day,

---

47   Marnie Palmer (2018): Page 137, *Goldfinger and Me: Bullets, Bullion and Betrayal*

the 'lovable rogue' – a successful 'Del Boy' – was travelling in First Class style and wanted everyone to know it.

Noye too, was on the move.

It was economy on Air France from Abidjan to Charles de Gaulle International Airport in Paris. The whiff of cordite from the civil unrest in the Ivory Coast precipitated his swift departure. He had a window seat. As serendipity would have it, another embassy official was on the same flight. Who better to assist you through immigration in Paris than an accredited diplomat in pristine business attire and with impeccable French? This was a piece of luck too good to pass up and, ever the opportunist, Noye took full advantage. When the fugitive said he was pleased to see the diplomat – he really, really was.

There was no special immigration lane for fugitives but in the company of his diplomatic friend he was waved through unhindered. Meanwhile, his photo ID remained on the notice boards of both the Interpol and immigration offices at the airport. He would never pass through the facility again. For the moment he was making his travel plans on the fly and for the moment the luck was running with him – but for how long?

The word was out that Palmer had assisted Noye and now the police were targeting 'Goldfinger'. There were two major police[48] operations tracking Noye and Palmer. One was still targeting the gold and the other was engaged with the manhunt for Noye and the Cameron killing. Heathrow Airport police observed Concorde landing, staring at the

---

48   Interview with Det. Supt. Ian Brown, July 2022.

grandeur of the plane and praying for a breakthrough. Around the perimeter, plane spotters tracked the landing of the iconic plane while airport police observed from air traffic control. Palmer's increasingly erratic behaviour at this time was driven by a two gram a day cocaine habit. In spite of having his own private jet and mostly his own private immigration channel, he never carried drugs on his person. This time was no exception.

Palmer and his wife Marnie, with their two small children, descended from the plane. While in the customs hall, awaiting baggage, with their youngest girl in Marnie's arms, armed police officers asked John to step aside and promptly arrested him. Marnie and the children got their suitcases and hurriedly dashed off home onto the M25 and then M40.

It was a smart plan. Track Palmer and find Noye. It made perfect sense to track Noye through Palmer and reveal the backdrop and detail of the Brink's-Mat raid and their involvement in it. Maybe they'd capture the gold and the fugitive in one fell swoop – or maybe not!

John Palmer wasn't bothered with the 'pull' by the police. He had talked himself out of far worse. As far as Marnie was concerned, and even to this day, she claims her husband had never met Noye.[49] At least that's what he told her and told the police. As she drove the children home in their Land Rover, Marnie was bemused as she was passed by a convoy of three police cars with her husband John in the back. He cheerfully waved from the backseat in between two officers,

---

49   *Goldfinger and Me: Bullets, Bullion and Betrayal*

entertaining the children in passing. "He clearly found the whole thing hilarious," she said.[50]

Marnie and her late husband John had a volatile relationship. After his death she disclosed that he had played Russian roulette with her − holding a gun to her head and pulling the trigger. The barrel, by way of mitigation, was empty.

Her divorce petition would call John, 'Unpredictable, volatile and frightening' − but at this stage in their marriage, his vast wealth and their gilded lifestyle was papering over the cracks. Those fissures were all too visible when Mrs Palmer − pretty, blond and tanned − arrived home and found her house ransacked by police officers. "John has been a naughty boy," one officer told her.[51]

She wondered if he had carried cocaine on his person, something he never usually did and Noye himself was surprised by the cocaine revelations.

"I honestly never saw him do a line," he said. "Never. He was always very sharp in business and yes, he was volatile, but I never put that down to coke. If he did it, he did it well away from his business partners."

Marnie holds a special place in her heart for the 'young John Palmer' − the one who wasn't on cocaine binges and the man she fell in love with. He increasingly became cruel and dysfunctional and treated Marnie badly in the aftermath of their divorce but, nonetheless, Marnie can separate the man from his drug habit.[52]

---

50   *Ibid*
51   *Ibid*
52   *Ibid*

The police weren't looking for drugs but were still searching for evidence of the Brink's-Mat gold and most importantly trying to get leads on where Noye was. While in custody at the Bridewell Police Station in Bristol, Palmer denied all knowledge of Noye. At least thrice. As Marnie, testifies, "Yes he could be violent, ruthless, paranoid and cruel... a womaniser and drug abuser" – but he was no grass.[53]

In a late-night Parisian bar in the company of some random American tourist, Noye sunk a cold beer. If he knew what Palmer had done in his name, he would have raised a glass in his honour. Was John looking after his own interests or Ken's? Maybe both of theirs. Either way Noye would not be calling him anytime soon. The die was cast in respect of his reliance on their relationship. He was flying solo from here on in.

---

53   *Ibid*

10

THE INVISIBLE MAN

The 7th arrondissement in Paris had a new resident. The district was the most sought-after real estate in the city and home to the Eiffel Tower. It was another luxurious bolthole in Noye's race from justice. This was his 10th temporary abode since he departed from the UK on May 20th 1996 less than 24 hours after Stephen Cameron died. His new home was typically Parisian. It was three floors up and compact. It was bigger than a pied d'terre and not quite large enough for a 'nuclear family' but more than sufficient for the solo occupant.

He was alone. Would there be an end to this isolation? Every moment felt like a void. Nothing was tangible. Every morning was a struggle and as a depression descended upon Noye, he did his best to break through.

He said: "I felt like an invisible man. Paris was a city where I had done little business. It never grew on me before and on the run, as the pressures increased, the city still didn't endear itself to me. Maybe I was suffering because I really missed my family, but I really thought that after a couple of months on the run, a deal for manslaughter would have materialised but it wasn't to be. It was getting me down."

Noye was now facing the realisation that being on the run was going to be a semi-permanent state unless of course, Kent Police and the UK authorities pulled off a major coup and tracked him down.

The police were hoping that Noye was operating in an information vacuum – he was not. They, on the other hand, were suffering from data overload. The police continued to be swamped with well-meaning calls from the public across the world, as well as erroneous and excitable rumours from their informer network. At the best of times, it was difficult for law enforcement to separate the wheat from the chaff but when your adversary is Kenny Noye, it was nearly an impossible job. Noye was hardly the Scarlet Pimpernel but he was proving equally elusive.

He sat alone in the Parisian apartment and ventured out for bread and cheese. The morning walk refreshed him. But Paris in August was too hot for the natives who fled to the countryside or abroad and he kept his walkabout to the early mornings or late nights.

He recalls: "I tried to think as a copper. What would I do to catch me? The first thing I would have done is charge me with a minor offence such as dangerous driving or fleeing the scene of a car crime and then issue a warrant for my arrest. It would be just enough to make sure that anyone who was helping me could be nailed for giving assistance to a criminal. If they did that then they could nail my family and friends and pull them in. That is where it would really hurt me!"

He ran a very successful, mostly legal haulage business from 1970 to the mid-eighties and he was au fait with transport routes across the continent. The Met and Kent Police may not have taken this into account. In the 80s and 90s, people kept phone numbers on pieces of paper or in their heads. Noye has a near photographic memory for figures and could tap up key contacts without having to involve anyone else who might turn him in.

For now, though, he needed to top up his readies. Reserves were running low. He had cut up the credit card Palmer had given him to avoid detection and was now close to running empty. It wasn't like the old days when if you were running short you could just print your own. Before he became a businessman and 'villain', he was a plate maker in the print industry.

"I left school at 15," Noye said. "I'd done a five-year apprenticeship, with indentures, the proper, proper old-fashioned apprenticeship, I'd done that in Fleet Street, Shoe Lane and went to London College of Printing in Elephant and Castle and I can tell you we were trained how to spot a counterfeit and also we had the skill to make counterfeit money as much as anything else." Obviously the College didn't appreciate this or know anything about it.

Noye made chump change on the side knocking off fake driving licences, truck permits, insurance certificates and a favourite – luncheon vouchers. They were the much-envied perk for employees of small businesses who did not have an in-house canteen. The distinctive green and white LV sticker could be used across the high street and in cafes up and down the country. Most fondly he remembers creating a Cambridge degree for one old friend. Singularly on the back of the perfect copy, the recipient got a 30 percent pay rise, a promotion, and a company car – a brown Rover from his employer. His friend went on to have a very successful career in business and eventually ran some Burlesque clubs, amongst other enterprises.

And then there were the fivers. The expert printer is not admitting to printing fivers and selling them for a pound each but that was the rumour, and it would be a startling surprise, if with his access to the finest Heidelberg presses and his skillset and mindset, that he didn't do it.

"I couldn't help operating in the grey area. If an opportunity presented itself, then I would adapt," Noye said.

Noye would soon have to consider doing deals on the road if he was to guarantee he had the funds stay one step ahead of the law. It wasn't just swerving the attention of the police it was trying to avoid in some instances his old Kent neighbours.

On one aimless walk near Place de la Concorde, he was convinced that he glimpsed Formula One boss Bernie Ecclestone entering a restaurant and considered saying hello but decided against it. He didn't want to make Bernie feel uncomfortable. Bernie was a Kent boy through and through and he was part of the entrepreneurial set from Bexleyheath. They knew each other personally but never did any business together. Ecclestone's first business was a spare parts enterprise and motorcycle dealership known as 'Compton & Ecclestone' which was beside the 'Mabel's Nightclub' which Noye bought.

Noye recalls: "I met him in 1967. I was about 21 and he was about twenty years older. He was a very impressive man.

I got planning permission to turn the nightclub into offices and then sold it to a pension fund. We never did business together, but he could turn a deal that man."[54]

Ecclestone would never have blanked Ken if he had clocked him on the run or otherwise. In any event, Noye crossed to the other side of the road and kept on walking without giving so much as a glance back in Bernie's direction.

There was danger lurking literally at every corner. How was he going to survive, if his neighbours were bumping into him in Paris of all places? It was time to make a call. But not to friends or family. Once again, he asked himself where the police would think he would bunker down and then avoid that location with a passion. He knew all his close friends and associates would have their phones bugged. It stood to reason. Noye was a home bird and it would make perfect sense to track his close friends and family and anticipate that at some stage, someone would get a little sloppy and give them a clue to his whereabouts.

There was one safe number – a burner – he could phone and he knew that assistance and not inconsiderable wisdom would be forthcoming at the other end. The man, Michael Lawson, in question was his 'Co-D' or co-defendant in the Brink's-Mat handling and laundering trial. Lawson was acquitted of the charges but made an out of court settlement with the loss adjusters acting for the Brink's-Mat insurers.

Lawson was one of Noye's best friends and the authorities knew that it was likely that he would be contacted and put measures in place in anticipation. They were ready. Lawson's

---

54   Phone interview with KN, November 2022.

burner rang. He too anticipated the call. The secret phone logs from NCIS would not show any telephone activity at this time. Lawson's burner was kept for this singular purpose and the arrangements had been made on the night before Noye departed the UK.

The conversation was short and to the point, "Call Mr Coffee and he'll take you to where you need to be". The enigmatic conversation was fully understood by both parties but anyone eavesdropping would have been none the wiser.

As it happens no one was listening.

The next day Kenny Noye bought himself a smart suit at a tailors near his Parisian apartment. Double-breasted and pin-striped. Sharp. Added to his new look was a brown leather briefcase. Wearing glasses with clear lenses, he looked every bit the businessman heading towards the Metro for a morning commute. This morning Lille was the transit point. Two hundred kilometres and just over an hour from Paris by train, Noye was on the next leg of his global adventure. It was a more rugged and precarious adventure than he would wish but he was always happy to be on the road (or tracks) again. For him it was basic physics. A moving target is much harder to hit.

Outside of Lille train station, Mr Coffee was waiting for him. Plans were afoot. But where would Noye be taken? Not even Noye knew. At the start of his escape, his family, Palmer and his coterie were au fait with some of his travel arrangements. Now even Noye was in the dark. In that respect, he and Nick Biddiss were on the same footing.

11

THE COURIER

The courier was a large lump of a man with a sweet tooth.

The package was a depressed English man on the road to nowhere. Outside Lille station, Noye's driver was sampling a baguette and puffing on a cigarette in alternate gulps. The courier and the package had never met before. Mr Coffee never drank the stuff. He did however, run a coffee shop in Amsterdam selling cannabis, or puff as Noye would call it. That was the destination. Mickey Lawson had arranged for Ken to be brought to the Dutch capital. Noye was nervous and scared. This was the heart of Europe and in Africa he may not have been safe from civil war, but he at least was safe from capture and from Interpol, for now. Lawson had strong connections to Amsterdam and got Noye a rent-free safe house in the heart of the city. Lawson some years later would run a multimillion cannabis route from Amsterdam to the UK. For now, he was only smuggling his good friend 'Ken' across the continent and out of harm's way.

The Volkswagen Polo was suitably low key, but the car was decidedly too small for the driver who squeezed his ample mid-drift between the seat and the steering wheel. Mr Coffee never gave his name and despite his excellent English, did not allow his conversation to stray too far from his mother or food – sometimes both.

"If it wasn't about his mother's cooking it was about the boxes of sweets he was going to buy for her at a special chocolatier on the French/Belgian border," Noye said. "You can't choose your company at times like these. I felt like I was sitting beside the singing nun in '*Airplane!*'"

In the smoke-filled headquarters of the incident room at Maidstone Police headquarters, Nick Biddiss got another ping on his pager. All his officers had pagers because Biddiss had taken away their mobile phones because the bills were too high. Nick personally paid for his own phone and wouldn't be without one. He had a message to contact Ken Cameron, Stephen's father for an update.

Biddiss said: "These are the most difficult of times. I just say call me anytime day or night and my door is always open. We are here for them and although there are specialist family liaison officers, the victim's nearest and dearest have got to look you in the eye and know you are doing your best. It was another week gone by and I can't tell you how frustrating it was to go to them and tell them that we were none the wiser nearly four months into the case. I woke up everyday wishing I could tell them something different."

His target was driving from Lille to the Belgium border. Noye was not himself. There wasn't a deal in his head. Gone was the snap, crackle and pop of his entrepreneurial flare. He was spinning in a void. Everyone at home was being followed, tracked and bugged and the prospect of life in prison dragged him into the darkest cloud he's ever fallen under.

"To be honest I was down," he said. "There were only strangers on the horizon and in my wake was a disaster. There was a dead man. His (Stephen Cameron's) family's life was ruined. My family's life was ruined. I was fucked. It would be easier if I just disappeared off the face of the earth – permanently. And most people now wanted that. Anyone in prison for nearly a decade knows how to solve that problem quickly."

For Toni and Stephen Cameron this was a wish they would happily visit upon him. And who could blame them, Noye thought. "They lost their son," he added. "Their mind's not for changing. I'd think the same in their position. Maybe I'd do them a favour."

Mr Coffee was oblivious to who his passenger was or what he had done or what battles were playing out in his head. Mr Coffee had chocolate on his mind. While on the road to Ghent in Belgium, he informed his passenger that he was taking a slight detour to a specialist confectionery store to buy a present for his mother. After he returned to the car from the shop, which was unhelpfully close to the local police station, he placed two large boxes of treats in the back of the car.

Kenny Noye recalls: "Jesus, I thought, they'll never survive the next three hours. It will be a massacre. I wasn't wrong. Of course, he offered me one and then kept snaffling them. I'd spent ten years locked up at Her Majesty's pleasure and here I was in this prison which was worse than anything I'd endured."

It did not get any better as the motorway signs announced

'Antwerpen'. Mr Coffee went through a menu of his favourite soups, sandwiches and even what to do with Christmas leftovers. By the time the small car entered the Netherlands, Noye decided to feign sleep to avoid the interaction with his driver.

Unbeknownst to 'Mr Coffee' he knew the port of Antwerp (Antwerpen) very well indeed. He fondly remembered it as 'the pot of gold at the end of his rainbow'. It was here where he shipped gold bullion before smuggling it into the UK and then sold it at a discount, without VAT, pulling in a guaranteed profit. It was a reliable VAT fraud. The old bank robbers of the 60s and 70s upskilled into white collar crime because armed robberies got 18-year jail sentences and the max for VAT fraud at the time was two years. It made perfect sense to Noye.

Initially, he had lent some villains some funds at ten percent return per month to start up the ruse and said: "I worked out that he was getting gold from Brazil and was flying the bullion cargo to Belgium as diplomatic cargo, but the super profit was getting it to the UK and selling it with VAT on top which was your guaranteed margin after smelting it down in the UK with some scrap gold. I decided to do it for myself."

And it was this in the end that was to land him in trouble in relation to the Brink's-Mat bullion robbery. If there was one person you needed to get rid of the gold in London it was Kenny Noye. He still denies that the gold he traded in was Brink's-Mat even though he paid insurers an estimated £3 million in compensation and was convicted of the crime. All the more reason you might think that he would, could and should admit it. But he doesn't.

The insurance loss adjusters for the Brink's-Mat insurers operated independently of the police and struck restitution deals worth close to £20 million after launching more than 54 civil writs[55] but by that stage much of the proceeds had been invested and was worth considerably more – one estimate put it at £80 million.

Noye said he made a confidential settlement to bring closure on it all: "They were suing me. They were suing my mum and dad, my sister. A complete and utter nightmare for me and my family. They were suing Mickey Lawson and John Palmer who were acquitted on Brink's-Mat laundering charges, but everyone was being hunted. I thought I'm going to end this. It'll ruin my legitimate businesses. In the end they got a lot of change and some, but it was over, and I thought I could move on."[56]

It was in Antwerp where Noye took possession of the gold from Brazil during the era of military dictatorship in the South American country. A senior figure in the army apparently had access to vast gold bullion reserves and Noye had to get it to the UK for an instant and guaranteed profit.

"Thirty kilos of gold is the size of a house brick," he said. "I was already moving freight across Europe and had trucks doing overnights on the ferry from Belgium to Dover with unaccompanied vehicles – with no loads. I had a dock pass in Dover and could pick up my trailer and leave without issues anytime. I just put the gold into a Tupperware box and hid it underneath the empty trailer and job done. I did this for

---

55   Page 162, *Goldfinger and Me*

56   Interview and transcript of KH and KN, June 2022.

about ten years. It was a sad day when the military lost power in Brazil."

Noye smuggled tens of millions of pounds worth of gold bullion from ports in Belgium to the UK. No wonder democracy was a disappointment to him. It cost him a lot of money.

His Brazilian fixer made the lions' share of the profits from the deal but a man in his position would be uncomfortable with loose ends. Noye was a loose end and knew it: "He wanted me to go on holiday to visit him in Brazil after it all ended and promised to look after me. I thought no chance. He'd probably knock me off. He was the only one at his end of the supply chain who knew he was at it and I was the only one at this end. If you knew how powerful and wealthy he was now you would know exactly why I didn't go and join him on holidays.

"There were diamonds as well which I could have had but they take a bit longer. With gold you cannot fail (except of course unless you get 14 years for laundering Brink's-Mat booty)."

The gold, which was found at Noye's West Kingsdown Cottage, and which formed the basis for the Brink's-Mat proceeds money laundering trial after the death of DC Fordham, could not be linked to the Brink's-Mat raid. "During the trial they tested it and in fact it was proved that it wasn't Brinks Mat. It was in fact Brazilian gold, but I got done anyway," Noye said.

Despite the gold connection, this was a side business for him: "Most of this was a hobby. My main business was haulage and property. But if a deal came my way and it stood up obviously, I'd take advantage."

The closer they got to Amsterdam the lower the speed limit came down, 100km, 50km and then 30km, all the while Noye's mind was racing. Was this a beacon of trouble or the safe bolt hole that Mickey Lawson promised. So convinced were the authorities that Noye was in Northern Cyprus or on the Costa del Sol, the underworld's hiding place of choice, that he just might be able to get into a rhythm – a routine. Noye enjoyed a routine and his prison time locked that into his psyche.

Now it was a new city and a fresh cadence. He immediately felt the vibrant pulse of the place as soon as he stepped out of the car. Maybe it was just relief to leave Mr Coffee behind or it was the prospect of a new beginning. Or maybe it was the sight of an old friend on the sidewalk. Over the shoulder of his long-term comrade in arms (probably not literally) was a tall shop window where the mannequins moved seductively and invitingly.

At last things were looking up.

12

A FRIEND IN NEED

If you needed a friend then Mickey Lawson was your man, likewise if you needed a cannabis smuggler, general swindler, fraudster or a second-hand car. He shared the dock with Kenny Noye in the Brink's-Mat money laundering trial in 1986 and with great court craft was acquitted. It was either his guile in the box or he nobbled the jury.[57] Perhaps it was a bit of both.

He was a man of huge appetites – only some of which he shared with Noye. He woke up every day to a large Scotch and a line of coke if it was available. He would hire three sex workers when one clearly might suffice, and he laughed from the moment he got up to the moment he crashed out. He was providing the logistical support on this leg of Noye's journey on the run. With John Palmer now out of the picture, Noye took a huge risk in drawing in the one person that the police were convinced he would tap up. "My mate was the criminals' crim," Noye explained. "He charmed the cops and he charmed the villains. For him, it was not just about Cops 'n' Robbers,

---

57   Interview with KN, June 2022.

the game and the deal – it was about having a blast every waking moment."

That was Mickey Lawson, Noye's best friend until he passed away from hard living and pancreatitis. Both men were thick as thieves – which they also happened to be.

"If I was out," Noye said. "I'd have got him sober and straight. I'd say to him. 'Come over to my yard I've got something to show ya.' And he'd say: 'No way – you just want to lock me up in one of the containers and put me in rehab.'"

Lawson's appetites were written all over his 5ft 7in frame. He carried a happy paunch, a good head of dark hair and an upbeat disposition. On one notable occasion Customs and Excise bugged a hotel suite he had taken for four days in Dartford. He alone shared it with four sex workers and enough drink and drugs to put manners on a heavy metal band, but such were the extremes of his behaviours and the graphic excesses on the soundtrack that the officers listening were convinced that he was pretending and mocking up events to provoke a raid, and so the officers never lifted a finger.

It was just something Lawson would do but, on that occasion, he was living life to the full. He was being true to himself. Although he was very much a 'Del Boy' character – 'This time next year Rodney we'll be millionaires' – Mickey was one several times over. After handing over several million to the Brink's-Mat insurers in civil damages – despite his acquittal – and having £2.5 million taken from him as 'Proceeds of Crime' ten years later by the UK authorities, he still had plenty left over.

Noye and Mickey were now sharing a fine apartment in the heart of Amsterdam where drugs and prostitutes were not in short supply. A buoyant Noye was happy to enjoy the delights of the city but he did not use drugs. Kenny Noye settled in for the long haul, but Lawson would come and go at regular intervals, bringing news and cash as required.

But Lawson was under surveillance. Nick Biddiss's team had arranged for all those close to Noye to be tracked, bugged and followed within weeks of his hasty departure. Both Noye and Lawson knew the limitations of the National Criminal Intelligence Service and the police and knew that both men probably had more resources to throw at counter surveillance activities than the authorities had available.

"Villains don't clock off," Noye said. "They don't have holidays or shifts, we're at it 24-7. To follow one person for 24 hours would take two pairs of officers on 12-hour shifts and the support staff for those officers and multiply that by all my associates, family and close friends and you would need a team of about 50 and that was separate to the officers on the investigation and the electronic teams. The police couldn't afford to track those close to me."

As much as the authorities tried to build the picture of an incredible battle between organised crime and the forces of law and order in their hunt for Noye, all Mickey Lawson did to swerve the police surveillance was to grab a car off the lot at his garage and drive to the nearest port and onwards to France. He even booked the ferry in his own name. Other than taking a circuitous route to Amsterdam, carrying a few burners (phones), it wasn't any more sophisticated than that.

Noye said: "Don't get me wrong. He could spot a copper at a thousand paces – and he went around a couple of round-abouts twice, stopped on empty streets and to see if there was someone on his tail but this wasn't some James Bond villain with a private army trying to outwit the world's nation states. It was Mickey from Hextable."

The authorities often discuss organised crime and based their assessments on a company structure as if there was a CEO delegating and directing a management team with a hierarchy and responsibility shared from top to bottom. The reality is that serious criminals are much more disorganised or, more correctly, 'opportunistic'. It is the chaotic flair and serendipity of these criminals and their response to opportunities that come their way that makes it so difficult to get a grip of them without supergrasses or undercover officers and a huge deployment of technological resources.

Nick Biddiss said: "We were taking mobile phones off officers and cutting back on overtime. We simply did not have the resources to mount a 100 percent foolproof surveillance operation on all the key people in Noye's life." But Biddiss was still confident that they would get their man before Christmas 1996 at the very latest. "Something would break," he said. "You cannot simply disappear off the planet. Eventually Noye would make a mistake and we knew that his family and friends would be his weakness. It always is."

The biggest threat to the operation were other operations and cases that were also being managed by the leading Kent officers. Biddiss was under extraordinary pressure. Two of his children were also police officers and his whole family understood the pressures of the job and it was to his family he turned too when the press criticised him.

"Our big break will come from someone close to Noye. He will be spotted, and he will be found," he insisted throughout the hunt. "His friends and family will be his downfall," the detective promised his team on the downtime days and afternoons over a few pints or at the golf course.

Danielle Cable and Stephen Cameron's parents meanwhile took off to the U.S. while these games played out. It could not be described as a holiday. It was a break, a breather, a moment but nothing was assuaging the pain they felt which was as raw and real as it was in those minutes and hours after their Stephen was stabbed. Danielle's mother, Mandy Cable, publicly called for Noye to hand himself in as she supported the £10,000 reward offered for information leading to Noye's capture.

***

Noye and Lawson were lifelong friends and the Kent crew were so tight that there were limited opportunities for infiltration. Supergrasses were thin on the ground. The authorities of course were also hamstrung by the fact that Noye had his own 'covert officers' in the police. Moreover, with the history of DC John Fordham's death fresh in the memory, great caution would have to be taken with any close-up surveillance on Noye or his associates.

After Mickey settled Noye into this apartment in the city, he returned to the used car lot in Dartford and mischief making in Kent. Noye meanwhile, found his groove quickly. He found a gym, a regular girl and travelled the city on a bike. At night he would seek out a couple of regular haunts and make friends as a fellow traveller among tourists and travellers. Fortunately, in the circles he frequented, names and backgrounds were not important – in fact many people were looking for fresh starts and were keen to forget their pasts in the haze of Amsterdam's coffee shops.

Noye was slowly developing his undercover legend. The secret to a successful covert persona is credence and believ-ability. You must keep as true to your essence and rely upon your real life to make your alias sustainable. So, when Noye settled upon the 'wide boy entrepreneur persona' he ensured that the apple didn't fall too far from the tree.

And that was working – for now. There was only one hitch. His flat was practically within spitting distance of the city's equivalent of Scotland Yard. And his photograph was on the walls of all the city police stations. Not one to be shy about coming forward, Noye left his bike outside one station and entered to report the bike stolen. While inside, he scanned the walls, and the office notice boards. He was a tourist in need. Who would expect a wanted fugitive to go into the lion's den? Only those who knew Noye well. And there it was. A clearly faxed over image. The grainy black and white image did not survive the battle with the printer's ink and Noye raised a quiet, near indiscernible, smile and walked promptly out without his heart skipping a beat.

He said: "If that is the best they can do, I thought, I could be wombling free for as long as I needed to be."

It was the judicial mugshot so familiar to us all and one of very few images of Noye in the public domain. The image was one dimensional, hard to discern and in the heart of one of Europe's most dynamic cities, it was decidedly ineffective.

As befitting his prison regime, his schedule was rigorous. At 9.30am every morning he would take his bike from the shared hallway in the apartment building and cycle to a gym in the Turkish quarter about ten minutes away. It was a low-key existence. The lifelong weightlifter put in a couple of hours there, careful to avoid the police officers who regularly attended.

As if by clockwork, at noon, Noye would come out of the gym and cross the road into the arms of an old friend. She would receive a visit from him at least three or four times a week. Inez, a Dutch, blue-eyed, blonde, 6ft tall friend of Mickey Lawson's – who had always been fond of Ken – was his paramour in Amsterdam. The pair got on famously.

Their companionship suited each other as did the time slots. She had some spare time in the day but as a single mum she had to collect the kids at school time, which suited Ken down to the ground. She was in between relationships and, while on the run, so was Ken.

Noye is happy to discuss women, but he never gives any details. In that respect, he considers himself more of a 'cad' who is on the nice side of naughty rather than a 'bounder' who would kiss and tell. The women he has had relationships with would likely agree. If not, they have certainly never spoken publicly about it.

The afternoon was for sending messages back to Blighty and receiving messages right back. It was for phone calls to phone boxes and coded phone calls outlining how and when

the next contact would be made. Although these were sur-
reptitious arrangements, as Noye was still not charged then
there was no encumbrance on anyone talking or speaking to
him. But naturally, Nick Biddiss and his team were scouring
for any opportunity to track Noye down. In forensic parlance
every contact leaves a trace, and this applies as much to communications as it does to any crime scene.

The very heart of Amsterdam is small and there was a
large concentration of British tourists and expats living there
or passing through. It was something he could not avoid.
Normally, he was not a regular museum visitor or ever went
to art house cinemas, but this is where he went to relax, safe
in the knowledge that he wouldn't be noticed.

He said: "If there was one thing I could be sure of – it
was that faces or people who might know or recognise me
wouldn't be sharing this space. I couldn't imagine Mickey
Lawson being here or any of the blue-collar businessmen in
our circle."

It must have been quite a sight. The fugitive, fresh from
sex with his Dutch girlfriend and surrounded with movie
posters of avant garde French films and a steaming hot cup
of coffee, with the day's papers in front of him. For all his
downtime, there was always the very real prospect of being
caught unawares and dragged back to the UK in handcuffs.

Shortly after his release after serving nine years and four
months (Noye counted his time like kids count their age)
on the Brink's-Mat money laundering case, he took his
wife Brenda on a cruise. It was to visit the US on a couple
of stops. So concerned was he that he might have his visa

rejected by the US authorities he flew over in advance so as not to ruin the holiday for his wife. As he was going through immigration he was called over for a conversation. "Sir, we need to ask you some questions? Have you ever been in trouble in the US before?" Noye said, "No". He could see the officer scanning his computer and getting more animated.

"'Have you ever killed a policeman?' he asked.

'I was acquitted,' I said.

'What is Brinks-Mat?' Before he had finished the question, I could feel the handcuffs on my wrists."

Anticipating the return trip, Noye had only booked a one-way flight to Miami so he wouldn't have to pay for his own deportation.

"'Sir, you'll be on the next plane home, he said.

'And what if the plane is booked full?' I asked.

'Don't worry we'll kick someone off!' he said."

Noye continued: "Two of the biggest officers you'd imagine marched me onto the plane. As it happens it was full. Everyone was looking. They sat me beside this woman who glared at me and said, 'It's because of you my husband has been left behind.' Next stop, Gatwick airport. When we landed, the cuffs were taken off and I walked off the plane into two plain clothes officers. 'How are you, Ken? Did you have any trouble, Ken?' they asked with heavy sarcasm."

Noye never looked up as he said "No" and walked on. Within a week, he had flown directly to Aruba, the second destination on the cruise itinerary, met up with his wife and proceeded to spend much of the time enjoying the company of two FBI officers and their wives who had no idea that their newfound friend was in fact an 'undesirable alien' in their own country.

Doubtless the next time he was in handcuffs, it would not have such a happy ending. In the afternoons he took off on his bike and cycled miles and miles around the city, looking at properties and taking in the cultural oxygen of the city, from Ajax's football stadium, the Johan Cruyff Arena, which was completed just before his arrival in the city. With over two hours of gym work in the morning and a couple of hours cycling in the afternoon, Noye was the fittest he'd ever been. Only professional athletes were more active.

Those long journeys were opportunities to consider his future and his past. Incredibly on one spin around the city he saw an Italian gentleman rather innocuously come out of his front door and walk towards him on the bike. "Jesus, who'd have thought it. I knew him. We met in prison and kept in contact. He was on the trot himself from a drugs charge and here he was. And here I was. I couldn't believe it and did what any prison friend would do – I kept on cycling and never looked back," Noye said.

13

THE SPANISH BOLTHOLE

When would he get the tap on the shoulder? Would he be wrestled to the ground? Or would it be the full-on blues and twos – an armed response unit or tactical team that would be drafted in? All this was part of Kenny Noye's daily mind map, more than five months since he departed Blighty in a hurry, fleeing inquisition for the death of Stephen Cameron.

For the moment he was comfortable that he was at least one step ahead of the law. Until that was…

Noye was trundling along at the end of his cycling route around the Amsterdam city environs and having just turned a corner, saw about two hundred metres ahead of him a roadblock nearly opposite his apartment building. The Dutch officers were armed to the teeth. Three police cars blocked the road with a fourth parked surreptitiously on the side of the road to catch anyone thinking of a quick U-turn and backtrack. "Fuck," he said. "Is this for me?" It was a significant police presence, and it would be more than sufficient to take him down.

Noye continued: "I couldn't see any easy way out. The bastards I thought, who's stuffed me up? What fucker? My mind was crackling a thousand miles an hour and I decided to cycle around and maybe outpace the singular patrol car in my rear. It made perfect sense. I could out-cycle them in the back streets and pedestrian areas, and I doubt they'd shoot at me in a public place, and I'm clearly unarmed."

Noye had weighed up the odds and then did so again. He executed a U-turn before he changed his mind and decided to front it out instead. "'I'll blag it out,' I thought. 'I'll chance it!' As I approached the line of officers, I got off the bike and walked up to them. One tracked me and my every move." Shorts and a sleeveless top and a bike was a disarming uniform of sorts and the lead officer looked him up and down. He then turned his head and nodded to a colleague. Good news or bad news – thumbs up or down – the decision was made. And then his colleague warmly waved him through with a salutation in Dutch.

A relieved Noye replied, "Dank u wel." No truer sentiment was ever uttered. The man on the run – the man whose photograph adorned the walls of police stations across Europe – was very grateful indeed. Another victory snatched from the jaws of defeat. Nick Biddiss would have to wait another day, he thought.

Noye added: "Were they looking for me? Who knew I was here? Maybe this was for someone else or maybe my goatee did the trick? I didn't know if it was another coincidence or if it was my 'great escape'."

For law enforcement it was a near impossible task to manage the decision-making matrix of a serious and dextrous offender like Noye because at these 'choke points'

– in military parlance – or at moments requiring critical judgement, Noye himself has no idea what he is going to do until he does it. His reactions at these junctions are instinctive based upon a lifetime of collective rule-breaking and opportunism.

Noye's next move would demonstrate this eloquently. He was out in a bar and musing about world events with the transient revellers and beatniks in an Irish bar behind Dam Square at the heart of Amsterdam, one Friday evening in November.

A Californian new age traveller, Skip, knew everybody and had an opinion on almost everything, including development opportunities. Skip was the quintessential hippie with his long hair and laid-back demeanour. He lived in Los Canos de Meca, near Cadiz on the Spanish coast, and extolled its virtues.

The innocuous conversation about the quiet area in the Spanish province of Andalusia, which was apparently ripe for profitable exploitation, immediately sparked the attention of the fugitive who was alternating between the names Mark and Mick. The company he was keeping didn't care. Noye's needs and wants met at this crossroads. Entirely by accident, the fugitive was considering a paradise of latent potential which would excite his addiction to the 'deal' and also, provide a low-key safe haven for him to hide away from the clutches of law. It was as if he planned it. He'd been nearly four months in the city and maybe it was time to up sticks. Noye cornered Skip and built up a more detailed picture of the area. He took down a couple of phone numbers and popped back on his bike.

By Monday, he was on his way. With little more than a couple of numbers on the back of a cigarette packet and a vaguely comprehensible lecture on property prices percolating in his head, he packed his bags and left Amsterdam for good.

***

Spain was a place he knew well but it was also a country where UK cops would expect him to frequent. However, this little part of Spain was a secret magnet for continental tourists but without the tourist traffic from the UK which posed the biggest danger to Noye. Canos de Meca is a small seaside village and a regular haunt for the rich and famous who would sneak down on their weekends from Madrid. The unspoilt windswept coasts boast stunning beaches, steep cliffs and rolling sand dunes against a pine tree backdrop. Neither Skip nor Noye knew that the waters around his prospective new home was the site of the Battle of Trafalgar, 193 years earlier.

Light on facts but fast on his feet, Noye had relocated from Holland to Spain in a matter of days and had placed a month's deposit on a picturesque cottage in the woods with a view of the coast. It was the perfect hiding place. The Dutch, Danish, and Germans populated the region, but Brits were a rare species. Scotland Yard did not count on Noye befriending a cannabis centred commune – they placed him in Tenerife or elsewhere on the Costa del Crime – but defying expectations and demonstrating sharp counter surveillance techniques, Noye went once again where he was least expected.

Mickey Lawson drove him down. "He never gave me any

advice," Noye said. "I said I was going. He'd never talk me out of it but would only help me. We took the road down. A thirty-six hours' drive – more than 2000 km through Belgium and France."

There were no border checkpoints, but Kenny Noye carried one of his bogus passports – he is keeping the details of that secret. He knew, however, that he needed a fresh one to be able to travel safely outside the EU if he had to escape to a non-extradition country in a hurry. The passport would have to be legitimate and survive a computer check. It would seem preposterous that he could engineer a new passport while on the run. It seems completely implausible that the Passport Office would issue a photo passport with Noye's likeness while he was one the most wanted men in the country.

Noye added: "If there is a chink in the system, I'll find it. That is my skill. Maybe it's a flaw but I was confident that I could pull it off. I knew I had to, otherwise my options would be very limited."

He had preparations in play, in the name of Alan Edward Green. The architect of this audacious scam was cannabis smuggler and bar owner, John Stone. He was also part of Noye's kitchen cabinet while he was on the run and took on the administrative task of solving this problem.[58] He lived in a flat above his bar in Amsterdam and was an affable, six foot tall and clean-shaven operator. Stone supplied cannabis to the UK but managed to escape the clutches of the law despite the fact that the police had substantial intelligence on him.[59]

---

58   Phone interview with KN, November 2022.
59   Interview with KN, June 2022.

Stone simply asked someone if he could take his identity. There was no pressure applied. The only pressure was time. Noye was now in Spain and needed a fresh identity document. It appears that Noye was concerned that the passport he was using may have been compromised and would have rung alarm bells if scrutinised by any border guards. From his modest flat in the centre of Amsterdam, he put in a call to a contact in Gravesend, northeast Kent.

Stone said: "He was a paraplegic and lived in Gravesend. He was in poor circumstances, and I asked him if he's been abroad. He said, 'No' so I said, 'Can I get a passport in your name? I'll give you five grand for it!' So he went, 'Yeah for sure.' I said, 'You've got to go to the doctors, get a photo and get the form signed by him.' He did that and then he came back and gave me the documents. I got my photo, forged the doctor's name on it, sent off for the passport and hey presto. It was my go-to passport on my travels."

In the Maidstone police headquarters, the team were fully aware of Noye's need for travel documents and his capacity to get them.

Nick Biddiss said: "Well, we knew he had the resources to forge documents and he was a former printer but while any passport in his name was red flagged across the world, we couldn't know what name any fresh passport would be in. We all wish we had the digital weapons we have now, back then – but we didn't."

The original Alan Green was arrested in due course, but the police didn't prosecute. Alan wasn't one bit apologetic. "He told officers that he didn't regret a thing and that his family had the best Christmas in years on the proceeds," Biddiss said. "The officers were decent and gave him a break, to give them full credit," Noye adds.

The processing staff at HM Passport Office who conducted the checks and signed off on the photo of Noye with his goatee, fair hair and glasses could not have contemplated that they were signing off on a document that would send the fugitive around the globe. It is hard to imagine that his likeness, which was nearly on every paper daily, passed the scrutineers by but it did.

Mickey Lawson dropped Ken off in Canos de Mecca and left him with the car before he then made his way back to Holland. Noye and Lawson were quite the double act.

Noye said: "On deals together, Mickey would joke and take the piss all the way through meetings, and I would try and play the straight guy. I'm sure some would just think these two are clowns. Then Mickey would start talking numbers, arbitrage and returns and then they could see we were serious."

Micky would take a bullet for Noye if it ever came to that but he'd rather not. Noye and Lawson were not gun-toting villains. No policeman, even the ones they didn't pay, would say that, but within the underworld they had heritage, connections, wealth and respect and when favours were being called in, that counted for everything.

It was the definition of soft power within this world. There was little need for the exercise of these power dynamics in this new chapter for Noye. He was Mick the builder and he had enough money in his pocket to lay low comfortably. But if he wanted help or to escape the hippie haven, then

Noye would only have to take a two-hour drive to Marbella and the Costa del Sol – the de facto capital of the British underworld. Is this a risk that he would take? Surely not now that he was safe and secure in a remote commune where the greatest risk was getting high in the cannabis smoke filled bars and restaurants of the village.

Noye's new home was a stunning cottage in the woods on the southernmost tip of Spain. Skip had arranged for Noye to meet Edith who had a furnished cottage for rent and all that was required was a month's deposit. In an instant, Noye was sorted. The landlady was a 'tough old bird' and lived in a large house adjacent to the cottage. For all Skip's 'flower power' cool and déshabillé lifestyle, he was a planner, and he couldn't have arranged matters better for Noye. He ran lucrative cannabis routes and encouraged all sorts to join him down in this idyllic setting.

It was along this coastline that he smuggled cannabis in from Africa. Skip had no idea that Noye (aka Mick the builder) was a wanted man. 'Mick' was connected, that was obvious, but Noye wasn't alone in having reasons to escape to this oasis from the world's troubles. It would transpire that his closest neighbour was a former Cold War spy, and his other neighbour was a drug smuggler, also on the run.

Within a month, Edith said that she wanted Noye out. Noye was convinced that nothing he had done would have provoked the sudden change of heart. It was nothing of the sort. Her husband had passed away six months previously, and she wanted to sell the big house and move into the cottage where Noye was residing. Without so much as blinking, the polite drifter asked how much she wanted for it and promptly arranged for it to be purchased. It would later end up in the hands of the architect of his bogus passport application, John Stone, who would later commit suicide in the house.

Edith was shocked to realise that this hippie associate, Mick the builder, could deliver on the property deal almost immediately. The big house was empty when Noye moved in. Edith took everything, including the light bulbs. The last time Noye had to furnish a house from empty was when himself and Brenda got their first home. All they had was two deck chairs and some boxes.

Noye's answer then was to hire a van, borrow a brown warehouse jacket and a clipboard. He pulled up into the loading bays behind a major department store and started issuing directions to load items of his choosing into the van and then drove it home. It wasn't until recently that Brenda found out that the brand-new furniture was of dubious derivation. This time he would not take such risks. He was on the run and would pay his bills.

His days in this secluded part of the world had a different rhythm to the bustle of Amsterdam. Every morning, it was coffee first thing. He patted the neighbour's dog Elsa and gave her a treat against the advice of her owners. And at a slower cadence, Noye set about planning his day. The gym, as in Amsterdam, kicked off around 9.30. It was run by two former Navy officers and was used by stroke recovery victims. In between sets, Noye would assist with the patients and support them with their exercises. For lunch he would drift to one of a couple of seaside restaurants and enjoy the local fare. There were no English papers available, but he could treat himself to *The Sunday Times* at the weekend. Noye is a sun worshipper and his house, Hollywood Cottage, in Sevenoaks, had its own solarium and sunbeds – but here Noye just laid down a blanket on the beach and drifted off.

In these quiet times, Noye's mind would drift to the disaster that brought him to this isolated location. He was alone. He was resilient and self-sufficient, but he was not a machine and sometimes his thoughts got the best of him. There was no unwinding the clock or bringing back to life, the young man whose life was so needlessly lost.

Nick Biddiss' days were markedly different. He awoke to Radio 2 and in between school runs, thought of little else except the hunt for Noye.

Biddiss said: "Every day was different. It was exhilarating and frustrating in equal measure. The case was like a campfire with its lingering embers, sparks and sudden flames which would burst unexpectedly."

His wife would wonder how he slept at night as he constantly planned and processed the latest developments at bedtime. "Honestly it helped me sleep," he added. "Turning over and over all the things we could do and all the leads which were coming in. It was like panning for gold and I just spent all my time hunting for that one nugget."

A man on the run had few friends. And that is the only way Noye would have it. He knew he was imprisoned in a jail of his own making but was making the best of it. He was lonely and sometimes bored but none of this would allow him to socialise beyond the narrow subculture of unconventional, off-the-grid drug smugglers and environmental peaceniks at the heart of Skip's circle. Noye's social life revolved around Skip and his wife, Raquel, but other than that he rarely interacted with anyone. Skip though would soon resolve this issue, at least in part.

He was key to the new love in Noye's life. Maria Hernandez (name changed) was a beautiful socialite in Madrid and was best friends with Skip's wife. Noye met her first in Amsterdam where his initial advance was rejected.

"Why do you want my number?" Maria asked Noye.

"I want your body," Noye replied, being explicitly honest. Skip took Noye aside and said that this was not the way that Maria wanted to be spoken to. Noye laughed it off and said, "Honesty was the best policy." His intentions, though, were rebuffed.

But after a couple of months in Canos, he got her number again and invited her down. Maria's father was a policeman under the Franco regime, and she owes her heritage to Lebanon and France.

Maria was beguiling and had been involved in PR promotion at nightclubs and bars and had had several very wealthy boyfriends. One of them, perchance, had arrived as Maria often did on the shuttle from Madrid to nearby Jerez de La Frontera about 85 km away. One night, Ken and Maria walked into a restaurant and sat in the corner was one of Maria's old paramours, a successful showjumper. She went over and introduced Ken to him. He was in the company of a Spanish actress. "I had no idea who she was," Noye said. It was Penelope Cruz. "Apparently she was well known." In that part of the world no one made a fuss over celebrities and that is why celebrities liked the place. Naturally, the accomplished actress would have no idea who Noye was or what he was fleeing from.[60]

He added: "She was very unassuming. Dressed simply – just jeans and a tee-shirt. She was down to earth and we drank and played pool till the early morning. With so much time in prison I had no idea who anyone was."

It wasn't the first time he failed to recognise the rich and famous. During a charity event at The Dorchester in 1994, after his release from the Brink's-Mat conviction, he sat beside Brian May.

The Queen star introduced himself, "Hi, I'm Brian!"

"Hello," Ken said, shaking May's hand in return.

"What do you do?" Noye asked.

"I play guitar," May replied.

"Oh, good for you and how is that going for you?"

"Hanging in there – hanging in there," May said, deadpan.

At the same event, Prince Edward was in attendance and was, by some happenstance, apparently introduced to Noye. Pleasantries were exchanged. In parting, Noye said to Prince Edward, "By the way tell your Mum, thanks for the holiday." A reference to his nine years spent at Her Majesty's pleasure which undoubtedly went right over the prince's head. It is a wonderful story and however unlikely, wags would certainly want the story to be true.

---

60   Phone interview with KN, November 2022, and transcripts from interviews between KN and Karl Howman.

Ironically, it always troubled Noye that inmates were held at 'Her Majesty's pleasure'.

"Who could take pleasure in incarcerating anyone? Surely, we should be held at Her Majesty's discretion," Noye, an ardent Royalist, said. He clearly had too much time to consider the esoteric point over the 30 years he spent in jail.

Noye and Maria began to enjoy nights out in the laid-back surroundings, where they would chill on the balcony over-looking the forest to one side and the sea in front and would often attend long lingering parties at Skip's place, where someone would put up an Arab tent.

Noye said: "Everyone would have their shisha pipes and while Skip would cook the fish nearly straight from the sea on the barbecue, one of the elderly neighbours would visit and would call Skip out out for all the vagabonds, waifs and strays hanging around – but she said that I was a lovely man. She must have been a very good judge of character."

Drugs would later kill Skip. While lifting bales of cannabis, he ruptured a hernia and, undiagnosed, he passed away from sepsis. "He was harmless and as close to Howard Marks as you can imagine," Noye remembered. "He didn't have a bad bone in his body, and he brought Maria into my life and I'm thankful to him for that…"[61]

Just before Christmas 1996, Noye drove back to Amsterdam. John Stone had something for him. Finally, he was collecting his ticket to ride – his new passport and his licence to travel the globe under the name *Green: Alan Edward: Date of Issue: 03 Dec 96.*

---

61   Phone interview with KN, September 2022.

THE SPANISH BOLTHOLE

Following a quick visit to his favourite call girl, Noye retreated to his Spanish bolthole. He decided he deserved a holiday – not that he was overworked but now, freshly armed with his new identity and a new love, there would be no holding him back.

14

THE HOLIDAY

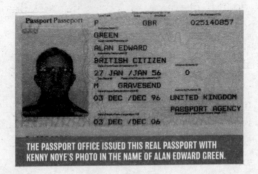

THE PASSPORT OFFICE ISSUED THIS REAL PASSPORT WITH KENNY NOYE'S PHOTO IN THE NAME OF ALAN EDWARD GREEN.

The Devil makes work for idle hands.

Noye was bored. He was idle. It could well have been argued that he is at his most devilish when he is in fact very busy – active. But now he was certainly not active unless you count avoiding capture for an impending murder charge or spending weekends with his new lover.

Noye was renting an idyllic cottage in the woods with a pristine beach a stone's throw away. His girlfriend came down regularly from Madrid to stay and he took other lovers during the week. He was looking at property deals, speaking to family regularly and keeping fit. He obviously needed a holiday.

He was comfortable on the run. Perhaps, too comfortable. This was either a tribute to his guile, or an explicit criticism of those hunting him down. He was living as if on a long-term vacation – just not the type of break that would be authorised by your employers unless of course you were self-employed – which he was. It was audacious and an insult to the police forces around the globe on the lookout for him. If Noye wanted to offer offence, then going on holiday was going to do it! If, of course, the police and Nick Biddiss were in the know – which they decidedly were not.

Biddiss, in contrast to Noye, was overworked. As the 'Principal Senior Investigating Officer' in Kent with more than 50 officers and civilians under him, more jobs were coming his way as the heat on Noye blew hot and cold. Noye was always in his eye-line but there were other cases unfolding day to day on his watch which would draw down his time and, in some cases, officers from the Stephen Cameron case.

He said: "I had an umbrella jurisdiction over all serious crimes in Kent. It was normal but not ideal to be running several murder cases all at once." This workload wasn't new to Biddiss, he was one of the Senior Investigating Officers on the 'Deal Barracks Bombing' in 1989 when the IRA exploded a device at the Royal Marines School of Music Building, killing 11 and wounding another 21.

While Kenny Noye was marshalling his progress across Europe, a gun fanatic living about 60 miles from Noye's home in Sevenoaks, was scanning 'Debretts', the guide to etiquette and high society, seeking victims. The offender, later described as a 'trained assassin' was as discerning as he was cruel. In November 1996, he arranged to meet wartime intelligence expert and former World War Two spy, Ken

Speakman, 84, at his home in Ramsgate, Kent. Under false pretences about buying antique guns, he handcuffed and tortured the pensioner placing the waist band of his dark blue dressing gown around his throat and, while looking his victim in the face, strangled the life out of him. The killer was skilled. He was cool and dispassionate. He gazed as he watched an old pensioner's life ebb away in the living room of his house.

Nick Biddiss was at the Maidstone headquarters in the Stephen Cameron incident room when he took an urgent call from the control room about a suspicious death in an affluent area in Ramsgate. "There are lots of things that go through your mind when you receive a call like that," Biddiss said. "You've got to preserve the scene and also minimise the risk to the public."[62]

The killer was a former Navy veteran and an ex-member of the French Foreign Legion but none of this was known to Biddiss, who was now on the hunt for two killers. Progress was slow on both fronts, but the most recent murder would take precedence in the short term. Noye was a known quantity, but he was not an assassin. In the small community of Ramsgate, a killer on the loose with firearms and ammunition was causing huge alarm. Juggling the two cases would prove challenging but comfortably within Biddiss's capacity. He would divide his time between the Dartford HQ for the Speakman inquiry and Maidstone for the Cameron investigation.

Noye's covert intelligence grapevine informed him that

---

62   *How I Caught The Killer*, Sky 2020.

Biddiss, his nemesis, was getting rather busy. "It made sense to me that if he was working on more cases then he was less focused on me," Noye surmised. "That would buy me time and maybe, just maybe, take a little heat off me."

For Biddiss, it was just a practical allocation of resources. He said: "Your cases are like children – you love them all equally, but you devote your time to the ones who need you most at that time, you don't divide your time equally."[63] The clues and tip offs on the whereabout of Noye were being followed up but the case was in a fallow period when Ken Speakman was murdered.

So, the time was right for Noye to go on holiday.

Morocco was a country which did not have an extradition agreement with the UK, but that's not why Noye went there. He and Maria, his girlfriend, wanted a quick break after Christmas and this was the chosen destination and a favourite of Maria's. It was accessible by ferry from their quarter of Spain and Noye had been there six months earlier on his way to the Ivory Coast. This time his destination was Tangiers.

It was their first trip away from their little hideaway. Every border represented a threat to Noye's freedom but having already had such success with his identity documents, he was reasonably confident. The border guards were vigilant, but they were not the real threat. That was a lot closer to home.

In fact, it was in the passenger seat.

Unthinking and perhaps a little distracted, Noye took his passport out of his pocket and handed it to his companion.

---

63   Phone interview with Nick Biddiss, November 2022.

His multilingual girlfriend lovingly caressed her Spanish and his UK passport. She patted his lap. As might be expected, just before their Shogun jeep approached the border checkpoint, she opened the passports for ease of access for the border staff. As the car edged in convoy towards the checkpoint, she gently gazed at her own photo and then her eyes drifted to the picture of her new partner. Then to the name on the passport. Alan Green? Alan who? Noye noted the rising hysteria. Here was a man she had shared her bed with. And on paper he was a stranger! She was panicking. It was beginning to show. "I can explain," Noye said. "Keep calm," he said, squeezing her palm.

This did not amount to reassurance. Nonetheless, Maria continued to hand the passports over to the border staff. But who was Mick? Was he Alan or Mick? She was scared and had every reason to be. In an instant her lover was exposed as a liar with a false identity. She knew him as Michael Mayne aka Mick the builder.

She had a choice to bail out there and then, or stand her ground. She considered her options. As the passport staff disappeared into their office, Noye rushed to make his excuses. He said he was on the run for tax offences and that his name really was Mick but that the passport was fake. "I'm wanted for a huge tax bill on a deal gone wrong. I'm just keeping quiet until my accountant sorts it out with the authorities," he said. A near tearful Maria drew her hands away from 'Mick'. He pulled away but Maria now was the least of his concerns.

***

The border staff had still not returned with their papers. Other cars had been checked and waved on but not the Shogun with the frosty couple in the front seat. He had received reports of increased police activity around his connections and his antennae were on hyper alert. The Moroccan security services had been notified by Interpol about Noye. Would the border staff connect the dots?

He kept his vehicle running and he was ready to drive through the port barrier to escape if it came to it. Maria was ready to run for cover too – she had every reason to – her lover and companion was living a lie – many lies. Noye was surrounded by jeopardy. You can take a holiday while on the run, but you can't ever stop looking over your shoulder!

The car was waved forward. Maria turned on her seductive smile. The young Immigration officer noticed the near 15-year age gap between the pair – paused for a lingering glance – and handed the passports back. Catastrophe averted.

For all the call girls, and occasional one-night stands, could this woman capture Noye's confidence and affections? Could he trust her? His long list of companions in England proved to be universally on message. None had a bad word to say about him. When the relationships ended, they never kissed and told, despite the inducements from the tabloids and undoubtedly moral pressure from the police. His Spanish companion was delivered a seismic shock at an acute junction and had held her nerve. He had some 'problem solving' to do and more than a little explaining, but this would prove to be a mere blip in their relationship.

After their close call, the couple stayed in a family run hotel halfway between Tangiers and Marrakesh. The women in the family chatted to Maria and Noye kept his company with the father of the clan. Noye celebrated the food and explained that in Spain he lived alone and could do with this standard of service full time.

"Very quickly, the man pointed out a very attractive twenty-five-year-old member of staff," Noye said. "He said if you can get her into Spain, she'd be delighted to be your housekeeper. I considered it. But before the offer was even contemplated Maria pulled me aside for a second – a brief chat. 'Don't worry about her,' she said, with a grin. 'I have a housekeeper for you – a big fat one!' I knew then that she had recovered from the passport crisis." Women were always his weakness and even with Maria, there would be others. He couldn't help himself.

Later in the stay, Noye spent some time with two of the daughters of the house in their late 20s.

Both were gorgeous and spoke impeccable English. Noye would not get a new housekeeper but he would collect a couple of mobile numbers which undoubtedly he would call when his two 'Moroccan Princesses' would go to Spain where their father had a very large and opulent house. The debate about whether he is a cad or a rogue is superfluous here. He was simply outrageous when it came to women and sex.

But would that be his ultimate downfall?

During one foray to a gym in Jerez, about an hour away from his Spanish bolthole, Noye quietly ventured in under the radar. Once inside, a beautiful eastern European woman came over and started chatting to him. She was full on. It was unnerving. Not shy or lacking confidence, he thought this woman was out of his league and, "This did not make sense. I looked at the exit doors and was waiting for the front door to be kicked in anytime. It never happened. I quietly left the building and sped back home".

Sometimes if it looks too good to be true then it might be your lucky day... or maybe not. With Maria, Noye was safe – for now! But for how long? After a week of luxury hotels, carpet buying and pool relaxation, the pair returned home without incident.

The only thing that could possibly get in the way of their friendship was another fake passport.

15

CLOSE ENCOUNTERS

Love hath no fury like a woman scorned. It was just as well then that Maria did not know that he had arranged to meet the 'Moroccan Princesses' in a restaurant halfway between Cadiz, where he lived and Gibraltar where he occasionally shopped. For a man in hiding, he wasn't entirely walking the walk or talking the talk. He was increasingly taking chances that a man on the run shouldn't take.

Nick Biddiss was, as ever, dealing with hundreds of sightings of Noye across Europe. "We would triage all the reports," he said. "Weigh up the veracity of them and act accordingly but we rarely sent officers abroad unless the intelligence was very good." There were also the regular late-night callers after the pubs were closed.

Biddiss added: "One person called from Brussels about 11.30 at night. And swore on his mother's life that he had seen Noye sitting right opposite him having a beer." Officers were sent to Tenerife, Cyprus and Spain but not to Marbella in the hunt for Noye.

"Marbella was the last place he would go," Biddiss explained. "There were so many faces and underworld characters there that he wouldn't risk it. And you have to understand that Noye wasn't universally liked. Some people might want to take him out and many would be happy to grass him up."

Biddiss was wrong but for the right reasons.

Noye would avoid all his old underworld pals and any others because he agreed with Biddiss that there was too much to gain for villains to turn him in. However, Maria, the nightclub promoter who lived in Madrid but knew Marbella well, wanted to bring Noye to her old haunts and Noye couldn't explain why he was reluctant. Noye never trusted any woman except his wife Brenda. "Obviously, I couldn't trust Maria with anything about my past," he said. "I was laying low and I couldn't tell her why I was on the run. She bought my story about hiding from the tax man, but I just rowed in with what she wanted even though there were real risks to being seen in Marbella. Usually, we went out after dark but it was still a risk."

The Costa del Sol became a crime haven after the century-old extradition agreement between the two countries expired in 1978 and became known as 'that part of Europe that fell off the back of a lorry'.[64] It was only reconstituted in 1985 to a large degree as a result of the flagrant behaviour of the UK gangsters on the Costa and the reporting of their antics back in Blighty. However, any villains who had made Spain their home could not be extradited retrospectively because the new law would not apply to them. If, however, they stepped outside of Spain for so much as a day or an hour, or even

---

64   Duncan Campbell, *The Guardian*

to Gibraltar as many did, then extradition could apply, and they could be kicked out. The retrospective law offered no comfort to Noye – but Gibraltar did.

'The Rock' is a British Overseas Territory on Spain's south coast and Noye was a regular visitor. He would cross the road border from Spain onto the Rock and do his shopping at Safeway. About once a month he went there for the English produce. In truth, he missed the British bacon more than anything. He would load up his Mitsubishi Shogun with cheese and other sundries and he also had a soft spot for cream soda.

He would often walk from there to the jewellery quarter to look for discounted Rolex watches. He didn't buy anything because the retailers would never take a deal. In the meantime, he would take in a coffee or a pizza while reading the readily available English newspapers. Sometimes, he would read updates on the police hunt for one 'Kenneth James Noye'. It was about an hour and half hour away from Cadiz and the border force rarely stopped travellers crossing onto the Rock. Noye savoured the 'more British than British' ambiance there. It was a home from home in the sun.

He only visited to do his shopping, but he was taking a huge risk – literally putting his freedom on the line for some bacon. The risk here was much more acute than anywhere else on the globe. This was British territory. No extradition warrant was required. It would only take so much as a hint of recognition by any member of the public – a quiet word to a policeman and then Noye could be immediately arrested. "I wanted my bacon. It was the one thing I really missed," he said.

It was on one of his visits to Gibraltar that he arranged to meet the two Moroccan sisters at an up-market restaurant about halfway between the Rock and Cadiz. He had his eyes on one of the glamorous women and he would later have a two-month affair with her, skirting around hotels in Marbella and avoiding Maria's suspicions at all costs. On this day, mid-course, a truck driver entered the restaurant. For obvious reasons, Noye always sat with an eye to the front door and the back exit. In his predicament, it was a wise precaution. In walked the man. Immediately, the stocky fella in jeans and tee-shirt, about 40 years of age, stopped. Stared. Halted. "I clocked him, and he clocked me," Noye said. "I knew it. He knew it. We both knew it. He did nothing. He turned about-face and walked out without saying a word."

Noye was more than eight months on the run and he'd been located, recognised and was maybe about to be caught. He saw the driver get into a UK registered lorry and drive off towards the Rock. What was he to do? He was in the company of two beautiful women, was awaiting dessert and coffee – and he did what you'd expect. He stayed put.

He said: "I figured if anything was going to happen, it wouldn't be quick. I didn't move. If it was to be my last moments of freedom, then let it be in the company of two stunning women. But better hope I'm not let out because if Maria finds out I'd be in real trouble." He returned home. He'd give that restaurant and the route a rest for a while. He could imagine the incident room in Maidstone when that call came into Nick Biddiss.

The tip-off would have been triaged and dispensed to the

'not bloody likely' drawer. That was his hope. But Biddiss was the least of his worries. Within a week, on a pre-arranged call to a public phone box in Kent, a message was passed to him. 'Mad' Frankie Fraser had news. Urgent. A truck driver had spotted Noye. He'd been clocked. The message was simple: "Tell Noye he was seen close to Gibraltar." Nothing more needed to be said. Noye knew that he was still safe despite the sighting. He could trust Frankie Fraser and even if anyone claimed he'd been spotted they'd never be believed. In any case, it was time to deluge the Noye hotline and Biddiss with a few bogus sightings. Perhaps this time, he'd throw in Russia. In total, the incident room received tip-offs about his whereabouts in 13 different countries. Biddiss was fully cognisant of the near certainty that Noye would be feeding distractions into the mix but each and every public tip-off would be filtered through the system.

Every Noye family event was a potential event of interest to the security services. These were potential magnets to Noye. Would he turn up? No chances were taken. The Noye clan was subject to all-encompassing surveillance. "We probably went to more weddings and funerals than Hugh Grant," Nick Biddiss said.

Noye's relationship with his Moroccan friend continued apace in the aftermath. After some assignations in and around Marbella, Noye decided to bring her to his house in the woods. It was night. It was dark. So isolated and deep into the woods was his house that his companion got worried. "'There's no house here,' she kept saying," Noye recalls. "I said there was. 'There is not!' she said, increasingly worried. You have to imagine that it was a lonely place and there wasn't even a hint of light from another house. 'Where are you taking me?,' she said. I'm sure she thought I was going to bump her off." Within minutes, the house emerged into view. Shortly after, she was making love to the person she was 'proof positive' was going to kill her just a few minutes before.

When Maria returned from Madrid, she took him dancing. One of the nightclubs was Olivera's, a place for the uber wealthy, yacht owners and foreign millionaires but thankfully none who knew Noye. He was nervous about going for a walkabout here but he was trying to please his girl. In his teens, he went to great lengths to woo a teenage crush. The object of his affections was a dancer and to ingratiate himself into her world, he spent two years learning ballroom dance, achieving bronze, silver and gold proficiency. In the end he got the girl. But the hard-earned prize wasn't worth it as Noye dumped her for being boring. Noye though, was sweet on Maria, despite his infidelities and she was anything but boring. Maria also thought Noye himself was full of surprises. First the passport and now this – he could dance. Who'd have thought?

One of her favourite restaurants was also in a problematic location. It was below the veteran 60's gangster, Freddie Foreman's flat. Noye had previously offered to buy it off Freddie. It had been on the market for two years and still was. Was there any chance that Foreman would come downstairs and see his old comrade? There was every chance.

16

CASTRO'S CHAIR

NOYE MOVED INTO A NEW BOLTHOLE, IN ATLANTERRA, NEAR BARBATE, CADIZ

There was no accounting for chance.

Noye had chosen a beautiful and discrete part of Spain to hide out but unbeknownst to him, others had the same idea. Noye moved into a new bolthole, in Atlanterra, near Barbate, Cadiz only about five miles from his original hideaway deep in the woods in Los Canos de Meca in the southwest of Spain. The property was a cliff top luxury location and more befitting a wealthy holiday maker than necessarily a home for someone trying to conceal their identity and dubious past. It had a view you could kill for, as one wag put it.

Nick Biddiss had predicted that Noye could simply not avoid the trappings of wealth including a fine house, active social life, women and fine dining. "It would be impossible for him to avoid these pleasures and as soon as he did, he would stand out and people would talk and that would put him at risk," he said. "Our problem and also his problem, was that Mr. Noye had access to more money than a Lottery winner."[65]

Was Noye building his own cage by settling down and putting roots down in this part of Spain? Sowing the seeds of his own demise? If he was, he showed no sign of it.

Noye wanted five-star accommodation for his gilded sojourn on the run. Parasailers took advantage of the cliffs to harness the sea breeze and updrafts and soared around his new home and the beaches below facing the North Atlantic Ocean.

His girlfriend Maria needed to be picked up at Jerez Airport just over an hour away. He'd been hunting for bargains for new furniture, and he was excited to show her his new lodgings.

It had been six weeks since he's seen her and there were several springs in his step.

That morning was a misty one in his Spanish paradise and obsessive to the last, he kept up his fitness regime with an early mountain cycle. "I was a creature of habit, and I knew that as much as I tried to, I couldn't really break the habits of a lifetime and most recently, the habits I grew into while in prison," he said.

---

65   Interview with Nick Biddiss, Channel 5 'Kenneth Noye' Documentary, 2000.

These habits are usually the downfall of most fugitives but so far, nearly a year after his disappearance from English shores, he was happily keeping himself to himself and keeping true to his normal regime. Every morning it was either a visit to the gym or a cycle. His other habit was women and currently, his obsession was Maria from Madrid. Either of these traits could be his downfall. He had the false passport, the goatee, the glasses but his undercover guise simply couldn't fall too far from the tree because otherwise it would be unbearable. He picked his lover up and made the 80km journey back home via Zahara de Los Atunes, a small town en route. As he approached the town, only 4km from their final destination, there was an infiltration of security personnel including the armed Guardia de Civil. This was highly unusual and Noye's foot weighed just a little heavier on the accelerator – you never knew if a speedy exit was required.

"My reactions are instinctive but when the area is swarming with police and soldiers you don't need any imagination to raise your guard," he said.

Noye had every reason to be concerned. He was carrying a passport in the name of Alan Green and was going by the name of Mickey Mayne in the company of a woman who didn't know her lover was a wanted man. Or at least this wanted! Surely not an army just for tax evasion!

Without alerting Maria, Noye skirted around the town and took a beach lane and avoided a checkpoint outside the key municipal building in the village.

"Why are there so many police?" Maria asked Noye. He shrugged his shoulders. "No idea," he said.

"I was more than a little relieved to have left the town. But as soon as I got to my village, there were even more police. I drove through the town without being stopped and took a turn toward my house and there were more police and as I drove up to my driveway there were Guardia de Civil everywhere – just outside my house. I drove on by. 'This is the takedown,' I thought as it had all the hallmarks of a dedicated operation. So, I checked into a hotel about ten miles away to lay low until I knew what was going on. Maria was a little confused obviously."

Noye went through the calculations – his synapses crackling. He knew what would happen next. Prison. Court hearings and extradition. He had mapped it all out. He was reaching out to the authorities through his agents of influence in the Metropolitan Police and the CPS, and offered to trade his freedom for a manslaughter charge but nothing had been forthcoming, either from official sources or through the back channels.

The police presence was troubling him hugely. He phoned Mickey Lawson to find out if there was news of any developments back in the UK. Were there any links with the Kent Police investigation and the armed officers outside his Spanish bolthole? Inevitably, Noye thought it was all about him. It wasn't vanity. There was a huge number of resources dedicated to bringing him in and this could be the moment when it all proves worthwhile. Mickey Lawson told him that the police had not made any inroads according to his sources, but he did warn him that Dennis New, John Palmer's wayward enforcer, was out to get him and told Noye that on no account should he go to Tenerife again.

Forewarned, it nonetheless did not protect Noye from the curiosity and bewilderment of his partner.

"Why are you not bringing me to your home?" Maria inquired. Even she would think that 'armed police' for a tax evader was a little over the top. Maria still knew Ken only as Mickey, a friendly builder laying low from the UK authorities. Noye deflected the questions saying that the house wasn't quite ready for occupancy.

He added: "I turned up the road towards my house the next day. Again, there was a presence in the area. Then as I came up to my house, I noticed there were still police officers outside the gaff. So, I kept on going. I drove right past and took Maria to a hotel for a second night. She was very confused."

For two days he drove past. Each day armed police surrounded the house, each night Noye and Maria camped out in a hotel just out of the area. "Eventually, I got Maria to ask one of the officers what the story was in a quiet part of the town," Noye said. "Somewhere I could have fucked off in the car If I had to! And to my relief, it transpired that a senior Spanish minister, the equivalent of the Home Secretary, lived right beside me, and the security was to protect him and not to capture me."

Ironically, the Spanish police had Noye in their sights and even helped protect him. In conversation with one of the officers when they became familiar with him, he was given a number in the event there were any security issues. "I was even recommended to carry a flare gun on my person and fire it in the air if I ever needed assistance and the police would immediately descend upon me to protect me as well," Noye added.

He was hiding from the police and here top officers in the Guardia Civil were affording him extra protection, naturally, under the guise of Mickey Mayne, the affable builder, when at the ports and main airports his picture adorned the most wanted boards.

He never got the flare gun. A wise move.

***

Nick Biddiss was having his weekly meeting at Kent Police Headquarters with the Assistant Chief Constable along with other officers. He drove to the headquarters in his police leased Ford Granada. Surrounded by white boards and stale coffee cups, senior detectives went through their policy and budgetary issues.

For most on-the-street investigators this was the 'boring stuff'. Nick was always a 'focus' because his inquiry was the highest profile murder in the country. His investigation was hot but stagnant. After the general paperwork and policy session was over, Biddiss was taken aside for a briefing and a catch-up on the latest. There wasn't much to add. The usual lines of inquiry were reported up the chain. "These sessions were to check up on me and the team as much as anything," he said. "To ensure the pressure was not building and to make sure that I was looking after the team and myself. It was a standard welfare check on me and the investigation."

Because there was little progress in the inquiry, it was due for an independent review within the force. Each decision and action would be reviewed by a senior detective outside. Biddiss never felt the pressure of such intrusions which is the mark of a good officer. It was standard practice.

Up to now the whereabouts of Noye was a mystery and any search continued to be hampered by the sightings that were coming their way, adding up to thousands over the course of the investigation. This was a focus of the review. Newspaper headlines read: **'Kremlin Join in Roadrage Search for Noye; Killer on the Razzle – Cheeky Fugitive Laps up Life of Luxury; Runaway Flies in for Quick Chinese – Noye Gives Law the Slip'**. [66]

"We were probably getting two or three sightings a week and there was hardly a European country where he was not spotted," Biddiss said.[67] "He allegedly went to South America and even had plastic surgery but what could you believe in the avalanche of information we were getting." The force had not conducted an international manhunt on this scale before and so the spotlight was on the investigative team.

Biddiss added: "They review everything, but it is not an admonishing task. It often comes up with fresh ideas and lines to push and follow-up. I welcomed these interventions and often led these reviews on other investigations which were struggling."

In fact, Biddiss, as the lead murder investigator in the county, had been called upon to review the investigation into the attack on Dr Lin Russell and her two children which left

66   *Ibid.*
67   *Ibid.*

only Josie (9) alive in an attack of random ferocity which took place in Chillenden in Kent in July 1996. The family had been enjoying a gentle country walk home after attending a swimming gala when they were attacked and beaten with a hammer after they were tied up and blindfolded. Throughout the hunt for Noye, Nick would often also stand in for Detective Chief Inspector Dave Stevens who was leading the Russell murder investigation. Likewise, Stevens would fill in for Biddiss whenever he took holiday leave.

Though now settled into his new holiday home/bolthole, Noye did not appreciate the close call with the Spanish police. He regarded Maria as his lucky charm and once again he decided to act on his belief that a moving target was harder to hit. At his Spanish girlfriend's suggestion, it was another Caribbean destination. The pair dashed off to Madrid from where they would take a long haul across the Atlantic.

If there were steps to follow, then Al Capone's were probably as good as any. Noye was just as enchanted with Cuba as Capone was 70 years earlier and he took great care to stay in the 'Hotel Nacional' in Old Havana, Capone's alma mater. Noye was an aficionado of the black and white genre of gangster movies often starring James Cagney and Humphrey Bogart. Havana was the perfect backdrop for any movie set. It was so rich and vibrant. Back in the day until the Cuban revolution in 1959, the island truly was a gangster's paradise, and their old haunts were a must visit for tourists. Original photographs from the era still adorned the walls of their hotel. Capone used to book out the entire sixth floor but for Noye and his companion a large room would suffice.

Neither had been to Cuba before. Its attractions were not a secret, but it didn't go unnoticed by Noye that it had no extradition arrangements with any other sovereign state. The hotel had a cast of characters and none more notorious than Noye.

In between the fine local rum, the pair toured the cigar factories and savoured the unique atmosphere and time warp heritage of Cuba but bizarrely on one occasion, he and Maria found themselves in the country's parliament building. Oblivious to the rules and any 'no go' zones – Noye found himself as a tourist in the heart of Cuban governance facing the assembly of 500 seats. He took the opportunity to sit in Fidel Castro's presidential chair and pose for playful photographs; Why not? Noye was not shy on the run. He was like a child on a sugar rush. Freedom, cash, and no consequences. Perhaps only in Cuba!

He said: "There was a door and I just opened it and next thing I knew we were in the seat of Government. Staring ahead was a row of fixed chairs belonging to the great and mighty and one stood among the rest, Castro's Chair. Maria was reluctant but I thought what the heck and persuaded her to sit in for the hell of it. You only live once."

Castro was still president at the time and there is no telling how the authorities would have reacted if Noye was caught. It was an incredibly risky prank, but Noye, as ever, pressed the accelerator rather than the brake.

But 30 minutes away by plane, in Montego Bay, on Jamaica's north coast, Noye was breaking the rules once again. At the nearby Bob Marley Mausoleum, he somehow avoided excommunication when he took the Gibson Les

Paul Special guitar from its display on the wall (one of only five remaining guitars belonging to Marley) and began to air play the rare memento for his amusement. Noye was a Marley fan but creating mayhem and another mad memory on the run was his true motivation for this sacrilegious act.

Initially, the security guard objected sternly but Noye then flashed some cash and the lips were sealed. He didn't stop there. Despite Maria's reluctance, he also took down a rare gold disc belonging to the late reggae star and posed for photographs with it.

It was the way he operated. Everyone had a price. Considering the crime for which he was being hunted for, it was a minor transgression, but the principal was the same.

Noye was staying in a luxurious bungalow in Montego Bay. He could walk out of the back veranda right into the turquoise sea. It was a stunning location. It was the only place which gave Noye pause for thought. It wasn't lost on him that there was no greater contrast between the prison cell awaiting him and the little glimpse of paradise he was currently inhabiting. He loved the mellow mood and the lifestyle. What a sight the pair made! A stunning brunette with silky youthful skin belying her 38 years and the lived-in face of the 52 year old villain.

It was not lost on Noye. He said: "Maria would kick up her feet. Enjoy a spliff and I'd have a beer with a reggae band playing by the beach. I'm sure that they'd ask what the hell is going on there. We travelled around. Without a credit card I couldn't rent a car, so I just bought one. A 'Mark V' Cortina which I was going to sell on the way out."

The hotel concierge changed Sterling and US dollars for him at a discounted price on the black market to complete the purchase. Noye would never use the currency exchanges at the airport because, 'they rip you off'.

The rental cars were of poor quality because of the import taxes and Noye spied an opportunity. He had no responsibilities and on the run, he had more time for his entrepreneurial eye. His appetite for the deal never wavered. Recognising a gap in the market he did a prospective deal to import cars onto the island. His number one priority was still acquisition – making money – even more than securing his freedom. He couldn't have both. Every interaction and deal left a trail for the police to follow but could Noye do both? Stay free and live the art of the deal?

Through a cannabis haze, he sank his Red Stripe beer. As his girlfriend had her hair braided at a family run beach-bar, he began to finesse plans to reach out to the UK authorities and offer to trade – his surrender – for a manslaughter charge. Of course, he could just stay exactly where he was. The police could not have imagined Noye in this realm. This part of his personality was not registered in his criminal profile at Scotland Yard. Nothing in his past suggested that he was capable of adaptation on this scale. Then, of course, Noye had never been on the run before. Had the authorities underestimated him again?

Nick Biddiss, though, was hotter on his trail than Noye could have ever anticipated. There was a holiday break in the investigation. The Detective Superintendent had travelled to Malaga and the Costa de Sol, literally in the footsteps of the most wanted man on the continent.

But Biddiss was not on the manhunt – he was on a break with his family, comfortable in the knowledge that this was one part of the world that Noye would not dare to come near.

17

CULTURE SHOCK!

"It was sold to me as one of the most isolated places in this part of the world. The postcards were pretty and peaceful and naturally that made it a good place to hide. A little piece of me was curious but most of me wanted to hide."

After a quick return to Spain with Maria, Noye decided to keep moving. He was now quite the trail-finder. Nowhere was off limits, except the UK.

When a Bexley boy, a former printers' apprentice, makes the San Blas Islands in the north west of Panama his temporary home, you know events must have taken a startling turn. This printer still has his original union card. He was a member of the Society of Lithographic, Artists, Designers, Engravers and Process Workers. It was a catchy title. Say what you want about Noye but he was a 'good union man' and his contributions card from 1968/69 showed his monthly payments guaranteeing him retraining and a job where the union operated as long as he kept up his payments even through those periods when he was in prison.

His payments ran uninterrupted until 2004, crisscrossing two significant jail sentences. The cosy union benefits largely died out with Margaret Thatcher and Rupert Murdoch's assault on the print unions in the 80s but Noye still has his original union card more than 50 years later.

There was no need for unions on the San Blas Islands.

Having previously become acquainted with Panama when legally at liberty, in the company of his wife and friends Noye was more than happy to use this as a spring-board.

He was enjoying absolute anonymity living among the Guas, the indigenous peoples of the islands and enjoying their hospitality. Noye was as unlikely an anthropologist as you'd find and perhaps this was why the police and international police forces were struggling to locate him. Even if they tracked him to the San Blas Islands, they would have their work cut out with 378 of them to search. Its name has its origins in the 1600s as a hiding place for pirates and thieves and Noye fitted in well, though that era of priva-teers and pirates had long passed.

He said: "There is not a family here who would not give you their last morsel. Visitors are treated as long-lost friends. I was humbled. They had nothing and yet were content and very happy to share."

Noye is materialistic. He is driven by accumulation. Every decision is a business decision. Here there was no place for such pursuits. Community, family, need-not-want were the driving forces. Noye was required to recalibrate his mindset. There were no potential property deals, no prospective development opportunities – it was an immersion into a culture and an outlook that was totally alien to him. He acquired property, girlfriends, influence and wealth with ease but that counted for nothing in this part of paradise.

Noye was travelling in between the islands by sailboat and staying under the thatched huts of the natives on this archipelago in Caribbean off the Panamanian coast. He stayed with one family on a large hut on stilts in the shallow turquoise waters just off a sandy beach. "Initially, they were suspicious of me," he said. "I was not part of a group and was too old to be a gap year traveller. But when they got to know you, they were wonderful."

He was taken out fishing on a canoe by the father of the household. Offshore, there were shoals of surface feeding tuna and plenty of snappers to catch. The Islanders are subsistence fishermen and only catch what they need to eat but the haul was ample for the family and extended family meal that night. He couldn't have imagined a more relaxing time. It was as if he hadn't a care in the world. He had packed all his troubles in his old kit bag and there were few enough smiles but here under the Caribbean sun and tranquil waters he couldn't help but decompress.

"What do you do?" The old man asked Noye.

"I buy low and sell high," he said.

"And what do you sell?"

"Anything and everything," Noye answered.

"And why would you come here on your own? Where is your wife?"

Noye felt safe in his company but there was no chance he was going to be honest. "I decided to try and find myself and India was just too far away so I came here," Noye said jokingly.

"Where do the Indians go?" said the old man. When the jousting was over, the pair made their way to the family hut on stilts.

For the hyper-masculine Noye, the matriarchal society on the islands was anathema. "The men marry into the woman's family and live and are literally trained by the father-in-law into the family's ways," he said. "That's not me but I did like the idea that each island had its own chief and that the boss-man would be in charge for life – I could live with that." The coconut was cracked open. The top sliced off and a good helping of rum poured in and Noye was given an island treat. Coco Loco: "Nothing like a bit of homemade hooch to lighten the load. I can tell you that drink was as good as you could get."

Noye was a rule breaker. He was the ultimate capitalist without boundaries. Here the economy was based on pastoral and social activities and for once Noye was not tempted to cross the line. Tourists are not allowed to collect coconuts because it is a community resource. The seas and fish are revered, and no scuba diving is allowed. Although a part of Panama, the Guas have a huge amount of autonomy and have preserved their traditional way of life, eschewing the western ways and influences that Noye had built his entire life on.

When Noye sees a rule he wants to break it because it's usually an opportunity to improve his position – to get a deal. But those outcomes didn't work here because they didn't matter. He was what criminologists call a 'criminal undertaker', not one who buries the dead but one who undertakes to 'sort things out' to 'get things done'.[68] In a capitalist economy – someone like Noye will operate as an illegitimate entrepreneur – stepping over ethical and legal boundaries – to achieve their aims.

"I operate in the grey, the blurred lines between the legal and illegal and I always have done," he said. "It used to be called the black economy, but I always called it the grey sector."

But none of that was relevant here. Your value – your status – was not measured by wealth so Noye in that respect, was impotent. Or perhaps he was free; released from the instincts that fuelled him from his early years.

It was 'Groundhog Day' for Nick Biddiss. Every month or so he caught up with Danielle Cable and gave her an update on the case. He said: "What was new? Nothing much. But my job was to be a sounding board for the family and loved one's frustrations and to absorb and support anyway I could. I can't tell you how frustrating it was to be offering no news because no news was bad news. At every stage Danielle was simply stoic and supportive and was unswerving in supporting the investigation."

In spite of the account offered in Granada TV's drama 'Danielle Cable: Eyewitness', which presented her as having a difficult relationship with the police and Nick Biddiss, Danielle was a constant source of encouragement to Biddiss and his investigative team.

Danielle had by now moved out of the Cameron's home. She and Stephen had lived with the Camerons for about four months before his death. It had been a comforting

---

68   *Journal of Theoretical and Philosophical Criminology,* July 2014.

bedrock for Danielle to stay with his parents while grieving but for the 18-year-old it grew a little claustrophobic. She moved in with her aunt, Michelle Cable, and her boyfriend, Sean Johnsone when the time was right. The departure was a blow to Ken and Toni Cameron who having lost their son now said goodbye to someone they considered like a daughter. Despite being apart, Ken and Toni and their late son's fiancée remained in close contact.

Noye was moved but not changed by the remarkable experience on the San Blas islands.

The low-lying islands were simply impossible not to fall in love with. While it did not change him, it did give him pause for thought. In paradise though, there were few public phones. In paradise he missed his family.

He missed his lovers.

And he missed his bacon.

18

THE BEST OF TIMES

The bolthole in Spain was now less a safe haven than a full-time holiday home. Noye was now arranging for his family to come in regular intervals to visit him. All visitors used their own legal names and passports and didn't have to go to any great lengths to swerve the attention of the surveillance they had been under since May 1996 when Noye was first mentioned as a possible suspect.

His wife Brenda did not speak to him often at the outset but Ken could contact her and did so occasionally. As time moved on, Noye's position hardened in respect of returning to the UK without a deal. And every day he was away the press had a go at him and made a deal less likely. "To begin with he just wanted to go away, get his head sorted out, and see what was going on," Brenda said. Brenda Noye took a few evasive manoeuvres to distract the police but never used any false documents. During his time on the run, she saw him three times. She brought him up to speed on the coverage back home and how that had made their lives 'intolerable'. She approved of his decision to hang out in Spain because, "I knew he couldn't get a fair trial in

England, and I knew it was self-defence and that nobody would believe him."

His boys, now young men, were more regular visitors from mid-1997, and Noye even bought three dirt bike scramblers for them all to mess about on the spectacular dunes and beaches nearby. He said: "I couldn't go to see my family, so I just brought them to see me. Obviously, they were aware that they would likely be followed but two years in and it hadn't happened so far. The key was avoiding all mobile phone contact as best I could. I made sure that they had done their homework. We made sure they weren't followed. Brenda came through Gibraltar, and I picked her up there. The key was making sure she could leave the UK unnoticed. As soon as she moved then likely the Met, Kent Police and MI5 would have been on her and when abroad, MI6 and Interpol."

It was a formidable force, if all those agencies were engaged. They would come on their own mostly and each would spend five or six days with Noye. There were no rented apartments for them to live in. They stayed with Noye in his new home. They hid in plain sight eating out every lunchtime and evening. Noye laughed at the thought of them cooking at home. "We were low key, but we were not hiding, bunkered down in a hole in the ground far from it," he said. "The boys and I would tear it up on the bikes and crash them too. My weakness was my family and so I broke those basic protocols and that may scupper me but for more than two years it was working." He had his freedom, his family and his lovers. He could have his cake and eat it too!

Speculation in due course would claim that he ferried himself and family out of a nearby airstrip on a private jet to fly in and out the UK using Bristol airport as his entry and exit point. It was simply not true. Despite the conjecture, Noye never returned to the UK mainland until it was forced upon him. Tales of him drinking with old lags in English pubs on the Costa del Sol because he was lonely for pints of Guinness were also baseless, according to Noye. Like tales of working with the Krays in the 60s, myths around Noye are a dime a dozen and must be treated with a little care and circumspection. Noye was taking risks, but he wasn't stupid. When his family weren't around Maria would attend for frolics and fun. With itchy feet he would occasionally join her in Madrid or drive to Amsterdam for a couple of days.

Noye said: "It was a happy time for me. The heat at home was dying down a bit and I felt safe in Atlanterra. Literally I couldn't ask for more. Before Stephen Cameron's terrible death this is the life I was trying to create. How ridiculous that I was forced to do it and that I was able to do it while on the run."

He could enjoy the swimming pool, the open air, the bike rides, and his female company. There were trips to Tangiers in Morocco and trips to festivals and fairs of which there were many in Andalucía. Too many to count.

Until he was assured of a way out Noye would continue to live his best life. "You have to live every day as if it is your last and someday, you'll be right," Noye always said. He was preparing to settle down. He had befriended neighbours and was preparing to settle in and relish his lifestyle among the European expats and beatniks lost souls in Atlanterra, in Cadiz.

He was still very much low key – but going to neighbours' house for evening drinks is not something we ever heard Whitey Bulger do when he stretched his time on the run to 16 years. Indeed, by this time Noye was 18 months on the lam, Whitey Bulger, the number one most wanted in the US, had been evading the FBI for nearly four years. He fled in 1994 and Noye in 1996. The Bulger story was in the public domain and Noye tracked his mirror public menace across the pond, through the newspapers and thought if Bulger can do it – then why not him?

Noye departed from Bulger's red lines. No family contacts. Bulger disappeared with his girlfriend Catherine Grieg. Noye was initially alone but found a girlfriend on the hoof. He couldn't resist the temptation and the longer he was on the trot the more contact he would have with his family and friends. By breaking Whitey Bulger's rule was there any chance he could outstay his American counterpart on the run?

Nick Biddiss spent his down time playing golf with a handicap hovering around the low 20s and popping off to the Kent County Cricket ground. Away from the case, he was running occasional lead on a number of murders including that of Lin and Megan Russell and the attempted murder of Josie Russell in July 1996 in Chillinden, Kent, which had little action until Michael Stone, a local drug addict, was arrested and charged.

As serendipity would have it, both Stone and Noye would

ultimately share a prison wing. Nick Biddiss's career was colourful, and action packed. His number one adversary though, was still one step ahead of the Kent detective for now.

"I always wondered what Biddiss was up to," Noye recalls. "It was nothing personal. His picture always accompanied many stories about me. The press pitted him against me as a battle of wits. I knew it was much more than Nick who was after me. It was the secret services and all the international agencies. I always got on well with cops – believe it or not."

19

THE EVER-TIGHTENING NOOSE

While Noye was living his charmed life on the run, the authorities were getting desperate. Every day that passed was an embarrassment. The police had taken more than three thousand statements and made over five thousand separate inquiries to no avail. There was pressure from every quarter, including Downing Street, to close this down. Simultaneously, Noye's police contacts, and others unnamed, were still attempting to strike a deal which would secure his return. The longer he was on the run the more likely a deal could be brokered – that was his thinking.

The deal would be an agreement to plead to manslaughter and a probable eight-year sentence instead of the likely 16-20 years that would come his way in the event of a conviction for murder. Crucial to this scheme was Noye's links to Freemasonry. He was 'on the square' – a Mason of long standing at a lodge in Hammersmith – and was nominated by two wealthy friends, Dennis Knobs and Frank Kenny, with the further support of many serving police officers.

One officer who nominated him would live to regret it and stole the book from the Lodge to avoid being linked to Noye. Another private members club in London had pages ripped out of a visitor's books after some members were concerned that there was a paper trail linking them to Noye and his dubious visitors.

Both proposers of new members would have had to be Master Masons of good standing and had to testify to Noye's good character before he was put to the ballot of members. The vote had to be unanimous before admission. Noye joined the Masons for business. "It was a business decision," he said. "I scratch your back and you… You get the picture. I got some of my best legitimate work from my lodge. There were a few police officers, lots of businessmen – it was good for commerce."

The 'First Degree Handshake' – hand greets hand. Right to right. The left arm rises and places the left hand over the embrace – 'covering your work' – in Freemason code. Out of sight, the imperceptible compression of thumb on the first knuckle of the outstretched hand, then telegraphs the bond. "How old is your mum (mother-lodge)?" is asked. "She was 20 before she was 90," comes the answer. The reply confirms both are in the 'craft' and the numbers used denote the exact lodge you belonged to; all of which could playfully be lost in casual conversation

Noye's Lodge was number 2090 which received its warrant (constituted) in 1885. Noye wasn't the only villain in its history. He would argue that the white-collar criminals are much more prevalent and pernicious. "The white-collar criminals aren't robbing banks – they're running them," he says.

One fellow member was a senior police officer, a Chief Superintendent with The Royal Protection Unit at Buckingham Palace. The Mason, who had shadowed the Royal Family for more than a decade, told Noye about the huge number of uncatalogued paintings growing dust in one of the extensive basements there. Brazen as brass, Noye asked, "Can't you get me a couple for the house?"

"I don't think so," he was told, with incredulity. To Noye, this was an entirely reasonable request.

"What a shame," Noye said. "They're just gathering dust and moths."

When he was arrested on the Brink's-Mat robbery and the murder of DC John Fordham, Detective Chief Superintendent Brian Boyce in the interview room greeted Noye with a Masonic handshake, which was reciprocated. Boyce, who was not a Mason, would claim in court that Noye offered him a million pounds to help him beat the rap but Noye vociferously rejected that idea. Those who know him would baulk at the idea of Noye offering this amount of cash to anyone. He'd rather do the time. In any case, the jury set him free and it cost him nothing.

Everywhere he went, Freemasons around the world, on the bidding of a secret handshake, would do what they could, to assist a fellow member of the brethren 'in distress', even if he was on the run. Noye's membership eventually lapsed under Rule 148 for non-payment, and he was subsequently expelled from the lodge.

But it was his relationship to fellow Freemason, Commander Ray Adams, the youngest inspector in the history of the Metropolitan Police, which has for more than 40 years raised concerns about corruption among police officers.

Adams most recently featured in a 2022 Channel 4 *Despatches* programme which for the first time disclosed that he misled a court in 1977 by claiming that Noye was a registered informer when police files demonstrated explicitly that he wasn't.

The effect of this declaration to the judge was to secure a suspended sentence for bribing a policeman when jail time was likely. Adams claimed that Noye was a "current active informant" even though Noye was not officially registered, an internal report revealed by C4 demonstrated. 'It is possible with hindsight to say the court, particularly the judge, was misled'. However, the report (Operation Russell) went on to conclude that there was 'no evidence which suggests these actions were for corrupt motives by police and in particular Adams'.

Noye was neutral on the report.

"Don't believe what you read," he says. "Corrupt cops will claim the people paying them are informants and grasses will always claim that they are managing and directing cops. All I'll say is that I am no grass."

Noye was interviewed by police three times while in custody in an effort to gather information on his relationship with Ray Adams. He didn't talk then, and he isn't talking now. Anti-corruption officers also travelled to Miami and the

Caribbean to talk to officers who had worked with Adams without finding any evidence to implicate the long-serving officer. He retired with hardly a blemish on his career and went to successfully consult on security issues related to broadcasting. There is no doubting the huge resources put into the investigations into Ray Adams without revealing any smoking guns.

He was the subject of two major corruption allegations and 11 other complaints between 1965 and 1985, and as his lawyers regularly advise, he was cleared of all allegations.

Corruption concerns around the Met have bubbled for decades and inaction or impotence has allowed the stain of bent cops to watermark the justice system to such an extent that the current Met Commissioner Mark Rowley has issued a hotline for members of the public to report concerns about corruption and crimes committed by the police. Perhaps, decades too late.

***

Noye is happy to discuss corruption in the manner that OJ Simpson discussed the murder of his wife Nicole – 'I didn't do it – but if I did – this is how I did it'. He believes that there should be an amnesty for those officers corrupted and those who corrupted them prior to 2000 to bring a door down on the decades long chapter of dirty cops.

Noye said: "You'll never get to the truth because no one wants to go to jail. But if you want to understand corruption then you must be able to talk about it without the risk of prosecution."

There is precedent for his suggestion of a Commission

and immunity for those who might testify to it. The Stephen Lawrence Inquiry 1999 was legally constructed to ensure that no one could be prosecuted based on testimony given at the inquiry.

"There are two types," Noye says. "Criminals paying police to let them off and police 'fitting' people up. If someone has been at it and got away with it for a while and they can't get a conviction, then they'll help one across the line. I hate that. But back in the old days, not me, if you got nicked you'd say do you know someone and they'd have a word and you'd be sorted. It might cost a drink or a big drink. Or someone might just want a future favour or a holiday and no money. Maybe a watch."

This is not a difficult conversation for Noye. It is a banal truth. It is the history of the underworld and the police over the last 50 years. Uncomfortable as it may be – the fantasy that the Met were the best and the most honest force in the world is a lie and when truths like this are told by (in his own words) a "villain" like Noye, then you know that there is a real problem with the ethos and ethics among the police of yesteryear, and likely today.

The price of corruption varies according to the task and the decade.

Noye said: "Back in the 70s a minor crime would be disappeared or resolved with a £1000 or £1500 bung but if it was a big job then you are talking much more. Then, a grand was a lot of money. In the era of 'Life on Mars' – there was a lot of fitting up and a lot of money given to keep out of jail. If you were lifted for an armed robbery that pulled a half a million, then you might have to pay £50k. That was the rules then."

Noye has been accused of corrupting police officers for decades and had spent 30 years and four months in prison talking to inmates who have paid bribes, bungs and treats to police officers, court officials and likely judges. Corruption could be his chosen subject on *Mastermind*.

"Officers can turn a blind eye, they might lose files, find evidence, lose evidence," he said. "Small mistakes or deliberate mistakes by police officers can have a big impact and that is as much about letting crims off as fitting some up."

Noye was confident in early 1998 in his Spanish hideaway that overtures made on his behalf and his police contacts would unlock the key to a deal which he could live with.

"If I got a manslaughter charge I could fight it," he said. "I am sure if I didn't leave the scene, I may very well have been charged with that but maybe not."

Nick Biddiss thinks that any thought of a deal with Noye and the CPS is unthinkable. "I cannot in any circumstances see it," he said.

Noye gave no details about who was operating and pulling strings on his behalf but you wouldn't bet against him having connections to at least keep the conversation going.

Was there a deep state negotiation at play here or was it simply a game of hide and seek?

While his 'proposed deal' was being negotiated Noye returned to his nomadic lifestyle and dispatched himself off to Guatemala, Central America. Why not? It was one of the most dangerous places for the lone traveller. Here life was cheap. He understood that he could easily be taken out for just a few dollars. He could be disappeared here. All those rumours he had set off in England that he was dead just might come to pass. Reports of his death could be all too true – if he stayed. He left within two days of arriving. He was safe from the police on the run in Guatemala but there is no point being free if you're dead.

Family and old contacts remain the link in the chain that those on the run cannot let go and this can lead to their downfall. Noye was no different. He loved his family. One day on a Spanish beach, near his Atlanterra house on a lazy August afternoon, a man walked up to Noye to ask him about a dog. The expats in this area were mostly Dutch or German. He knew quite a few of them. Of course, there were Brits, but they were few and far between.

Noye said: "I could tell he was a copper. He was English and smelt like 'old bill'. He said he'd lost his dog. I thought it's coming on top here, but I backed myself for about another week or two and I knew that everything would be sorted." He asked himself was it a chance encounter? Was there an informer in his ranks? Was Noye getting complacent? It may have been all three.

He had family at the house, and they had a couple of days to go so he let the uncomfortable moment pass. But at what cost.

His mind reached back to another moment that he knew had placed him in a vulnerable spot. The Andalusian region is an equestrian Nirvana. Earlier in 1998, at one major centre near Canos de Mecca, Cadiz, a show jumping competition was taking place. As his bad luck would have it, a Spanish friend of Noye's who owned a ranch nearby wanted to visit and persuaded Ken to attend with him. "I didn't even want to go," Noye said. "Nothing against horses but I had better things to do. Anyway, we go and we're having a drink and I turn around and I see them. A North London couple on a day out. 'Hi Ken,' the man said. 'Hi, John,' (name changed) I said. My friend knew me as Mick and was out of earshot. Pleasantries were exchanged."

The elephant in the room was of course the fact that they knew more than anyone that he was one of the most wanted in Europe, at the very least. A polite dance then ensued when each asked the other how the family was.

Then while he was chatting, his mobile phone rang. For more than two years he avoided using any mobiles "but I was a cunt" Noye said, admonishing himself. "It was my son. As I answered it, I knew that this was a link, a connection and a mistake." It was a rookie error.

When Mary's husband drifted closer to the show jumping arena, she moved to Noye and in a whisper said, "Listen, Ken if you're ever caught, it's not us. We'd never tell. You've got to trust us on that."

"Sure," Noye said. John returned a bit closer, and the pleasantries resumed but the couple were nervous. Nervous of recriminations.

Noye played out the permutations on the chess board. Just how reliable were John and his wife, Mary, the two London socialites with legitimate business interests. If it was 'Mad'

Frankie Fraser, he could count his discretion as he had done earlier on his adventure but perhaps he was expecting too much from these two straight members of society.

* * *

Noye believes that back in North London, the couple accidentally disclosed his whereabouts at a dinner party one evening. The wine was flowing. It was late in the evening, and the company was good. One of the party is thought to have said, "Have you heard, Kenny Noye is dead?"

Which was met with this response: "I don't think so, we saw him randomly in Cadiz, Spain. He is very much alive."

The news would have had a lot of currency that night but back at home, the couple must have reflected that maybe it was not such a wise move to throw themselves into the centre of an international manhunt. The last thing they had wanted to do was meet Noye on the run and as sociable as he was, meeting friends from home was the very last thing he wanted. And yet, it was hard to undo this moment.

Perhaps the couple called the police themselves and there was no dinner party but sometime in early June 1998, Nick Biddiss was brought a piece of intel that came in through the usual channels.

He recalls: "We triaged it and after a few inquiries, phone calls, and the like, an officer came back to me and said this might have legs. As the old guard used to say: 'This lead gave us a hard on.' We don't say that anymore."

The husband in due course would give a statement, likely with some trepidation.

There was no witness programme for this businessman.

There was no hiding place for him and his family. Their statement to the authorities, which would never see the light of day, would connect Kenneth James Noye to Canos de Meca, near Cadiz. But would it be enough for Nick Biddiss to locate him and then capture him? Evidently.

Noye let himself down in one other respect. He phoned home to a selection of phone boxes from a public phone in Zahara, a small hamlet within a couple of miles of his own house. Looking back, he would identify these two moments as self-inflicted wounds.

Was this the tip-off that sent Kent police officers to Cadiz to hunt the fugitive down?

In June 1998, Nick Biddiss had turned his focus to this part of the Andalusian coast, but he is not telling the 'why, who or the where' of the intelligence. Some reports suggested that Noye was located by a post box he was using in nearby Zahara to receive mail. Biddiss dismisses this as does, more importantly, Noye. "I never had any mail sent to me," he insists.

Other reports named supergrasses and underworld snitches as responsible for this critical tip. None appears to be true.

As Biddiss is disclaiming any role by MI5 or MI6 in the investigation then the arrows continue to point to the horse show in Cadiz. Of all the places that might lead to his capture. It wasn't a brothel. It wasn't a murky pub on the Costa del Sol an hour or so away or an underworld super-grass – it was a random show jumping event that did it for Noye.

Nick Biddiss was at a crossroads in the case. He could not confirm the information unless he had officers on the ground. He said: "I had to make a decision. We couldn't risk letting this information out of our hands. We had to keep it close to a chosen few in the force and not even the Chief Constable knew." He rightly was concerned about leaks, if not to Noye, to the press. "I decided to send two officers over there to conduct surveillance on someone who we believe killed two people including a police officer. And we had to send them over incognito without informing the local Spanish authorities. It was a huge risk for me and a huge risk for them, notwithstanding the potential diplomatic incident that would ensue if something went wrong."

This decision weighed heavily on his mind but two officers were despatched to Madrid and then onto Cadiz on the hunt for Noye. On the July 7th 1998, the two Kent officers flew into nearby Jerez airport, picked up a car and headed towards Atlanterra. On the morning of July 10th 1998, Noye left his house and drove down towards a crossroads that would take him to his gym a couple of kilometres away. Trussed into the roadside verge of one tight bend, the Kent officers had the bonnet up, tinkering with their car.

Oncoming vehicles had to slow down to pass. At 8.30am, just as he was leaving for headquarters, Nick Biddiss got a call: "'It's him, boss, it's him!' they said. 'Are you sure?' I asked and they said emphatically: 'Yes.'" Biddiss told them to go right to the airport and come back home. He picked them up at Gatwick and got the lowdown.

Biddiss said: "I said most importantly, 'Do not tell anyone' and to their credit – they never did. That information was worth a lot of money to some people."

Noye had not spotted the two men either. He never even looked at the occupants of the car. He never glanced at the men who would dramatically alter the course of his life.

"I would have been on the way to the gym in Cornhill not too far away," he said. "I was being a little reckless. Maybe the two years have given me a false sense of confidence."

Over the next few weeks Nick Biddiss would work out a plan with the CPS. He would orchestrate the identification on the ground by Danielle Cable then an arrest warrant for murder if that ID was successful and then the takedown by the Spanish authorities.

Noye had family over in the following weeks from late July to mid-August. Nick and his officers were now working with a local officer in Cadiz who was helping to plot Noye's movements over that month while the paperwork was being sorted out. There was a buzz in and around Biddiss's office in Maidstone. Only a tight few were aware of the progress in the case. "If you didn't have to know – you weren't told," Nick explained.

Biddiss contacted Danielle Cable and told her that he might need her at a moment's notice to identify Noye. She was up for it. The identification of a perpetrator in a public place in a foreign location had never been attempted before. The CPS lead Elizabeth Howell said that it would suffice with the rest of the evidence for an arrest warrant for murder, but first Danielle must ID Noye. The ID expert at the force was a stickler for detail. He worked effectively within his ID suite but how would he perform outside in the open, in the public and in another county? Biddiss said: "I talked through the requirements, and it was good to go. He had cleared two weeks for a potential trip to Spain. When it was green lit a couple of problems raised their heads. Danielle Cable's parents were off in Cyprus and had taken Danielle's passport with them in a suitcase. Disaster.

Biddiss would end up bringing Danielle to the passport office for an emergency one, the day before departure. The other issue was that the specialist ID man who had promised full availability had a crisis. "I said, 'What's the issue?'"

Biddiss recalled: "He said, 'You know Nick that I breed Shih Tzu dogs.'

'Yeah,' I said.

'But what does that have to do with the ID gig?'

'Well the bitch is in heat and she's due to be serviced in Manchester tomorrow.'"

Biddiss asked if someone could take her instead but, apparently, the dog could only perform if the ID specialist was present. Consequently, the identification and takedown of the most wanted man in Europe was put off for a day. Nick demanded a photo of the frisky pups as a price for the favour. In due course he would get it.

Eventually, Danielle, the ID specialist and a chaperone, travelled to Cadiz on the 17th of August 1998. The trio were over there for ten days before the ID was secured. Officers knew Noye's movements and his favourite haunts.

"The task was to get a location that would facilitate easy identification without exposing Danielle to danger," Biddiss said. "We couldn't act until the ID officer was happy it was the right location and the right time."

Noye's movements had changed since his location was confirmed on July 10th but while it caused some drama, the team working with some Spanish officers from Cadiz quickly re-established his routine. "The officers had scoped out three favoured locations for the ID and would act when the watchouts signalled, he was there. We had to get a location of Noye's choosing but of our liking," Biddiss said.

The group were going undercover as tourists. It was not a difficult disguise in this part of Spain, in the middle of summer. On August 27th, Noye and his girlfriend, Maria pulled up in their Belgian registered Shogun outside the Il Forno, an Italian pizzeria in the hamlet of La Muela about 11.00pm. It was a quaint town squeezed between the Sierra mountains and the sea and its traces of the Islamic occupation in centuries past made it alluring for visitors.

"It was a normal night. We took our usual seats and there was nothing unusual," Noye said.

Spanish surveillance officers meanwhile called in the ID team with Danielle in tow. There was a corridor and a very dark space where Danielle could look into the restaurant without being seen.

Biddiss explained: "It had the effect of a one-way mirror. We brought her in. Noye was sitting with his girlfriend. The ID manager spoke to her in the manner as if he would have done in a standard ID parade back in a UK police station."

The ID officer added: "I asked Danielle to stand at the open window and view the whole restaurant from that position. I told Danielle not to stay in the window for too long and try not to draw attention to the fact that she was looking."

The situation was anything but standard. Danielle froze. This was the moment of truth. If she failed, then the arrest warrant would not be forthcoming and Noye would remain at large. Officers were afraid she had panicked.

The ID Officer, who prefers his name not be used, said that it was on her second glance around the room when she recognised the man sitting at the end of a table. "She started to get physically distressed," he said. "I knew that she'd identified Kenneth Noye. I thought: 'Someone is going to look up and say why were those people hanging around that window, or did you see that blond girl.' I was very concerned that we ought to get out of there as quickly as possible but not draw attention fleeing the restaurant."

"That's him. That's the man I saw kill Stephen," Danielle told the team outside the restaurant.

The job was done. She was whisked away and the next morning she would fly home.

"You know I saw a woman looking at me," Noye recalls. "Holding a gaze and I wondered. I never recognised her. But maybe she did me?"

It was a pretty woman catching Noye's eye. Normally, it wouldn't cause him much concern and today it didn't either. He sat and continued his meal.

The team immediately contacted Nick Biddiss back in Kent. "We were elated," the ID officer said. "Only half the job was done but we had the team in place. A team of Spanish officers were on the ready but there was the small matter of the paperwork – the arrest warrant." That was all they needed to begin extradition proceedings against Noye. Newspaper reports later state the wine glasses used by Noye were whisked off to Madrid for fingerprint analysis and forensic tests but that never happened, according to Nick Biddiss.

***

8.30am, Gatwick Airport, Friday August 28th 1998

Biddiss quickly de-briefed Danielle Cable before she returned to her parent's home. Biddiss now had to get the arrest based on the successful ID past the Crown Prosecution. He phoned Elizabeth Howell at the CPS only to find she was on a Channel Tunnel train with family headed for a day trip to France. Biddiss didn't need her authorisation but wanted her tacit support because it was a very unorthodox operation. Noye was getting antsy and, just maybe, any further delay may mean he flees before the takedown.

10.30am, Folkestone

Nick arranged officers to contact the train operator and get Liz off the train with her family. He met her on the platform at Folkestone. "She wasn't altogether pleased with me, but she was with the ID and the prospective arrest," he said. It was now good to go and Biddiss phoned ahead to Dartford Magistrates to say that an emergency hearing would be required.

12.30pm, Dartford Magistrates Court

The court was in full flow dealing with parking and speeding offences. Biddiss marched into the building. He was waved through security and walked into the court. At his request, the room was cleared. Nick asked to speak to a single magistrate.

"One of the senior lay magistrates presided," Biddiss said.

'Mr Biddiss what is this about?'

'I am seeking an arrest warrant for the murder of Stephen Cameron.' You could see him buck up.

'Oh, right!' he said. I gave him the statement from Danielle and discussed the CPS advice and he agreed to authorise it. As he signed it, I requested that he not actually put it into the docket until Monday so prying eyes would not see it and speak of it.

'So, we'll see it in the news tonight, Detective?'

'Maybe over the weekend,' I said."

9.30pm, Atlanterra, Cadiz, Spain

Noye was trying to hurry Maria. He had made a booking at the El Campero restaurant. "They knew me well and I always had a seat with my back to the wall," he said. "I could see the entry and exit points and I knew that if I was late, we'd still get a table, but I'd lose my favourite spot. I didn't think anything was going down, it was just what I did."

As he left the house late, undercover Spanish police officers from the serious and organised crime unit, the UDYCO, tracked the car as it made its way to Barbate from Canos de Meca. Officers did not know of the booking but knew once Noye took this route it was likely only one or two locations. When the team lost him en route, another picked him up further down the road.

10.00pm, Barbarte, Cadiz, Spain

"Maria and I got out and went to the restaurant. We were late. As I thought, I lost my table. We were placed out in front on the veranda. I was facing the bar but had no sight of the entrance," Noye recalls. Nick's team were on the ready.

"The Spanish officers were told that he had killed twice before with a knife and I can assure you that they were taking no chances," Biddiss explained. Two Kent police officers, the same officers who identified Noye on July 10th, were on site to confirm to the Spanish team if Noye was present.

The couple were spotted by the surveillance team and the plans were put in place for a quick snatch and grab. "The specialist officers wanted to scope the location out inside first, so they all went in for a drink at the bar," Biddiss said. He was getting regular updates on the phone.

Noye had ordered a bottle of Rioja and a Mediterranean Tiger Prawn salad. "The Rioja came but the food hadn't, and I noticed three well-built Spaniards come to the bar," Noye said. "They were wearing shorts, and each ordered a half a lager each. I thought they're fit – I haven't seen them around here. I let it go. They drank up. Walked past our table and then went out of vision."

The snatch squad were ready to pounce. British officers were only allowed to observe as the Spanish officers cordoned off the perimeter of the restaurant to prevent escape.

10.24pm

"I felt a hand around my neck," Noye recalls. "As one put me in a headlock, the other two officers took hold of each hand

and put me to the floor. Before the handcuffs went on, I put my finger to my lips and nodded at Maria and said 'Shh-hhh.'"

Nick Biddiss got a call immediately. "'I can tell you Nick, he definitely knew he was being arrested,' the caller said. We were elated. After two years and three months we got our man." Maria Hernandez simply disappeared into the night. The police had no issue with her. She was irrelevant and she had no idea why her man was dragged off by plain clothes officers.

Noye was fucked off. The gig was over. He kept beating himself up over all the clues he had missed and the basic mistakes he had made: "I had resigned myself to going back to face a manslaughter charge but not murder. Now the decision was out of my hands."

He was taken to the local police station and at 2.00am was moved to a more secure prison, El Puerto de Santa Maria maximum security jail in Cadiz, about 30 miles away.

8.30am, Saturday August 29th

The *News of the World*'s Ian Edmondson was onto the story first and contacted the Kent Police press officer. The story would occupy news headlines for months to come. Biddiss phoned Danielle Cable to confirm the capture but she knew it was coming. At that stage, Ken and Toni Cameron were none the wiser about the details but they knew that Danielle was whisked away on a secret task related to the case. "I knew it would break and wanted them to know first," Biddiss said. "Ken would usually answer and rarely went out, so I was surprised when Toni answered. 'He's out,' she said. 'Well, can you tell him to come back. I really need to speak to him. I'll be there for two o'clock.'"

Noye had a sleepless night in a cell which was completely dark. He was in the company of another man who slept on the floor and didn't move from the moment he entered and left the cell that morning to meet with the English officers. Ken thought he was dead. The two Kent policemen introduced themselves. Noye was asked: "Do you wish to return voluntarily to the UK?"

"No," was the answer. The extradition process would ensure that he could only be prosecuted for the charge he was extradited on and nothing else and on that basis most defendants insist upon extradition. The holiday was over.

2.00pm, Swanley, Kent

When Nick Biddiss arrived at the Cameron home, the press was already camped outside. Flashes went off as Nick walked towards the door. He went in and they hugged him away from the cameras. There were tears and cheers as Toni and Ken celebrated over a cup of tea and biscuits. Another time they'd share a drink. "I told them there was a long way to go yet," Biddiss said. "We had to get him over here first.
'But we got him,' said Ken.
'We have Ken, we have. Finally.'"

20

THE SPANISH DEFENCE

"Tonight, Kenneth Noye is being held in the Southern Spanish city of Cadiz after being arrested for Stephen Cameron's murder," the BBC announced in the evening news.

Nick Biddiss gave a short statement: "Kent Police have been in liaison with the Crown Prosecution Service for the past number of weeks and with the assistance of Interpol this arrest has been effected."

It was treated as a vindication of his work and his determination.

"Let's not forget that Noye was his ultimate prey, having been pilloried in the press, it was quite a coup to get his man," Gary Jones, the *News of the World* man who broke the story more than two years previously that the police were looking at Noye, graciously said.

Appearing in Spanish courts looking like a man, as one newspaper reported, who'd just stepped off a super-yacht rather than handcuffed from a prison van, Noye would fight this extradition battle like every other – to the last. His liberty was gone and so was his £500 pair of Cartier sunglasses. A police officer who attended his arrest and helped escort him to the local prison had also helped himself to his designer frames.

Even today, it rankles him that the officer who took them off him on the day of his arrest was wearing them the next day. He saw him as he was being brought back to jail in a van with blackout windows. 'What a cheek!' Noye thought, with a tiny hint of admiration. While his lawyers worked on his defence to the extradition, Nick Biddiss went to visit the British Ambassador in Madrid to thank the embassy for their assistance.

The embassy has one police officer and an officer from HMRC to deal with drugs and criminal issues with British offenders, primarily on the Costa del Sol.

As he entered the majestic building, he noticed something which he could not allow to rest. He was directed to a lift and made his way to the third floor where the UK Ambassador was waiting. Pleasantries were exchanged. It was clear that the Ambassador had not been fully briefed because the police officer had a day off. The office overlooked the street and fluttering in the window and across the eye line of the Ambassador was the British flag – billowing upside down. "Is there anything I can do for you Detective, we are so ever grateful for your efforts?" Biddiss was asked.

"Yes, please," he said. "Can you put the flag the right way up!" As he left, he chuckled as the local staff were hastily correcting the diplomatic faux pas.

Shortly after, the embassy sent its consul, Carlos Formby to visit Kenny Noye at Valdemore Prison, the maximum-security jail in Madrid, as it often does in high profile cases.

The two hit it off very quickly, according to Noye. Formby, who was an avuncular man with an interesting heritage. His father was a vice consul and one of his relations was George Formby, the champion of the ukulele and leading entertainer in the UK throughout the 30s and 40s. "He was a lovely fellow but kept talking about George Formby," Noye said. "He asked me if I knew about him, and I said no and then he continued to fill me in. Eventually, I had to interrupt and say, 'Thanks for the history lesson but what about me?'

'Do you want to go back home?' He asked.

'No time soon if I can help it,' I said.

He was with me for about an hour and gave me his number and said, 'Call me anytime if you need help.'"

A preliminary hearing on Noye's extradition was scheduled for November 1998 in the Spanish High Court. A full hearing would be held the following year but for now Henry Milner, Noye's lawyer was telling the court and all who would listen that Noye was not at the murder scene and would never get a fair trial in the UK.

The press had gone to town on Noye and all who knew him. They were in the enviable position of being able to report as they wished because he had not yet been charged. The newspapers would take every advantage naturally. Having lost his designer glasses, Noye was fighting to hold onto his car and the £6,000 that he had on him when he was arrested. The passport he had used for much of his travels in the name of Alan Green was seized, but this would be passed to the UK authorities. Eventually, when his car was returned and collected by his family, the expensive stereo was missing. "No surprise there," a frustrated Noye exhaled. He was settling into a new routine.

Following one of the extradition hearings, Noye was so frustrated by the apparent gentle acquiescence of the Spanish judges to the extradition request that he took it upon himself to write to the judges and give them a little piece of his mind. Normally, such communications come through lawyers, and they are naturally nervous of such contact because it is a crime to denounce the judiciary. Noye said: "They were just rolling over. I had enough so I got one of the guys on my wing to translate my thoughts and put it down in Spanish." Noye may have put too much trust in the translation but the next thing he knew he was taken from his cell to serve a three-month stint in solitary confinement. "The warden told me that I had broken the law and the judges were furious. I had denounced them and I could get two years in jail," Noye said. "I said bring it on, anything to delay my return to the UK."

Toni and Ken Cameron made a public intervention and called for Noye to voluntarily return to face justice: "Noye, if he is innocent, should return home and defend himself. He cannot be afraid of the truth – if he is innocent." The press ran with it. Maria, Noye's girlfriend, arranged to visit him and would do so weekly. "You've been on the news all the time," she said, on her first visit. "They are saying you killed a policeman."

"No, I got off that. It was self-defence," Noye replied. "It's another murder they want me for."

"Another?" she exclaimed. She was genuinely unaware of

the criminal heritage of her boyfriend but she was right in one sense, as Noye risked being retried for the death of DC John Fordham.

His defence counsel, John Mathews QC was frank about it: "Someone attacks a police officer with a knife and stabs him to death, an unarmed police officer; and if you string those facts together the general perception is how can there be any justification for that. But he was acquitted on the grounds of self-defence."

Mathews said that the acquittal counted and mattered, but not in the court of public opinion or in the media: "It is not unreasonable to say there must be the gravest suspicion that he could ever get a fair trial as a result of the publicity."

The press coverage of him after his arrest and during the extradition proceedings was unrelenting. Noye could do little about the coverage and it was even more reason why he would fight the enforced deportation with every sinew in his body in or outside of solitary confinement. On his lawyer's advice though, he would stop corresponding with the judiciary.

21

TO THE LETTER OF THE LAW

In the recreation area in the Valdemoro High Security Prison, Kenny Noye was writing an important letter. The red tiled structure – with fading cement 20ft walls – jumped out of the dusty farmland surrounding the penitentiary which housed both male and female prisoners. The jail, open for just six years, was not ageing well despite its relative youth and was based upon the Panopticon or all-seeing concept and drawings of Jeremy Bentham in 1785. The inmates were monitored in each wing from a bubble room where officers could witness and record all their movements. There were literally no hiding places in this prison. Fights broke out all the time, but Noye was never targeted or felt the need to engage. Officers would let the fights run their course and then come down from their bubbles and hand out disciplinary papers to those involved. In British prisons, officers would run in with truncheons to break it up but in Spain it was a little more relaxed.

Noye was preoccupied with preparing his defence and had just said goodbye to Henry Milner who had visited the previous day. Now he was on the offensive.

Today there was less writing and more dictating. But not to his lawyer!

'*Dear June.*

'*Thanks so much for your lovely letter. It was very kind of you...*'

As inmates walked through from the mess to the recreation area and passed the book lined walls of the secure penitentiary, Noye was encouraging a tall German to put his best pen forward in the interest of love.

The pen pal he was responding to, joined a plethora of women who wrote to inmates in prison, and in particular, to Noye.

Noye said: "I'm not alone but I got my fair share. I was always concerned if they were journalists, so I'd ask them to send some intimate photos which they usually did. Axel, a tall German banker who had run off with £40m from a Swiss bank, was on my wing and he had beautiful handwriting and he wrote my letters on my behalf. I swear I'd seen it happen in *Porridge*. But it was my words. Axel was just the scribe. I was still the poet – you better believe it."

Kenny Noye continued: "This worked until Axel was released. The Swiss authorities had offered to drop the case in return for half the money. He refused and said for a first offence he would only get two years and had already served 18 months in the Spanish jail and would not hand over a penny. The Swiss dropped the case and he was free but I was stuffed. Suddenly, I had to write my own letters which didn't quite carry the same romantic mood." You didn't need a handwriting expert to know the script had changed – but not the scribe.

Noye added: "The women questioned if I was writing to

them or if someone was masquerading as me. Usually, a phone call would sort it out."

For most of the women, it is an attractive proposition to have a relationship particularly with lifers because the women can control the dynamics. Often these women seek out these relationships because they have suffered with previous partners but with their new boyfriends behind bars – they subconsciously feel a lot safer – because they can safely dictate the trajectory of the relationship.

Noye was cautious about responding to his unsolicited mail. It was an old tabloid trick to write to cons and build relationships and then eek a headline out of it. Most of the high-profile cons were aware of this stunt.

Noye was sending romantic letters to several women simultaneously and still receiving visits from Maria, his devoted lover on the run.

Inevitably, some of the women would find out that they were being two and three timed and would write to Noye to threaten to cut him off unless he was exclusive. Noye would never agree to such an arrangement and was unashamed about his proclivity for female company, and lots of it.

Two thousand kilometres away, a party was in full swing on John Palmer's yacht in the balmy climes of the Balearic Islands. Helicopters, jets, and boats were the playthings of the rich and infamous and Palmer was more than happy to display the trappings of his ill-gotten gains and in particular, his beloved 100ft, £7 million boat – The Brave Goose. Noye had spent plenty of time on the boat, but it was the only yacht he ever got seasick on. Its slim 100ft hull simply did not agree with him and he only stayed over when it was tied to the dock. Languishing in one of the worst jails in Europe, Noye could only dream of such an occasion and with him facing life imprisonment back in England he knew he might never be seeing a party outside of a prison ever again.

On board was Palmer, his Spanish lawyer, and Noye's trusted lawyer, Henry Milner. The well-regarded defence lawyer was working on Noye's extradition defence and was returning from Madrid after a visit with Noye. His client was understandably jealous about the soirée on The Brave Goose to which in any other circumstance, he undoubtedly would have been invited to.

Himself and Noye were still banking on maintaining the defence that he was not the perpetrator and that he would not get a fair trial in the UK. Both were fully aware though, that they had a battle on their hands. This night, Milner was taking soundings from John and his Spanish lawyer. Palmer had avoided extradition from Spain under a different legal regime initially evading arrest on the Brink's-Mat case before ultimately fleeing to Brazil where he was deported to face trial which ultimately ended in his acquittal.

Palmer though had ulterior motives. More than anything he wanted Milner to attend a poker game he was hosting. This was a serious game and Milner had a reputation as a good card player although Bridge was more his forte.

Palmer was a long-standing client and paid well – Milner was delighted to take up the offer of what was always going to be a memorable evening.

Palmer's favourite tipple was a brandy but, on his boat, he

always took great pleasure in cracking open a good bordeaux from Chateau Palmer, an esteemed vineyard going back over a hundred years and with absolutely no connection to John Palmer. By coincidence, the wine had a distinctive gold label which always tickled him. As if on command, the vineyard also created a second label wine called 'Alter Ego de Palmer', which was exceedingly popular and a lot more palatable than John Palmer's alter ego, by all accounts – and certainly his estranged wife's (Marnie Palmer).

This evening, it was the Chateau Palmer 1983, a £600 bottle. The wine critics were full of praise for the pale ruby, sweetly perfumed flavour and 'its fragrant nose of berry, fruits, cedar, pencil shavings, leather and a soft, exotic spiciness'.

Also, on the boat that night were some local businessmen from Tenerife where Palmer still had everybody from the police to the airport in his pocket.

Palmer's yacht had a crew of six which included a Dutch captain, a couple of mechanics, serving staff and a chef. At the end of the meal, a poker game broke out which continued until early the next morning. "It was dealer's choice with Texas House rules which means cash only – you put up or shut up," Milner said. Palmer took everyone's watches to ensure they couldn't see the time and try to quit early. It was typical of the man. John's Spanish lawyer was wiped out and had to go ashore to replenish his reserves. Milner was begging for the night to end when he was $800 up but was $500 down when the session finally ended. Departing, Palmer told Milner to be sure to send Noye his best. He probably meant it too. Noye was practically family. Milner would return to England and try to engage Nick Biddiss and the CPS and persuade them to agree to a manslaughter charge, which would certainly provoke Noye's acquiescence to a return home and an end to his fight against extradition.

Unbeknownst to Milner though, Biddiss had other things on his mind. The Kent Police force was his family. He had given two of his children to the force where they were serving with distinction. His other family were the victims, the witnesses he supported and shepherded over a 30-year career. He got his man. Noye was locked away. Inevitably justice would now run its course. He was positive that the extradition proceedings would bring Noye home but there was always a chance that it would not. It was out of his hands. But there was one more thing he had to do, before he could retire with good grace and a clear conscience.

Few outside the force knew that he was about to sign off and drop out from the investigation for good. Nick had plenty of opportunities and had nearly bowed out earlier when he got the offer of a senior job in New South Wales, Australia. The hunt for Noye kept him in the country and in the job. He didn't want to leave until the task was completed.

But his departure would come as a shock to many and undoubtedly, a real blow to one person, in particular.

There was one person he had to see before he handed over the reins of the investigation to DS Denis McGookin, the officer who would cradle the case 'hopefully' to the Old Bailey and to a jury. Biddiss contacted the force's liaison with the witness protection programme. Danielle Cable had been in the capable hands of Nick's officers when in mid-August she identified Noye at Il Forno Pizzeria, close to where Noye lived deep in the woods upon his first arrival in the area.

Biddiss had been a rock to her throughout and he needed to say goodbye in person. Just weeks earlier, Danielle was whisked into witness protection. The Kent force had received a 'viable threat against our main witness' and she agreed to go into the witness protection programme. It was her decision, and it was taken solely by her, now as an adult.

Biddiss had shepherded the investigation with deft skill and sensitivity and he helped manage the expectations of the then 19-year-old who was, by now, in a new relationship. At the drop of a hat, she had scrambled to Spain with Kent officers to support the case against her boyfriend's killer. It was a task that her mother knew would change Danielle's life forever.

Biddiss said: "Mandy Cable was not happy that I picked up Danielle when herself and her husband were on holiday. There was no intention to do that; it was just the way the cards fell. But Danielle's mom was rightly really worried that this identification and witness protection would change their family's lives forever. And of course, she was right." She was very protective of Danielle and understood the full impact of this decision on Danielle's and all of their lives.

Her father, James Cable (1957-2020), a former European lightweight boxing champion, was less emphatic and more content for Danielle to make her own decisions.

A meeting was arranged. Biddiss said: "I had asked for it and Danielle agreed that it would be important for us both.

She was happy for the handover to chat and sign off, on what had been a traumatic few years. I just felt it was the right thing to do."

Biddiss was given a full briefing in advance. He was prohibited from asking her about her new home, life or anything that might identify her. He knew this of course, but protocols were protocols. There was a complete firewall between the witness unit and the investigative officers.

Cable had a change of name, look and home. Nothing about her life was familiar. Today, Biddiss, Danielle's anchor in the difficult waters of the country's most high-profile murder investigation, was jumping ship. He had been in the Kent force for 30 years and three weeks and was only a week from his full retirement. It was the end of one journey for Biddiss and just the beginning of a very different path for Danielle.

The case was in the best shape it could be in. Noye was in a high security Spanish prison. Cable was in a very different 'prison' – witness protection. At the Lakeside Shopping Centre, in West Thurrock, Essex, over Kentucky Fried Chicken, the eyewitness and the detective were parting ways.

She had lost her fiancé, her home, family and now her rock in the police – the one person who held her hand through every lead, potential breakthrough, newspaper headline and ultimately the capture of Kenneth Noye. Two officers from the witness protection unit accompanied Danielle. It was odd for Biddiss because it was so anathema to the ways they had met previously. Then it was open and relaxed over tea at her home or in a coffee shop but this was artificial and constructed, understandably because of the very recent circumstances of the death threat against her.

"It's not ideal but it's the job," Biddiss said. "It was sterile and not the way I'd imagined it. I couldn't even say 'Hi Danielle'. I didn't know her new name and I couldn't say her old one. It was difficult and strange and obviously, it was equally so for Danielle who must have just been getting to grips with her new predicament. We chatted about the journey we'd been on. She was proud that she'd done right by Stephen. It can't have been easy. In fact, it was a huge commitment. Her life had moved on. She was doing well, all things considered."

"Thanks Nick," Danielle said. "I know that my Mum wasn't happy, but I did it for Stephen. It was for him. It is what I had to do. It wasn't you but I know it was what you wanted."

"There were no recriminations," Biddiss added. "She was just determined and resolute."

No one among the throngs knew the drama unfolding in the innocuous surrounding of the shopping mall. It was the handover. Having been at the end of the phone 24/7 for Danielle since the day Stephen died, Nick would now be absent. In the event of a trial, he'd be a bound witness and couldn't see anyone's evidence so he wouldn't even see her then. This was the last time. The last dance. The last chance to say thank you! "You did a great job. We're all very proud of you. You should be very proud too," Nick told Danielle with more than a little emotion in his voice. The pair hugged. As she and her security officers departed, the pair quickly became lost in the maddening crowd. He would never see or talk to her again.

22

HOMEWARD BOUND

The Madrid prison was tough by UK standards, but Noye had fought a hard battle to stay there. It was in all truth a hopeless task. The delay did however have some strategic benefits. For the first time he was able to review the 32-page file that Nick Biddiss had prepared for the Spanish courts. His Spanish lawyer was emphatic that there was no evidence that Noye was even in the UK when the murder took place and that the publicity he had received in the ensuing years on the run and in the Madrid prison, would make it impossible to get a fair trial. Noye was hedging his bets. The Spanish would not adjudicate on his guilt or innocence but only decide whether he should be extradited on the back of the warrant issued by the Kent Magistrate in his closed courtroom to Nick Biddiss before Noye's takedown over a romantic dinner.

In a courtroom with judges puffing away in the dock, Noye's lawyer, Senor Palayo Honrnillos stated his case. Maria was at the Audiencia Nacional Court to support him, and they connected when they could. Uncuffed in the dock, Noye pleaded with the three judges. Noye remembers: "It was as bizarre a scene as you can imagine. I was made to do the perp walk on the way to the hearing to give the cameras the pictures they wanted. In the UK that wouldn't happen. I was always shy about publicity." Photographs of him outside of prison or a police van are rare. Not for him the famous 'David Bailey – Kray Twins' photo project (1965). Noye added: "'Trial by media' was my defence. And it was clear to me that the ID by Danielle Cable was so unusual after nearly two and a half years, a thirty second fight and all my pictures on the news during that time, that there is no way that could stick here or in the UK."

All were reasonable arguments, but the Spanish judges had enough of the circus around Noye, they were well aware of the history of Spain giving sanctuary to killers, gangsters and drug dealers from the UK prior to 1985 and would not be the laughing stock of Europe again on this matter. There was a warrant, and the Spanish had no authority under EU law to deny it, the lawyer for the UK authorities claimed. Biddiss wasn't quite sure that it was a done deal: "Anyone dealing with the Spanish over the last few decades could not be sure of anything, but I had my fingers crossed and so did Ken and Toni Cameron."

On March 25th, 1999, Noye was given official notice that his application against extradition had failed. Fuck it. The news came in a letter. It was all over bar the paperwork which would take two months.

Noye said: "Once I lost, I knew that meant that I had to decide upon my strategy in the UK. What would I do? Would I say nothing? Would I claim I was never there? Or would I claim self-defence which is what I always believed happened, but could I risk it? Who would believe me? I was leaning towards just saying nothing and leaving it up to Biddiss and his crew to place me at the scene. That was my preferred route. And it had the benefit of being consistent with my Spanish defence."

Noye was homeward bound, and he had some decisions to make. That could wait until he kissed British soil again. On May 20th 1999 – exactly three years to the day since he took off on the run – he was returning to the UK. DI Terrance Gabriel, with his stocky build and greying hair, was tasked with escorting him while Noye's prison car and security team would not leave until it received notification that the plane taking Noye back to Blighty had landed and refuelled.

Noye was strip searched at the prison by State Police and a trolley of his personal possessions were brought with him. Noye asked where his television was. Inmates had to buy their own sets and he wanted his nearly new and expensive television to be left for collection by Maria, but he suspected it was held back by the screws so they 'could nick it'. Kenny Noye was not having it.

He said: "Get the Governor. I'm not leaving here unless my TV is on that trolley." Two fit young officers from the 'Guardia Civil' thought about taking on the then 51-year-old who was match fit after nine months on the yard doing weights for five hours a day. They thought better of it. The Governor was called, and arrangements were made for Maria to get his TV.

DI Terry Gabriel arrived about noon to take Kenny Noye

home and extraordinarily, the aircraft that was tasked with the job, was HM Queen Elizabeth's personal aircraft. So concerned were the UK authorities that Noye and Palmer had penetrated the police and other border agencies that normal procedures could not be followed. With the support of the military and the Royal Air Force, they commandeered a plane from the Queen's fleet of aircraft, formerly The Queen's Flight (No. 32 Royal Squadron) to bring him home. Exclusive permission from Buckingham Palace and the government was granted for the move.

Just after 1.30pm, Noye was driven in an unmarked blue saloon car. He was handcuffed and in the back with an armed officer in blue security garb on each side. A glass partition separated the prisoner from the driver and his passenger.

The car with six armed outriders drove onto the runway to where the Queen's jet was waiting with the steps down. The escort vehicle drove within feet of the plane. Thirty armed Special Forces soldiers from the Spanish Military surrounded the plane. 'What did they think I was going to do?' Noye thought.

The burly Guardia Civil policemen handed Kenny Noye over to DI Gabriel who directed him onto the plane. He would wear handcuffs throughout except in the event he needed the toilet. Two officers sat in front of him and another on the right of him blocking him in.

Noye arrived in Madrid three years or so ago in John Palmer's private jet. He spent the night in a five-star hotel in the company of a beautiful woman. Now he was leaving Madrid in the same style on the Queen's plane but the accommodation awaiting him would not be quite as salubrious on the other end.

The short haul plane has only recently been retired to the 'South Wales Aviation Museum' but their biography of the plane makes no mention of the passenger this day.

Halfway through the journey, sitting in plush leather seats and handcuffed, Noye gazed at the splendour and thought: 'Where did it all go wrong?' From a Spanish prison to the Queen's Plane. In the bathroom, he saw a powder puff encased in gold, presumably used by Her Majesty. It would be more than 20 years before he would use a private bathroom again, let alone the Queen's.

"I could have nicked it except I was going to Belmarsh," he said.

In an extraordinary move, European traffic controllers at the request of Interpol[69] and the UK Government also introduced a 200-mile blue corridor – an aircraft exclusion zone to prevent any interference with the Bae 146 carrying Noye. His mood was not distraught. Perhaps, it was as one source claimed, because a deal was indeed done behind the scenes and Noye had arranged his own capture. Was this a 'Machiavellian' plot too far? Those who knew Noye wouldn't put it past him. Under extradition arrangements, Noye could not be interviewed in flight and anything he said could not be used against him.

He said: "It was a civilised flight. I figured I wouldn't be in this luxury for very long. It was a life you could get used to. It certainly wasn't 'economy' on Easyjet."

---

69   W Clarkson (2000): Page 323, *Killer On The Run*

There was little or no chit chat on the plane, but Noye recognised one of the officers as one who in the days before he was arrested walked up a lane and looked a bit lost. Noye caught his eye. Held the gaze and then said, "Did you ever find that dog?" The officer offered a soft smile in reply.

Without fanfare, the plane landed secretly at the airport it had set off from, RAF Manston airfield in the Isle of Thanet in Kent. Noye would not spend any time there. Once on terra firma, at 5.30pm, DI Terry Gabriel explained to Noye with a clear and crisp delivery: "I am arresting you for the murder or Stephen Cameron on the 19th of May 1996."

It was a profound moment.

There were cheers down the line when he quickly passed the news to Ken and Toni Cameron. Nick Biddiss heard the news on television. He was a little annoyed that he had to find out that way. Now working in the corporate sector, he felt a little emotional and not a little pride that his nemesis was back to face justice.

All his work would deliver him to the Old Bailey where he would now be held to account. Noye had his rights read out to him.

"I told him that he didn't have to say anything but that it might harm his defence if he didn't mention something he would later rely upon," DI Terry Gabriel said. "He made no reply."

"Ah, of course, I was saying nothing until I spoke to Henry (Milner) and John (Mathews QC)" Noye says now. DI Gabriel and his team then escorted Noye to Dartford Police station. As he entered the holding area, CCTV caught him in handcuffs and as he turned to catch the red light of the camera, he looked directly into the lens. This rare video shot of him remains the 'go-to' footage for news producers and media picture editors.

There after a snack, the Kent police officers went through the formality of explaining to him why he was being held. Just before 7.00pm, Noye was asked if he wished to say anything:

"I told them no reply unless my solicitor is present. They knew the score. It was all a bit of a blur. One second, I'm touring the globe and the next thing my universe is a 6ft x 6ft cell."

The following day, magistrates at Dartford who had issued his original murder warrant received the subject of the warrant back more than 10 months after it was first authorised. Then it was one magistrate in closed session – this day, three lay magistrates manned the bench. After a perfunctory hearing, the case was moved to the Crown Court, and he was sent to HMP Belmarsh to face the most secure conditions of any jail in the country. He had never served time there before.

Noye said: "When I arrived, it was overkill. Kent Police told the prison governor, John Knight he was going to have his hands full and there were 16 screws ready to greet me and looking angry and aggressive. I insisted on going into solitary confinement because I wasn't having some prison grass inventing some confession or nonsense. It wasn't normal but they agreed."

Noye was out of sorts but he was beginning to prepare for the penal grind and steeled himself for the prospect that he may never live another kind of life.

He added: "My legal team came to see me. It was decision time. I was at a crossroads. Deep down I knew I was fucked no matter what because of DC John Fordham but John (Mathews QC) my barrister said that if I was honest about the events then it was at the very worst a manslaughter conviction. I was advised that this was the best course. Honesty was the best policy. I figured it was too and then agreed to change my position – my Spanish defence – and admit that I killed Stephen Cameron in self-defence and then fled the country."

Following his return to the country, John Palmer, never shy of a bit of publicity, gave his tuppence worth, and in rather disparaging terms distanced himself from his good friend. The man who spirited Ken out of the country would deny knowing him, ever meeting him and ever looking after him in Tenerife. He denied him thrice. 'Kenneth 'bloody' Noye, I never knew him, I don't want to know him. If I was harbouring him then why not get him!' the indignant entrepreneur told a newspaper.

It was every man for himself. The rats were leaving the sinking ship.

Two months later, on July 6th 1999, Noye was returned to Paddington Police Station and Henry Milner was present to oversee an ID Parade. The passengers and drivers of vehicles who were witnesses to the events of May 19th 1996, were brought into ID Kenny Noye. Kent Police did not know at this stage that Noye had already decided to admit to being present at the scene. Thirteen witnesses came individually into the ID parade room, behind a one-way mirror. Only one couple picked Noye out accurately. He was second from the end in a line of eight white men in ages ranging from their mid-twenties to late-fifties.

Alan Decabral, a Rolls Royce driver who phoned the emergency services, was one of the witnesses who failed the ID. He said he saw Noye walk past him with a smirk on his face after the stabbing, one of the few who got a close up view of the assailant on the day. This was devastating for the prosecution, but they got bailed out when Noye made the ID irrelevant by sensationally admitting to being present at the attack, and to being the man who put a knife into Stephen Cameron.

Kenneth James Noye pleaded 'not guilty' to murder, citing self-defence, and a trial date was set for the March 30th 2000. It wasn't a rerun of the DC Fordham trial but that is how many would present it.

Deja-vu was not sufficient to capture Noye's mood. He shook his head. "Not here, again."

23

PRE-TRIAL

The mention of the Old Bailey evokes nostalgia and romance involving the grand victories of Rumpole and other grandies at the front row of justice.

It was the centre of remarkable dramas over the centuries, including being destroyed by the fire of London in 1666. In the pantheon of justice, *'Regina v Kenneth James Noye'* more than held its own for drama, intrigue and tension. The wood panelled walls of Court Number 2 would house this murder trial which was scheduled to last for just two weeks.

"My Lord there is a real and present danger if protection is not given to the Jury," Mr Justice Latham was told at the Old Bailey, on the afternoon of Thursday February 10th 2000.

In the absence of the press, the judge was hearing submissions about whether the jury should be protected or not. Noye's legal team were concerned it was prejudicial and softened the jury for a conviction. The prosecution determined that the threat of jury nobbling was very real and there was little risk of prejudice to Noye with protection. It swings both ways, the prosecution claimed. With protection, the jury may be more inclined to acquit because they may fear retribution if they convict. One's natural instincts were that a protected jury would leave a stain on the accused character – deserved or undeserved – and the court was inclined to agree with that.

This pre-trial hearing was the first key legal battle in the jousting between the two adversarial legal teams. Earlier in the morning Detective Superintendent Dennis McGookin had applied for an intelligence summary to be excluded from eyes of the defence in an ex-parte Public Interest Immunity hearing –that is without the defence being present. Only the judge would see this intelligence which provoked the unexpected application for jury protection which was heard later that day just a month and a half before the start of the trial proper.

"Is Mr Noye a person who has influence in the criminal fraternity?" Justice Latham asked the crisply dressed officer. "Is he in a position to call upon assistance within the criminal fraternity in dealing with this matter we are dealing with?"

"He is my Lord," McGookin said.

Jury nobbling has long been a noble art among the criminal fraternity particularly in the 70s and 80s. But it was a game that both sides could play. Criminals would nobble juries and during trials, the police would nobble the juries right back into line. This secret battle could never be discussed nor disclosed but it happened.

The state in this instance was relying upon secret intelligence which Kent Police had garnered over the Christmas period which suggested that moves were afoot to contact witnesses and prepare to nobble the jury. Their intelligence would not be disclosed to the defence but DS Dennis McGookin did tell the court that in the two previous trials involving Noye, namely the Brink's-Mat money laundering trial where he was found guilty and the John Fordham murder trial where he was acquitted, "There was no evidence of jury interference".

Although Noye was never accused or involved in jury nobbling, he knew exactly how it worked. He recalled that back in the 70s, there was hardly a jury in an armed robbery trial that wasn't nobbled. It wasn't a sophisticated process.

Noye said: "Once the jury is nominated. They look at the jury and think, 'Oh, he's a powerful person, and looks like a powerful person who can convince the jury to find them NOT guilty'. So that's how it all starts. And the police played the same game. They look at that jury, they want someone who's got a bit of power to convince the jury that he's guilty. That's what the police used to do all the time. It was like the wild west. It doesn't happen anymore and hasn't really done so for thirty years. In the 70s, after a whole spate of trials involving armed robbers resulted in acquittals when the evidence was overwhelming – it was cracked down upon. Some verdicts just stank. Those cases were bound to raise eyebrows."

Prison lags often spoke of the good old days when one didn't have to worry about the evidence, just the jury.

Noye added: "They'd pick one person. Follow them home. The offer would have to be delicately put. A thousand pounds was the going rate. To make sure, they'd pay off three to eliminate a majority verdict, but the instructions would also influence the other nine. Those three would be told that there were others on their side but would not be told who their fellow bent jurors were. Rarely would a juror refuse. All the juries need is a little twinkle of doubt and hey presto – a NOT guilty verdict. But that was the old days."

Noye was called into court to give his views to Judge Latham about the jury predicament for his own trial. "How can I have a fair trial with police guarding them outside their homes… 24 hours a day? There is no alternative but to think I am a violent man," he said.

He recalled in the Brink's-Mat case that the jury were not supposed to be fraternising with the police protection unit and yet they were going out drinking, shopping and eating out together. In one instance, he said, a female juror appeared to fall for one police protection officer and asked for him to be her permanent security shadow over a trial potentially lasting a month. "Since I heard, she got engaged to him," Noye said, as he pleaded his case for more than an hour – against the advice of his legal team.

Noye revealed for the first time that the issue of jury interference or inappropriate contact between the police and jury members two months into his Brink's-Mat case nearly resulted in a mistrial. He said: "Judge Lowry said to me: 'What do you want to do about it?'" Offering him the choice to dismiss the jury or proceed with firm directions in his summing up, Noye chose to proceed and was convicted. Perhaps he should have taken up the offer for a new jury!

The real concern for Noye was that the Metropolitan Police would provide the security and after the death of DC Fordham, he said every police officer and, in particular, the

Met wanted to send him down any way they could. The die was cast with the secret intelligence and as with all his previous trials over the last 20 years, the jury would have full military style protection throughout the course of the proceedings.

The judge came to his decision. "Jury protection is bound to carry with it the potential for prejudice to the defendant, and he (Noye) has expressed eloquently and if I may say so, moderately, and effectively, the concerns," he said. But with the secret intelligence issues in mind, he ordered a protected jury for the trial.

"I knew I was fucked," Noye said. "You start with protection and then you are fighting an uphill battle."

***

A contingent of 14 police motorbikes, three bulletproof Range Rovers, armed officers and a police helicopter followed the prison van that took Noye to and from high security HMP Belmarsh, for the pre-trial hearings. The imposing prison, built in 1991 on the grounds of the Royal Arsenal in Woolwich, London captures most of the inmates from the Old Bailey and is renowned for its Category 'A' inmates. However, over the years 'guests' have also included writer and politician Jeffrey Archer and former Conservative Minister Jonathan Aitken. Inside the clink, Noye's mates on his wing were causing him some trauma.

One was a drug trafficker prescribed lithium to manage his moods. The other was a mercurial gangster who flipped and started shooting at the police after a routine traffic stop over road tax. He had a light trigger on his temper and was so incensed by some minor slight by prison staff that he went on hunger strike. Such protests were part of the Irish Republican ethos but rare outside of the political arena. Noye had spent time with IRA inmates in prison in the 80s who had gone on hunger strike but also were part of the 'dirty protest' where inmates instead of slopping out would daub faeces and urine on the walls of their cells.

"I was just worried that my pal would escalate his protest and start shitting on the walls and stuff. I would not have put it past him," Noye said. The prison staff were concerned and knew the inmate had a loose tether on reality. He was a serious and volatile prisoner in the jail housing the most dangerous offenders in the country.

In a window to how prisons work backstage – and that is with the innate consent of the occupants – Noye was asked by the prison governor to intercede and to persuade the self-starving inmate off his hunger strike. He said: "The governor John Knight called me into his office. I was someone he could deal with. Prison officers used to call me a straight shooter – knowing that I'd never used a gun. But when faced with a problem such as the hunger strike they knew that I was a likely answer."

Noye went in to broker a deal. It mirrored his activities outside; brokering, bartering and negotiating as a problem solver and deal maker. But inside the 'nick' he was being asked by Knight to sort out something which the governor knew was not in his ability to resolve.

Knight noted in Noye's prison record that he 'was on the placid end of the inmate spectrum'. He knew Noye was the ideal intermediary. He was no Boutros Boutros-Ghali but he had a track record of dealing with difficult inmates on his wing. In 'prison-speak' he said that Noye, "Had a mature attitude towards confrontation and difficult situations."[70]

After some discussion, Noye struck a deal with the fasting inmate: "If there was a deal to be done then clearly, I was the best broker. I just asked him what he wanted. What would end the hunger strike? I talked him round to a reasonable solution."

When he told Knight that the protest would end in return for five bags of peanuts, it was met with incredulity. The nuts were duly served and the 'fasting' ended. The hunger striker though was not altogether happy. Kenny Noye only gave him four packets of the KP peanuts and kept the fifth packet to himself. "I brokered the agreement, and I took my slice of the action," the wide boy entrepreneur said – content with his 20 percent. And that was the way Noye rolled.

***

In the run up to the court case, Kent Police were making arrangements for witnesses when Nick Biddiss got a frantic call from Ken Cameron, father of Stephen. Ken was panicking. Nick had been retired from the force just over two years when the anxious father phoned.

"Nick, you promised me that I'd be looked after," Ken said. "The police have told me that myself and Toni have to make our own way there without any support or protection." Ken and his wife Toni were witnesses for the prosecution. Ken had been called within minutes of the stabbing

70   John Knight transcript evidence, R v KN, 10th April, 2000.

by Danielle Cable and drove immediately to the scene. He witnessed his dying son being placed into an ambulance – blue lights blaring – on the way to the hospital.

"They can't do that. It's an outrage. The jury gets protection, but we don't," he said.

Nick told Ken that he agreed he had made a promise and that by hook or by crook he would fix it. Like Noye, Biddiss was a problem solver and in that singular respect he was not too dissimilar to the defendant.

"I made the promise and although now outside the force and excluded from the investigations I knew I had to sort it out," he said. Biddiss wrote to the Chief Constable David Philips and said that he had made a promise to look after the parents and support and protect them throughout any trial and he was shocked that Kent Police would not honour that promise. "I told the powers that be that if they didn't pay for it, then I would – out of my own pocket," he said. Kent Police relented and Ken and Toni Cameron were promised support throughout the trial by the force.

Biddiss always distinguished himself by looking after the victims and that is why the Cameron family have always been unstinting in their praise of the detective. As they prepared for the grizzly details of their son's death to be played in front of the nation's media, they steeled themselves for the weeks to come. On every May 19th since the death, Biddiss always phoned Ken and Toni to offer his condolences. He continues to contact surviving members of the family on the anniversary of Stephen's death.

And that was the way he rolled.

24

THE TRIAL

There was a hush in Court Number 2 when Danielle Cable was brought into court. She had not been seen for nearly two years in public as herself. She lived in a new location under a new name with a new partner. Her hair, her home and her entire life was turned upside down. Her father Jim, in a rare contact before trial, had told her just, "tell your story straight and all will be fine". There was immense pressure on her. It was not just the moral imperative to right the wrong in the witness box of the death of her fiancé but also to deliver evidence that would salve the still open wounds of the still grief-stricken parents of Stephen.

Millions had been spent on the investigation by police forces in the UK and abroad and every police officer and many members of the public believed that Noye still had to pay for the death of DC John Fordham. This burden must have been close to unbearable as she took her oath and commenced her evidence.

Danielle initially appeared relaxed when she entered the dock on the afternoon of the first day of the trial to testify to the most traumatic experience in her short life. Despite being in witness protection she gave evidence in open court without screens to protect her identity. She never caught Noye's eye throughout her two hours of evidence but regularly connected with Ken and Toni Cameron sitting close by. Four years on, she was now the same age as her fiancé was when he was killed. The judge and the barristers would treat her with great care and respect, knowing that her presence here was borne of great tragedy.

Her look had changed and now she was engaged to a soldier. They had planned to marry later in the year and her new man came with the blessing of Ken and Toni Cameron, it would be reported later.

Invited to sit to give her evidence, she chose to stand. Noye looked on with keen interest. He was wearing a grey open necked shirt and cardigan.

The questioning of Danielle began shortly before 3.00pm:

"How old were you at the time?

"Seventeen."

"Were you working?"

"I was working as a waitress."

Danielle explained that she left school and was living with Stephen Cameron at his parent's home and had been doing so since the start of 1996 or so. She started out confidently but became more troubled as she approached the nexus of her evidence. Her voice became softer and the timbre crackled as she recalled the key events. She told the court that a jeep type vehicle (Noye's Land Rover) cut her up at the Swanley Interchange on the M25. Stephen gave a disparaging look towards the driver of the Land Rover and that driver (Noye) came out of the car heading toward the Red Rascal van she was driving. She said the two men met in front of the van and that Noye punched her boyfriend in the face "hard". She said that the punch was unleashed once Noye came within an arm's reach of Stephen.

The press corps were rapt with attention as they knew that this woman's copy would occupy the next day's front pages, radio and TV bulletins. Tears were being kept determinedly in check but a subtle tremble was visible as she held a handkerchief in her hands. This setting and the scene are why legal dramas dominate the television schedules.

Stephen started shouting. "He was telling me to get back in the van because I was shouting and screaming for him to get back into the van," Danielle said. "He was telling me to stay back."

"And that was before you saw the knife?"

"Yes."

After some scrapping, she said she saw Noye, "fumbling in his pockets… I guess he (Stephen) saw it I don't know". Her previous statement was read to her to confirm her evidence: 'At this point I noticed that the man (Noye) had a knife in his right hand. I had a clear unobstructed view of the man with the knife. When Stephen walked towards him, the man lunged at Stephen with a knife.'

"He was clutching his chest," Danielle said. "He said, 'He's stabbed me Dan.'"

"Take down the number plate," Stephen told her. Her voice was aching. The prosecutor gave the details in the question and Danielle kept her answers quite contained:

"I was screaming and crying for someone to help me." She said Stephen was still standing while Noye got into his Land Rover and then, he "sort of stumbled to the driver's side of the van and to the ground".

She was in the dock for just over an hour. The fight between the two men lasted about 30 seconds. The legacy for all involved – the grieving family – endure for a lifetime.

Danielle said: "What stands out in my mind is him standing there with a knife in his hand and Steve coming forwards with blood everywhere!"

Defence barrister Stephen Batten QC put to her the suggestion that in the circumstances, she was very reluctant to describe her boyfriend as the aggressor in the fight and that this was natural.

"Is it not a fact that you told the police far less than you really saw because you find it difficult, totally natural, to believe that any of this was Stephen's fault?" he said.

"No, I do not believe it was Stephen's fault at all," she replied. "That is not what I told you," she added, emphatically.

She also batted off suggestions that Stephen, who had practised kickboxing and worked as security at a bowling alley in addition to his electrician work, was kicking Noye on the ground. And she dismissed any suggestion that Stephen was ever violent or hit her as Noye's QC politely pressed her. She was steadfast and resolute.

Danielle was very competent in the box. As good as any witness in her circumstances. The prosecutor Julian Bevan QC spoke to her difficulty as a witness.

"Have you in fact made any efforts to try and forget these events of four years ago?" he asked Danielle, who replied, "Yes, tried to put it to the back of mind, maybe not forget completely."

Mr Justice Latham signed off with a heartfelt thank you to Danielle for the "clarity of her evidence". She was the only witness on the first day of this trial. She would be whisked away back into her safe house having performed robustly on a day she must have been dreading for the last four years.

"From all reports on the news, it was clear she was good in the box and gave a great account of herself," Nick Biddiss recalled. He was a bound witness and so could not speak to those at the court but of course followed it in the press.

Noye was brought down to the holding cells to have a quick chat with his legal team before being returned to HMP Belmarsh. Once the jury had left, Prison Officers put handcuffs on him. Three officers marched him down steps with white tiled walls into a long corridor. An armed officer stood on sentry duty, Courts Number 1 and 2 are the 'murder' trial courtrooms and the Category A inmates have their quarters close by.

There are 19 courts over three floors and 70 cells in the basement. The River Fleet trickles past underneath. This building has history. And the murder trial of Stephen Cameron would now be among the tens of thousands that these walls could speak of.

Thousands of inmates would have walked the same corridor as Noye that day and some were marched on their 'dead man's walk' to an execution in the open square outside Newgate Prison which was connected to the court house.

Noye's cell was a steel door double lock cell with a porthole for officers to keep a view on their charge. At every lunchtime he was fed in his cell by court staff and in the evening back at HMP Belmarsh. Initially, he was only permitted to meet his legal team behind a glass partition but Judge Latham, the presiding judge, told his staff that it was unacceptable. That ruling allowed Noye open access to his team during breaks and after the day's proceedings.

"I thought she gave good evidence," Noye said of Danielle. The legal issue under the microscope distilled down to the question: was Noye in fear of his life when he took out his knife? If that was the case, then he had an argument for self-defence. He had a chance at an acquittal. It worked before. Would it do so again? Noye's legal team were upbeat – they were still in the running. They were in with a chance. The mind of the jury could be swayed by small moments that pointed to motivation. The legal team were still of two minds whether Noye should give evidence himself. He was insistent. His team were not so sure.

There was no issue really with who launched the first blow because other witnesses would cancel out Danielle's testimony and say that the younger man was getting the better of the older one and also that Stephen Cameron was the aggressor. There was other contradictory evidence with one witness, Susan Watson, saying that she only saw punches being traded. One travelling in a red Ford Fiesta saw the younger man grab the collar of the older man; another said that the older man was backing off and "was getting what he deserved for throwing the first punch". A tanker driver with an elevated view saw two men out of their vehicles "discussing things". As he approached it escalated into pushing and shoving and as he got even closer, it grew more and more violent. The driver, Jonathan Saunders, had to swerve because of the trajectory of the two men on the road. His tachograph recorded his speed at 10mph. As he passed, he said "it was a level fight". He was the first to contact the emergency services with a 999 call.

Another witness, Amanda Whelan, a lecturer and a mom of two with her children in the back of the VW golf, said that the two men were "trading blows" and the younger man was kicking at the older man. She said that Danielle was hysterical and trying to pull Stephen away from the fight. She witnessed a flash of a wristwatch she thought and then saw the older man drive away towards the Dartford Tunnel.

It was a "ferocious" row she said but her husband still drove on as she managed the excitable kids in the back seat. She contacted the police after seeing it on the news. In closing her evidence, she remembers a Rolls Royce close by. She didn't see the occupant. If she had done so, she would have definitely remembered him.

Everyone who saw or met Alan Decabral would never forget him.

***

He was one of the key witnesses who phoned 999 at 1.25pm after witnessing the fight. "My Lord, may I call Mr Decabral?" Perhaps someone took it literally because his testimony would watermark the case from the moment his mobile phone rang in the box. "Mr Decabral would you mind not taking a work call at the moment?," he was admonished by the prosecution barrister Julian Bevan QC. He was the sixth witness to be called on the second day of proceedings.

ALAN DECABRAL WAS A KEY WITNESS IN THE PROSECUTION OF KENNETH NOYE

He stood for his evidence. Without fat-shaming him, any chair he used would have needed support. He was a 'man monster of a fella', an imposing figure with long hair racing towards his shoulders and away from his forehead. The 40-year-old was not ageing well. His déshabillé appearance looked like he was burning the candle at both ends – and in the middle as well. Court evidence and process can be a bit tedious, but no one could take their eyes off Alan Decabral.

His evidence differed from other witnesses in that he saw the knife and then Noye stab Stephen Cameron. He alone suggested that there was a scene in which Noye was pulling at the door and Cameron was inside trying to get away. And he alone suggested that Noye hid the knife from Cameron. In respect to the knife used, the prosecution was making the point that if a flick knife was used then it required three actions A – getting the knife B – opening the knife and C – using the knife. The more steps required, the more steps the offender has to retreat from his course of action. The more steps required, the less sustainable was Noye's self-defence claim.

"I saw the guy put his hand in his trousers like he had some key thing or something on his belt which was in the way. I see him tugging at something as though it was stuck in his pocket but it came out and he put his hand behind his back," Decabral told the court, demonstrating the action.

He said that Cameron would not have seen the knife. Noye had claimed that he held the knife out to deter an aggressive Cameron but Decabral said that he had a good view of Noye's hand and that the knife wasn't open at first, suggesting it was a flick knife. He said: "It seemed to open… then I saw a flash because it was a sunny day… and then I realised it was a knife because I could see the sun glinting off the blade."

He told the court that Stephen Cameron "staggered back and fell against the front of the Rascal (van) and I heard him telling the girl (Danielle Cable) to get the number of Noye's car".

"After the stabbing he (Noye) turned so he was facing me and I could see him shut the knife with both hands… he put it in the right hand pocket in his leather jacket. He then walked past my car and he went like this, [making a nodding expression]…that was as if to say: that sorted him out… like you've got yours, mate." It was a devastating testimony. The jury were agog. It was day two of the trial and the courtroom was stunned at the apparent callousness of Noye who was expressionless throughout.

Decabral added: "I thought I was dreaming… as soon as I saw the knife and I saw him get stabbed… I reached down for the phone and dialled 999." He then described in detail how he chased the Discovery heading towards Dartford 'PDQ', he said before clarifying "pretty, darn quick". He said that he wrote the number plate down on a Rothman cigarette packet which he lost but he had given the full number to the 999 operator. Decabral was palpably enjoying his moment in the limelight.

Decabral claimed to have given the full licence plate to the 999 operator while witnessing the fight. He also claimed that the call was going in and out of coverage. He said that he was taking his car for a spin, testing a repair on his Rolls because it had been overheating but then a friend called, he drove to Lewes when he came upon the fight.

Decabral was robust until it was pointed out to him that he didn't call 999 immediately but about ten minutes after the incident at 1.25pm; that he didn't give the full number to the emergency operator and that the call was uninterrupted and not "breaking up" as he suggested. There was no doubt Decabral was on the defensive when challenged about his recollections.

"Do you use recreational drugs?" he was asked by Stephen Batten QC.

"Yes," he replied.

"Had you that morning?"

"No."

"Are you sure? Sunday morning?" Batten asked with an arched eyebrow.

"Well Sunday is Church," Decabral said. "I had just taken my kids to church. I try to keep straight for church."

"Mr Decabral, you are free to go," Judge Latham told him after a long stint in the box.

"Cheers," he replied.

With a glint in his eye, the judge said, "You can turn your phone on now," provoking a moment of levity in the proceedings.

Noye's legal team recognised the brutal power of the smirk while leaving a man dying in the gutter. It did not help a self-defence plea. It may prove an insurmountable account.

Journalists did not report the inconsistencies in Decabral's testimony, but they did report the phone calls and the alleged expression on Noye's face as he walked past Decabral to his car.

'Noye Smiled as he Fled the Scene' shouted *The Guardian* headline. Newspaper sub-editors alight on the key words that imprint on the psyche of punters and mimic the moments that – by osmosis – seep into the mind of the juror. They called it right. Decabral's description of Noye's apparent gloating after killing a man half his age – with a screaming girlfriend nearby – was a compelling and alluring image that was hard to offset against his other statements which had suggested Stephen Cameron was the aggressor and gunning for a fight.

Additional testimony from the pathologist Dr Michael Heath about the Noye's knife movements and incisions suggested that these were aggressive and not defensive actions. The pathologist was emphatic and experienced. When asked about his years of experience he flippantly said, "I have a number."

"Can you give me a number, so?" prosecutor Julian Bevan QC asked, surprised at the unusual response and tone in a trial of such gravity and trauma.

Eventually his enquiry would elicit an answer of 22 years. The performance quality of the curious Dr Heath gave a hint that this may not be the last we might hear of him. The eminent Home Office pathologist's evidence further undermined Noye's claim of self-defence. The trial was occupying the news headlines for nearly two weeks. And it was all one-way traffic against Noye. Few could have doubted the outcome.

The exhibits officer in the case was asked by Judge Latham if Stephen Cameron had any convictions. The answer was no. In view of that answer, Judge Latham asked Noye the same at the commencement of his examination. "Do you have any convictions for violence?"

The answer came swiftly and emphatically. "None."

Noye's evidence and his view of events never deviated from his first thoughts in the hours after the murder which he shared with his family and a chosen few. The court and the press were fascinated to hear it from the man himself for the first time.

Everything about the trial was extraordinary, the revelations, the drama, the media circus. It placed the justice system under extreme pressure, *The Guardian* reported. There was an unprecedented level of security for witnesses – and for Noye. Even the fact that Noye had his near £250,000 legal bill paid out of Legal Aid would prompt complaints and the Home Secretary threatened to target him for proceeds of crime. There was also discussion of possible efforts to retry Noye for the murder of DC John Fordham which would have required a change in the double jeopardy rule that prevented defendants from being charged twice for the same crime. The Government recommended a change in the law a year later and in 2005 the legislation was passed after a campaign by *The Sun* newspaper.

Noye said: "It was impossible for me to get a fair trial. If I was acquitted, then they would have gone again for me on the Fordham case. I just felt that they would get me no matter what. My lawyers all agreed that if it was anyone else it would have been a manslaughter charge. I just felt it was much easier to convict me than anyone else."

In HMP Belmarsh he was contemplating his chances of success. "I was a cunt for carrying a knife, a fucking idiot," he said. "Whatever happened I was going to get the wrong end of the stick. I should really have just stayed in the nick (prison) because nothing my defence did was going to change things. So, I was kind of resigned to my fate as the trial came to its conclusion."

The Cameron family were breathing hatred for Noye, understandably. They always would. They did their best to connect with the jury and were desperately hoping for a conviction, as retribution for the loss of their son, whose life was cut so tragically short.

"No parent should lose a child before they pass, and Stephen was just 21," Ken Cameron said. An acquittal would have felt like losing Stephen all over again. "It's the hope that kills you. We were confident that it was going our way, but you can never tell with a jury."

In his summing up, before he sent the jury out, Lord Justice Latham told them that the crux of the case was the question of self-defence: "Might Mr Noye have been acting in self-defence when he used the knife? Or do you think when he got out the knife it was to confront Stephen Cameron or even up the odds, so he did not leave the scene a beaten man? But even if you conclude he may have believed he needed to defend himself, you still have to consider the very important question of whether the use of the knife was really out of all proportion to the incident."[71]

It was a fair summing up which Noye's legal team had no criticism of. The question of provocation (by Stephen Cameron) and self-defence (in respect of Noye) was left entirely in the hands of the jury. The court of public opinion had rendered its verdict in the pages of the tabloids but now the jury would have their say. They were taken to a hotel by jury bailiffs and would sleep under armed guard. Noye would also have armed guards in HMP Belmarsh.

But where would Kenneth James Noye next lay his head?

---

71   Court transcript, R v KN, 13th April, 2000.

25

JUDGEMENT DAY

It was a Friday morning verdict.

Juries never wanted to let a verdict interrupt a weekend if they could help it. After a trial, lasting two weeks in Court Number 2, Old Bailey, London EC4M 7EH, the four men and eight women on Friday morning were invited to return a majority verdict.

On April 14th, 2000, after just 8 hours of deliberations, the foreman of the jury answered the judge's question. To the charge of murder, he answered, "We find the defendant guilty."

"Yes!" Stephen Cameron's parents shouted in vindication in court. They were sat in the press box but closest to the jury. During the trial, Noye's legal team had asked for them to be removed from their proximity to the jurors. Noye also objected to the family and jurors acknowledging each other every morning. The judge refused. In the DC John Fordham murder case, also in the Old Bailey, Noye's legal team succeeded in removing DC Fordham's widow from the immediate precincts of the jury box. But not this time.

"They (Ken & Toni Cameron) nodded good morning, and after the verdicts, they acknowledged each other again. I wasn't happy with it. But what can you do," Noye said.

At midday, Lord Justice Latham spoke directly to Noye but his words went around the world: "The jurors, having found you guilty of murder, as you know, there is only one sentence I can impose and that is life imprisonment." He could have delayed sentencing to another day, but the drama demanded immediate closure. A 'book stop' to the theatre that commenced at an ordinary roundabout off the M25 nearly four years previously. The judge had to engage with Home Office guidelines in respect of a murder conviction including various levels of mitigation, if any.

Consequently, Noye was sentenced to a 16-year minimum sentence with no relief for the nine months he'd spent in the high security jails in Cadiz and Madrid while fighting extradition back to the UK. The judge in sentencing adjudicated that there was no clear intention to kill but to cause serious bodily harm; a lack of premeditation and an element of self-defence, though "falling short of a full defence" to the charge of murder. Life did not mean life in this instance but with Noye now 53 years old, it certainly felt like a permanent end to his life in any meaningful sense.

Following the verdict, Noye was brought down to the cells at the bottom of the Old Bailey and had a chat with his QC, Stephen Batten, and long-term solicitor, Henry Milner. His legal team had succeeded with the previous self-defence plea in relation to John Fordham but not this time.

There was no talk of appeals. It was too raw for Noye.

He was fuming: "The extradition agreement was based on a manslaughter charge and not murder. In any event, it should have been a limited, restricted sentence, not an open-ended 16-year tariff, which could mean that I might never be released."

The assurances that were apparently given to the Spanish authorities by the CPS and the Foreign Office had been quietly ignored.

"I've not been convicted on the evidence but for the death of John Fordham," Noye said.

There is no doubt that the death of DC Fordham overshadowed this trial and indeed, Noye's life here and forever more.

Outside the Old Bailey, as Brenda Noye, hailed a cab and escaped the glare of the media, the Cameron family were jubilant. The ordeal of the trial in the end was worth it. Ken Cameron said: "It really was hard. But for Stephen's sake, you keep strong. It shows you how far they were struggling to dig up so much rubbish about Stephen. He was a normal 21-year-old. He had a temper – I had a temper when I was 21."[72]

Detective Supt Denis McGookin, who led the investigation following the retirement of DS Nick Biddiss, gave a press conference. Biddiss was not called as a witness by the prosecution or defence and was not invited by McGookin to any after-trial drinks. Biddiss was inelegantly excluded from the inquiry in retirement, even though he was the officer who

---

72   Press conference with CPS & Kent Police after conviction, 14th April, 2000.

had skilfully cracked the case for Kent Police. "It sometimes happens. But nothing gets in the way of the fact that we got him to court and let the jury do their stuff," Biddiss explained.

To the hungry press, the cultured accent of McGookin emphasised: "Kenneth Noye ran, but he couldn't hide."

Danielle Cable, now 21, heard the verdict on the news bulletins from her safe house. A police officer within the witness protection unit phoned her with the exact details from the courtroom. In a quote released to a daily newspaper, she said she was initially surprised at the verdict. "I was overjoyed," she said. "I could not believe it at first. But it will never bring back my Steve. I just hope he is looking down from heaven and smiling. This is for him."

The police sirens in the background of the Old Bailey beckoned the police convoy carrying Noye back to HMP Belmarsh to begin his life sentence. In the prison van were six prison officers and a principal officer with inmate CB9123, otherwise known as Kenneth Noye.

The van was followed by a police helicopter and armed outrider motorcycles. On the way to court that morning, Noye entered the van in handcuffs. He sat down. On the floor were six bulletproof vests. The prison officers asked the PO (principal officer) if they should wear the flak jackets. "I don't know, you better ask Noye," he said. "They looked at me inquiringly," Noye said. "I would if I were you.'"

Noye had an aversion to bulletproof vests for himself. On his return from Spain in the company of the Kent police officers, the security team demanded that he wear a jacket. "Why?"

Noye asked. "Who's going to kill me? Who's going to take me out? The only defendant who wears a jacket is a snitch, a grass."

***

In the melee after the conviction, Biddiss, so long the key cog in the investigation, was now observing the victory mayhem. He had been in court for the verdict and was clearly moved by events. It was with relief and a little satisfaction that he inhaled the proceedings. Slipping quietly away, he took the tube to Victoria train station and then made his way to Swanley. He was in a contemplative mood. His day wasn't over. Four years earlier, his odyssey commenced. His obsession was ignited and today, the promise he made to Stephen Cameron's family was fulfilled. He hopped into the car and went to Stephen's simple grave, nearby, in St Paul's churchyard, in Swanley.

The gravel crunched underfoot as he headed to pay his last respects for Stephen and perhaps to draw a line under his last case.

"It was emotional," he said. "I spoke to him. I have to say there were tears welling up and I told him, 'We've done it. We were with you all the way and we got there in the end. You were always in our thoughts. We all wish things turned out differently, Stephen.'"[73] As he wiped away a tear and made his way out of St Paul's cemetery, a local young cub reporter came up to him. "Excuse me," she said. "But I just noticed you spent a little time at Stephen Cameron's grave and my editor asked me to find out who visited, to make contact and get a quote from family or anyone connected to the case?"

73   Interview with Nick Biddiss, November 2022.

"Well, he is a good editor," Nick said.

"So, what brought you here?" the earnest young reporter inquired, not recognising the man who had lived the investigation for nearly four years and the man who brought the fugitive home.

Pausing, Biddiss said: "Nothing, I was just walking by."

The pager was gone. A text arrived on his phone as he sat in his car preparing to leave the cemetery. He was taking a breather to compose himself before going home. The message was from Toni and Ken Cameron – 'We're having takeout. Come round for a drink. What do you want to order, we're having fish and chips. You can have fish and chips or fish and chips!' Ken Cameron's text read. Later that afternoon, Biddiss and the couple shared fish and chips and reflected on the journey they took together – a journey no one wanted. The three savoured this victory of sorts and the couple, Toni and Ken, were demonstrably grateful for the compassion, dignity and passion that Biddiss – a straight and honest policeman – displayed throughout his involvement in the case.

He added: "It was the end of the road. Closure for me and in part for them but of course, there would always be a gaping hole in their lives. We'd always remain close and in contact but this night they made me feel like extended family, savouring the same relief and bringing down the shutters on this chapter." For Biddiss and the Camerons, the takeout was a deserved, cathartic occasion on their undulating path towards peace of mind – something which they would, in truth, never achieve.

For Noye, there was only resignation.

ITV News brought the news to the nation. It was the lead headline. Dermot Murnaghan opened: "Good evening, Kenneth Noye is starting a life sentence," in a news script that was replicated on all the news bulletins that night.

In Bridge Cottage, Sevenoaks, Kent that evening, a phone rang. It was a recorded message: "The person calling is an inmate in Her Majesty's Prison. If you do not wish to take the call, please hang up now." His loyal wife, Brenda answered.

"Ken, I'm sorry you were never going to get a fair trial?" She said.

"No chance," he said. "If I was done for manslaughter, I'd have got 10 years and out in six. Now they'll never let me out." He just managed to finish the sentence before the pips on the phone told him the money on his phone card had run out.

Noye would find himself in a very different prison regime to the one he left on his release in 1994 from the open prison in Latchmere House in Surrey, where he could arrange weekends off by exerting a little soft diplomacy on the 'screws'. He would now be placed in a Special Secure Unit where natural daylight and human contact with any other inmates would be denied to him. Throughout the night, the lights in his cell would turn on for a security check every 30 minutes. He would be alone. Isolated. Never forgiven and never forgotten.

There was a very real prospect that Noye would never see the outside of a prison again. There was a real prospect that he would leave Her Majesty's Prison Estate in a coffin.

26

WHAT IF?

Overlooking the topography of the crime, the hunt for Noye, the extradition, and subsequent trial, Nick Biddiss came to some extraordinary reflections once it was all over.

It comes with the freedom of someone long retired and with the wisdom of a grandfather and elder statesman of the law-and-order fraternity – and maybe a couple of long walks on the golf course.

"During the hunt it was my job to place my mind in the mind of Noye as much as it was his mind to get inside my head," Biddiss said. Today, the thought that washed over his head was: 'How could Noye have avoided the conviction and the 21 years in jail for the murder of Stephen Cameron?'

"I accept that if it was anyone other than Noye, it would have been a manslaughter charge most likely," Biddiss explained. "And there was a tiny gap between murder and manslaughter which is why we leave it to the jury who always have the final decision."

In that way he echoed John Mathews QC, Noye's former barrister and other observers. However, what he said next would shock Noye: "The truth is after denying that he was present at the interchange and being the man who stabbed Stephen Cameron in Spain to the Spanish judges, when he came to the UK, he changed his position. We were shocked. The reality is that there was very little evidence against Noye except for all the actions he took after the murder."

Danielle Cable failed to identify Noye from a "very good likeness" in the weeks just after the death of Stephen Cameron. Likewise, Alan Decabral, the other key witness, couldn't do it. Biddiss added: "But as Noye had already admitted his presence at the fight then it wasn't an issue. If he had maintained his stance that he wasn't there at the interchange, the case might have been simply unprovable. If he had maintained his denial then the key evidence against him was his early race to leave the country and his she-nanigans around the car. The disappearance of the car, the replacement of it with another one similar on his driveway and all his efforts to disguise his involvement with the vehicle were key bits of circumstantial evidence. However, if Noye had done nothing other than destroying the clothes he was wearing during the attack, there was very little chance he would have been convicted."

It was, it *is*, a startling revelation.

Biddiss was claiming that most of the evidence that connected Noye to the crime was generated by Noye himself, after the crime. Had he done *nothing* – literally never lifted a hand other than deny the crime, then the police would have struggled to even charge him.

Biddiss said: "He had fallen into the same trap that I had done after I was first told about the fight. I thought that with all the witnesses, all the cameras and the sheer visibility of the crime on one of the busiest roundabouts in the country, that the amount of evidence would be overwhelming. On that sole point myself and Noye agreed – but we were both wrong. But by acting on that false assumption – albeit a logical and likely scenario – then Noye sowed the seeds of his own conviction. In the event of a blanket denial it would have been only circumstantial evidence that linked him to the crime. There was no DNA to link him to the scene. The number plate identified about 17,000 similar vehicles and identification evidence in the middle of a trauma can be very unreliable, leaving Danielle Cable's evidence on this point debatable."

The telephone mast evidence showed Noye's mobile in the area within 6km of the crime scene but there was a great deal of contention about the accuracy of that evidence. While Noye was in the pub about 8km away, three separate masts – Brands Hatch, Swanley and Sevenoaks – connected to his mobile over a 20-minute period for separate calls. At the time it was not the exact science it was made out to be and arguably not enough to link Noye to the crime scene.

With Danielle Cable having already failed to identify Noye two weeks after the murder, an identification more than two and a half years later with Noye's face all over the newspapers was going to be easy to challenge.

To Noye, this truth was painful.

He never accepted the murder verdict nor indeed, the murder charge, and consequently his jail time was difficult to tolerate. Indeed, he was sore that he was extradited for manslaughter but convicted for murder and this was a fresh revelation. For someone who was credited with great court craft in the past; to be confronted with the fact that he was the architect of his own legal demise was doubtlessly unsettling for him.

Noye says: "I followed my legal advice. Everyone told me that we would get a manslaughter charge and, on that basis, I decided to admit my presence there. I was happy to tell my side of the story and I thought I should have been acquitted."

In retrospect, the state was lucky to get a conviction but it's never over until it's over, and a range of appeals would inevitably be forthcoming. 'Over' was always going to be a fluid proposition, like a red light at three o'clock in the morning.

"It is funny sometimes if a criminal overestimates the case against them then they build their own case for the prosecution. That's what happened here. We got lucky," Biddiss said with a relieved demeanour more than 20 years on from the conviction.

Noye was phlegmatic: "It is yesterday's news and I've moved on. They were always going to get me. I am at peace with the events and how they turned out even though I still believe that I was wrongly convicted and my conviction was held to a lower standard than others which were challenged and were quashed."

The die was cast on April 14th 2000, when Noye was convicted. But would it stand the test of time? Nobody worked harder on their appeals than Kenny Noye. Even in the isolation of the Special Secure Units, the most active jailhouse lawyer in the country was the 'Cat AAA' inmate

– Noye. He would later order transcripts of the two-week trial at the cost of over £10,000. When he refused to share them with the prosecution in a subsequent appeal, the CPS went to the High Court to force him to share the paperwork. Everything has a price. Everyone has a price and Noye simply could not abide giving the Crown Prosecution Service a freebie.

Of course, if he had done absolutely nothing he would have been free to spend his cash on something more exciting than trial transcripts.

27

FALLOUT

June 1999

Customs and Excise swarmed on a suburban house in Pluckley in Kent. The house had been paid for with £250,000 in cash.[74] Assisting them were armed officers from Kent Police. Armed resistance was a distinct possibility. The officers were taking no chances. Bulletproof vests, Glock 17 9mm pistols, ballistic shields, stun grenades and G36C 5.56mm semi-automatic carbines were part of the arsenal. The target deserved every bit of the preparation. Adrenaline filled the veins of the loaded officers. This is what they trained for – this is what they loved. Trained not to shoot – it was all they ever wanted to do and today the forefinger hovered on the trigger. A sniper marksman (they were nearly exclusively male) surveyed the scene with a standard issue bolt action rifle. The kit promised a Hollywood scene of deadly precision when in fact, studies showed that trained police marksmen only hit 35 percent of their targets. Still, if you were the target, you wouldn't fancy those odds. The tactical team was

---

74   Ann Decabral Statement – Decabral Bundle (6-1-6) – Appeal, October 2001.

faced with a serious offender. They were faced with a very big problem. The target was a twenty-seven stone former Hells Angel.

The curtain in the downstairs window twitched. The door was smashed in seconds later. The man-mountain was wrestled to the floor and handcuffed. It took four officers to lift him up off the ground and manoeuvre him to the police van. Inside the house was an Aladdin's Cave of contraband drugs, cash, and firearms, enough to lock one away for a long time – maybe even for 16 years.

The 40-year-old self-described businessman had a reputation for dealing in cars and vintage guns but what the search teams found was much more menacing. Police found an arsenal of 56 weapons, including machine guns, as well as 36 grams of cocaine and £123,500 in cash. Officers also located a Mercedes that had concealed compartments in the petrol tank which was undoubtedly used to transport drugs. A specialist team used ground penetrating radar and a scanner to check for other contraband in his garden. His properties had been the subject of search warrants many times before.

"The unforgettable Mr Decabral," as the judge referred to him when summing up the evidence he gave around ten months later, was arrested, and brought in for questioning at Dartford Police station.

His estranged wife and mother of his two children brought him cigarettes and clothes before being released on bail. After an eventful children's birthday party at Butlin's Bognor Regis, Alan Decabral received a conditional discharge for the unlicensed guns, the drugs and illicitly gained funds from Rochester Magistrates Court.

Decabral, who was known in the underworld as 'Tiger' had all his guns returned to him, as well as the £123,500 in cash before his starring role at the Kenny Noye trial. Kent Police, however, insisted upon destroying the drugs and held onto his Mercedes with its secret 'smuggling' compartments. The S-class left hand drive, 4-door Silver Mercedes with German number plates had false panels in its doors and a hidden storage cubicle in its fuel tank.

These events played out in advance of his role as a star witness in Noye's trial for murder In March 2000. Eyebrows would have been raised, at the very least, at the trial if this was known, but it was not. Decabral had witnessed the killing and phoned in the sighting on a recorded 999 call about ten minutes after Noye and Cameron came to blows on the motorway roundabout.

Crucially, his evidence testified to Noye's demeanour and notably he said that Noye smirked as he walked away having stabbed Stephen. It significantly undermined Noye's claim to have acted in self-defence. This may have been the difference between a manslaughter verdict or a murder one.

Extraordinarily, Henry Milner and Noye's counsel had limited knowledge of Decabral's colourful background and no idea about the police raid which would have raised the rational suspicion that Decabral may have gilded his evidence in return for a remarkably soft landing before the courts.

Indeed, Noye's lawyers may never have known without…

April 3rd 2000, Old Bailey

A female teacher's assistant called the Old Bailey court in a frantic fashion. "Can I be put through to the Noye court-room please?" she said. The reception staff tried to explain to her that it wasn't possible. "I have to insist, I have important information relevant to the trial," she said. The front desk ultimately relented and gave her some time. "My husband has just given evidence on Friday and it's all lies," she said.

"Who is your husband?" she was asked.

"Alan Decabral."

"Everything he said was a lie," she told the court reception.

"I'm afraid there is nothing I can do with the court still sitting," the receptionist told her that she should call Noye's barrister, Stephen Batten QC. The trial was still in full flow and undoubtedly an intervention at this stage of this magnitude could have caused a mistrial or even an acquittal. The prosecution did not disclose this key evidence to the defence and despite the call from Mrs Ann Marie Decabral to the court with more than ten days of the trial to go – the defence would never find out until some months after the verdict.

Upon the advice of the court, she sought out the lawyer's phone number but got a different Mr Batten – the wrong number and the wrong lawyer – and was dismissed as a raving lunatic. "Are you the gentleman representing Noye?" she asked the man on the other end of the phone. "I am Mrs Decabral, Alan's wife. Alan lied in his statement, and he doesn't even live where he says he lives… I believe he has done a deal with the police."

The man told Mrs Decabral; "You're mad and you don't know what you are talking about." The confusing exchange was extraordinary bad luck for Noye. His legal team could have made much hay of this.

And so mid-trial the prosecution swerved a trapdoor of its own making. Ann Marie Debabral thought that Noye's legal team had rebuffed her intervention when nothing of the sort had happened.

In the trial, Alan Decabral told the court that he witnessed Noye stab Stephen Cameron twice in the chest and that he then walked by him and nodded, "As if to say, 'that's sorted him.'" He then told the court that he didn't stay at the scene of the attack because he wanted to follow the Land Rover being driven away to note down the registration number. His wife had a very different version. He was a very effective witness and described as "charismatic" by Noye's QC, Stephen Batten.

His wife begged to differ. "He was driving away from the scene because he didn't want to be stopped by the police," she said. "Alan had been on his way to Lewes, in Sussex, to drop off a consignment of cocaine. He told me that he used the car chase as an excuse because he feared being arrested." Decabral had told the court that he was a recreational drug user but Ann Marie said that he was not only addicted to cocaine but that he was a "big time dealer".

"It got so bad he had nose bleeds all the time," she said. "But he never offered me drugs. 'One junkie in the family is enough,' he once told me."[75]

---

75   Sunday Mirror, July 16th, 2000

In fact Decabral phoned his wife shortly after the 999 call and told her that he had told the police he had given chase to the perpetrator when in fact he went on to complete his drug run. At the time though, Mrs Decabral didn't believe him: "Alan had a tendency to exaggerate. I believed he had seen a row but nothing [else]."

Mrs Decabral said that Alan had given a statement about what he saw the day after the death of Stephen Cameron. The officers interviewed Alan in the family kitchen while a consignment of drugs were quietly locked away in his upstairs office. Ann Marie said: "He did an E-fit and was more than happy to help. After he gave his statement he told me that if he ever got arrested in the future this would be his bargaining tool and he would use it accordingly."

July 18th 2000

Three months after the verdict, Ann Marie wrote to Noye in Whitemoor Prison where he was in the highest security category, 'Cat Triple A'.

"I spent 24 hours looking at that letter thinking about whether to send it. I knew it could change my life forever," she said. "I knew there was an appeal and I wanted Noye to know the truth. But I also reasoned that if he needed my help he would not hurt us."

Noye's lawyers were appealing on the grounds that the pre-publicity meant that he could not have received a fair trial.

In the letter, she told him that she had information that could assist him. She said she had crucial information about the evidence her husband gave in the dock and offered her contact details. The letter was filtered through the screws and immediately entered into the intelligence files on Noye. Likely, it would have also been passed to the Kent Police.

Noye says: "I was astounded by the news. Of course, I knew that Decabral was lying about me apparently gloating after the fight and his evidence was all over the top. I had no idea about his criminal background. No one knew on my legal team. Obviously if we did, it would have been raised. I was facing a life sentence and got a minimum of 16 years."

During the trial, Noye had given evidence under examination that he had been afraid that Kent Police would nobble witnesses but accepted the proposition put to him that Kent Police acted properly. "Basically, yes. A few bits and pieces, but I am quite happy," he told the court. He wasn't happy now.

Noye immediately contacted his lawyer, Henry Milner. He also asked his son Kevin to reach out to Ann Marie to check out this incredible claim. Could this be true? Is this the flaw in the prosecution case that could get a retrial and get the charge downgraded from murder to manslaughter and the sentence reduced from a minimum 16 years to a likely eight years with five to serve? Is this the intervention that could see an acquittal and show evidence of prosecutorial malpractice?

"All these things went through my head," Noye says. "It should have been a manslaughter charge all day long and this could mean that I'd be out of jail before I was 60 rather than in my 70s. It could mean that I might be out before I die."

It was nothing short of an incredible development.

August 3rd 2000

Within two weeks of Ann Marie's letter to Kenneth Noye, she took a call. "This bloke said: 'Hi, I'm Kevin Noye, Noye's son.' I nearly dropped the phone."

A meeting was planned for just 30 minutes later. Having promised so much would she turn up? In just a few minutes, the answer would become clear. On the grand surroundings of McDonalds in Eltham, Ann Marie told Noye's eldest son her extraordinary story.

She said: "I was so nervous that Kevin said he could tell it was me from 20 yards away. We sat in his car, and he asked me what information I had and why I wrote to his dad. I told him that Alan had lied under oath, and he asked me if I could prove this. I said 'Yes.'"

The convent-educated Ann Marie, who had left her home in Ireland when just a teenager, told Kevin that she was worried about his father. "He said, 'Why would my father want to harm you?'" Ann Marie added.

Alan Decabral, meanwhile, was talking to some newspapers: "Giving evidence against Noye had a devastating effect on my life. I split from my wife because of the stress, and I haven't seen my children for a year. I haven't done a great many things I am proud of in this life, but I am proud I told the truth. I did that for Stephen and because it could have been my son."

Alan had in fact split with his wife Ann, considerably earlier, before the armed raid on his house in June 1999. Decabral never told the press that throughout his marriage to Ann Marie he had an entire secret family and two other children. He never told his own parents that he was married to Ann Marie. He told his wife that in fact his father was dead and his mother was from Trinidad. However, they were both from London and very much alive in Wimbledon. He claimed he had a brother who was killed when a car he (Alan) was driving as a young man crashed and exploded upon impact. His parents, he claimed, said they would never forgive him. Yet he never had a brother, he wasn't a churchgoer as he told the court, and his claim that he spent six years in the army was a lie. You couldn't make it up – unless you were Alan Decabral.

Ann Marie's evidence was not just the rantings of a woman scorned. Police intelligence in the months before he gave evidence stated that Alan Decabral was 'strongly suspected of being actively involved in the supply of Class A drugs in the London area'. Customs & Excise Officers had spent months following him before the raid on his home so Ann Marie's view of her husband was shared by them.

Ann Marie told Kevin Noye that Alan was a serious criminal trading in guns and drugs. From the time they first met when she was 16, in 1984, the then slim Alan was awash with cash, driving a Cadillac and bringing her on a champagne lifestyle of Concord flights and Orient Express train journeys. It was all, she told Kevin, fuelled by criminal activities which centred on bootlegging alcohol and cigarettes and reactivating guns for use by the underworld.

Their marriage broke up as his drug habit and involvement in the drug trade ramped up. She told Kevin of the raid on the house shortly after his father was extradited to the UK after his nine months in a Spanish jail.

"I just wanted to set the record straight. Alan lied and your father should know. He was raided by police and found with guns and drugs, and he was let go. I couldn't believe it when I realised what he told the court. It's just fair that you should know. That your father should know," she told Kevin.

It was clear that the story was credible. Her home telephone records confirmed her account of her ringing the Old Bailey, trying to tell the court of her husband's alleged lies and of the accidental call to the wrong solicitors.

It was an explosive discovery, something that defence briefs dream of. Henry Milner, Noye's solicitor, called the revelations "sensational". From this moment forth the conviction was in serious trouble. The increasingly erratic Alan Decabral, with his shoulder length thinning grey hair, was claiming death threats from a number of quarters including Kenny Noye. The police deemed these to be bogus. He had refused the police protection initially offered to all the state's key witnesses in the trial but now appeared to be making up threats against his life.[76] The flamboyant threats would not look out of place in *'The Godfather'* as he alleged in one instance, that three bullets had been pushed through his door. The only thing that was missing was a horse's head in his bed.

After the trial, it also transpired that the convertible (a very appropriate adjective) Mercedes – with the hidden compartments for smuggling drugs and other contraband which had been seized by Kent Police – was returned to him, raising

---

76   Tony Thompson, *The Observer,* 14th October, 2000.

suggestions that it may have been a reward for his testimony. The car was returned despite objections by Her Majesty's Customs and Excise, whose intelligence had precipitated the raid.

Decabral's complicated life got more so over the summer when another police raid found cocaine and another prohibited weapon, crimes to which he subsequently pleaded guilty to.

The testimony from Decabral's own wife would have been "absolutely devastating" if he had known about it, Stephen Batten QC, who led the cross-examination of Alan Decabral said, with certainty. The suggestion that Kent Police had withheld the Mercedes until after the trial would also have changed the whole interrogation of Decabral in court as Batten explained: "It would have given me something that I could make stick. It was quite clear from his statements that Decabral was a major threat to Mr Noye and in fact when he appeared in the witness box, he was strangely charismatic. If I had the information about the Mercedes, then it would have changed my tactics [during the trial] completely."

Batten said that the damaging claim of the "cocky smile on Noye's face" would have been fiercely challenged if he was aware of Ann Marie Decabral's evidence. Batten said he would have challenged Alan Decabral's objectivity and, "I would have suggested to him that he had in fact received favours from the police". This was quite a damning statement from a senior lawyer who alternated between acting for the CPS prosecuting murders and acting for the defendants in other cases such as Noye's.

If he had known the full extent of Decabral's arrests and seizures had been known then the "cross-examination would have come from the angle that for the totality of his evidence Mr Decabral embarked upon a dishonest enterprise of giving a partially true story, but a greatly embellished one".

The star witness for the prosecution in the murder trial was fast losing his glitter.

October 5th 2000

"Please don't kill me. Don't shoot," Alan Decabral pleaded. His killer fired through the open car window.

"Then the next thing I knew he was slumped at the wheel of his car, just outside a Halfords store," one observer reported. "The poor guy was screaming for his life." The shoppers at the Warren Retail Park in Ashford in Kent were startled by the noise and then shocked by the execution. His new partner, Susan Quinn, was shopping with him and discovered his body in the car. She identified him to police amidst tears at the graphic and distressing scene of her dead lover.

Alan Decabral, 41, was the last to give evidence for the State in the Stephen Cameron murder trial but the first to die. A Home Office pathologist prosaically stated that he died from a gunshot wound to the head. It had all the hallmarks of a professional hit. The lone gunman fled. Never to be seen again. Decabral died slumped in the passenger seat of a Peugeot 205.

Noye's 'Get Out of Jail' card was dead.

28

A LIFE BEHIND BARS

"EXECUTED IN COLD BLOOD".

The phrase speaks nothing to the crime; the hitman who killed him or the criminal that Decabral undoubtedly was. The temperature of blood has long been attributed to emotion or a detachment from it, since before Shakespearian times.

The 'hot blooded' Decabral though held so many secrets that trying to isolate suspects would prove nearly impossible. Following his now discredited evidence against Noye just six months before his death, it was entirely predictable that Noye would be the prime suspect in his murder. Indeed, those who ordered and carried out the hit may very well have been relying upon that conjecture to deflect from their involvement.

Despite the convenient tabloid talk citing Noye as a suspect, Kent Police knew, with more than a hint of certainty, that he didn't and couldn't have done so. What killed Decabral was hope. He hoped the drug barons who brought his consignment of cocaine would pay him the £1.5 million agreed; he hoped that the drug smugglers from Germany would not call in the £1 million debt he owed them for the drugs they gave him on tick. And he hoped none would jump the gun

– with one. It was an unholy trinity, and it was not going to end well.

He bet that the publicity around him as a witness would protect him. He bet that people would believe that he had a cordon of steel around him. He bet that he was too dangerous a target for a quick hit. He lost.

Kent Police say the case remains open and subject to regular cold case reviews. The force never did interview Noye in prison about the crime and for very good reason; he was incarcerated in the most secure accommodation in HM Prison Service.

"It was the UK's equivalent of Guantanamo without the waterboarding – I was in full-time solitary confinement for five years," he said. "It does wreck your head but they want to break you and the more they wanted to do that the more I became determined not to be broken. It fuelled my resolve."

Every breath he took, every phone call, letter and even every interaction with prison guards was recorded and passed on a weekly basis to police intelligence officers.

Even if he had wanted to kill Alan Decabral, there was no chance that he could have orchestrated it, in these conditions. Moreover, as Henry Milner, his lawyer said: "This murder would have been judicial suicide for his appeal."

The Special Security Units, which had been criticised by Amnesty International for cruel and inhumane or degrading treatment, made it impossible. This was a marked contrast to Noye's last time in prison when visitors were allowed to bring in cooked meals or takeaways to inmates, and prisoners were entitled to a pint of lager or half a bottle of wine every day.

He longed for the times his father would drive up from Kent to HMP Brixton with a curry for him and extra takeaways for some of the IRA inmates who did not have family close.

In the SSU, inmates were deprived of sleep, woken through the night, and constantly disturbed. Each cell had five locks and he had no human contact with any individual with all visitors separated by a solid glass partition. The specially constructed unit was for those at great risk of escape. There was constant noise and light pollution and despite little or no contact with either inmate or officers, he was regularly drug tested and searched.

The unit was so oppressive that the prison officers were required to have monthly psychological assessments for their own protection, but not the inmates.

Initially, the government denied Noye's account of his experiences in the unit but when he provided a regular diary of his life in the unit, the government's position became untenable.

January 2004: Noye Prison Diary - Whitemoor SSU

'Prison Service Director. Unit visit. Asks how I am doing? I say every half an hour the light goes on. Officers smash on the steel door, checking on me, and they deliberately disrupt any peace and quiet. I ask if there is anything he can do about reducing the noise and light pollution. He says he'll see but the rules are the rules. He then asks, "How am I feeling?"

I tell him straight: "You see those planes flying overhead (from the nearby American Air Force base) I can't wait for the day when one of those lose it and come crashing into the prison and take all of us out in a big explosion including you."

"That's a bit harsh," the director said.

"Well, you asked how I was feeling! I said.'"

***

The conditions in the 'Special Secure Units' were simply insufferable and inhumane and that's what ensured their closure. Not for the last time, Kenny Noye took on the Home Office in court and won. He was the last inmate to be removed from the units. To Noye it was another small victory to savour. In terms of penal reform, it was quite a triumph, albeit an unheralded one.

After the decommissioning of the units in 2004, he was moved into the next most secure setting – Category 'AA' – at some of the country's most notorious jails and would stay there with serial killers, terrorists, and assorted humanity until well passed his retirement age.

Nick Biddiss' retirement was an entirely different prospect. He was keeping abreast of matters and busied himself by playing golf and attending to cricket and grandchildren. After the conviction, it was said that he would never have to buy a drink whenever there was a police officer around. He said: "It only happened once. I was in Streatham and walking to a building site and a PC on duty stopped me. I'm saying to myself, 'What have I done wrong?' 'You're Nick Biddiss,' he said. I nodded. 'I'm buying you a drink right now,' he said."

The Cameron verdict was seen by every officer as a retrial of the DC Fordham murder.

Even still, Biddiss was only one drink up, not that he was counting.

The drama in Danielle Cable's life had abated but there was more to come.

In late 2002, Mandy Cable, Danielle's mother, and former Det. Inspector Ian Brown were having a private meeting at a Kent country club. Danielle was not present. Brown, a former Metropolitan Police 'Flying Squad' officer was commissioned by Granada TV to connect with Danielle and broker a deal in respect of a film about her experiences. Negotiations were in place for the producers and lead actor Joanne Froggatt, the former Coronation Street actor, to meet Danielle to discuss the role. The meeting was not to be an interrogation. "I wasn't allowed to ask her anything about her new life, but she told me she was happy and moved on," Froggatt explained.

"She didn't think of herself as anything special in any way, even though she'd been through this horrendous ordeal and came through the other side. I was struck by her strength of character," Froggatt added. The film, *Danielle Cable: Eyewitness* follows the events from the road rage fight to the conviction of Noye in 2000. In a statement supporting the film Danielle said, "The film brings an end to a difficult time in my life" and said that Joanne "seems to have shown much of the way I felt".

In Whitemoor Prison, in Cambridgeshire, there was one inmate in the Special Secure Unit who did not watch the *ITV* 90-minute drama.

Noye's appeal of his conviction at the end of 2001 was based upon the suggestion of a sweetheart deal between Alan Decabral and Police – that he bartered gilded testimony against Noye in return for near immunity against prosecution related to the armed raid on his house. Michael Mansfield QC, Noye's counsel, also raised the pre-trial publicity and the heavy security around the jury.

The appeal judges could have reduced his conviction from murder to manslaughter and his sentence from a minimum of 16 years in jail to a possible six.

In essence, the judges rejected this appeal on the grounds that even accepting Decabral's evidence was tainted, it wouldn't have mattered. The jury alone decided that you don't bring a knife to a fist fight and that Noye's actions were not proportional to the threats he faced.

"Kenny Noye Public Enemy No.1 is a creation of the press. Anyone else would have won their appeal but not me," he said.

Noye's time in prison would be littered with legal actions against his conviction, his conditions and the length of his sentence. In March 2011, he watched by video link the proceedings at the Court of Appeal in London, awaiting a verdict on his conviction which this time was referred to the Criminal Case Review Commission, the body concerned with unsafe convictions. As he entered the video suite, one police officer said "So you're going home today."

Such was the general view on the strength of his case.

The Cameron and Cable families were more concerned than ever that Noye would walk. The case was built this time upon another flawed witness. Dr. Michael Heath, the pathologist who conducted the first autopsy just hours after Stephen Cameron's death, had been discredited and a number of convictions where he gave evidence had been overturned and sent back for retrial. Could the same happen to Noye's conviction? The removal of Dr. Michael Heath and Alan Decabral as legitimate witnesses undermined the case against Noye – but would it be enough?

The family and undoubtedly Danielle Cable, were on tenterhooks. So was Noye. The judges read out their verdict. As it progressed it was impossible to determine which way they would go. In the conclusions, the judges said that even in the absence of the discredited witnesses, the jury would have come to the view that Noye had not acted in self-defence and therefore the murder conviction was sound. Noye had already served 12 years in prison and would be faced with nearly another decade inside.

In 2015, his close friend and protector when he first went on the run, John Palmer, was killed by a professional hitman – a double tap to the head. Palmer, it transpired, was under surveillance at the time of his death by the Serious and Organised Crime Agency (SOCA), now the national crime agency, and had been for 19 years.

The reporter who broke the story, was the veteran *ITV* reporter, Roger Cook. He delivered epic TV exposes on Palmer in the 1990s and was the proposed target of a hitman in the employ of John Palmer as a result. The threat to Cook was very real at the time but in the game of life and luck, Roger Cook won and John Palmer lost.

While still in prison, Noye was visited by the Essex murder detectives after the bizarre death of his friend. Initially, police believed that Palmer had died from complications arising from a recent surgery only for two bullet wounds to be discovered about a week after he was assassinated.

"We know you didn't do it," they told Noye. "But we think you have information about the people who probably did."

Noye said: "I told them that I always got on well with John. We complimented one other in business. We took the edge off and it worked. But I'm sorry I can't help."

Shortly after the visit by the Essex detectives, the Parole Board's decision to send Noye to an open prison was refused by Justice Minister Michael Gove. "It was me versus the government," Noye said. "I took them to court again. The minister went for me because he wanted headlines but that's not justice. I didn't have a blemish on my record. They said I was at risk of absconding – where to? I was nearly 70 years of age."

His challenge in the courts was eventually successful and his path to ultimate release was set in train.

Over the years he's seen it all: "I always said everyone has a price. I'd be in a prison and screws would come to me and say, 'Anything you need Ken? I can get it for you'. Phones, sims, drugs, anything you want. I'd say no. You'd never know if it was a setup or not. Sometimes they'd say how much they owed and offer to sort you. But no chance. I'd have been a mug if I did that and got caught."

Love is never too far behind as he took on a new girl-friend on the outside who visited him religiously every week. Intriguingly, he also ran a pen pal dating agency between cons at Whitemore Prison and Send female prison in Surrey. With the assistance of an inmate at the woman's unit, he would pair prisoners off with each other and they would write sweet nothings or "filth", as Noye says, to each other to keep themselves amused while locked up. *Love Island* meets Alcatraz it wasn't but you get the picture. None of his pairs survived beyond their release – to no one's surprise.

It seems every decade throws up new information about the life and crimes of Kenneth James Noye. In June 2019 he was released with few restrictions, save the occasional probation meeting and a ban on leaving the UK. He served 21 years for the murder of Stephen Cameron; six years more than the minimum Judge Latham sentenced him to on April 14th 2000.

Today he lives his life to a rigid timetable.

A legacy of 30 hard prison years.

One ritual is his two hour gym sessions. Daily events which would task most people, let alone someone well into his 70s. He plies his fitness trade at his local private gym, a bastion of suburbia. With his black Adidas trainers, tracksuit bottom, and mismatching sweatshirt, he wouldn't look out of place in a prison courtyard. He has a couple of regular training partners (some ex-police officers) and is friendly with those who share the space.

As a qualified fitness instructor (prison had some benefits…), he advises on weights and is very congenial and attentive. And people respond to him. One couple, in their late 20s help him to troubleshoot his iPad. He is surprisingly open. Some know who he is – others don't. One member arranged for a press photographer to catch him leaving the premises. It made its way into the *Daily Mail*.

"I know who he is," Noye said. "He doesn't know I know. He probably got a couple of grand. It is part of the price I have to pay for my notoriety."

In the press, he is a pariah. Stories appear showing him with a new partner, or new car, or even **'Roadrage killer Kenneth Noye poses with Elvis impersonator as he enjoys freedom at pub'**.

On the street though, people come up to him and ask for autographs and photos. "I never knew the term selfie until people asked when I came out." he says. "There is no hint that they are terrified of me. Maybe it's because I'm old or maybe they don't believe all they read."

It's nearly 60 years since, as an apprentice printer, he first forged Cambridge degree certificates – and allegedly made fake fivers on the side. The world has transformed greatly since he was sentenced in April 2000, but he remains largely unchanged.

Twenty-five years after the manhunt began; would Nick Biddiss, upon reflection, have changed anything in his investigation?

"Hindsight and all that," Biddiss says. "Not much!"

For Noye, it was a very different matter. "If I could unwind the clock I would change – change everything!"

29

POSTCARDS FROM THE PAST

At 8.00pm early November 2022, Kenny Noye phoned a number that he hadn't seen for more than 20 years. He had tried it before in the previous few months but with no reply. Was he being blanked? Did she never want to speak to him again? Hands free on the M25 he called again.

Then Maria Hernandez answered. "My God, it's you," she said. She was his lover on the run and was with him as the Spanish police arrested him on the back of the UK warrant.

"How are you, Ken?" she asked.

"'I'm fine, I can't leave the country, but I am well, how's life treating you?" he said.

"I have grandchildren I look after now but I'm happy," she said.

They spoke as if it was yesterday. "Do you remember 'Castro's chair?'" She laughed.

"And do you remember Bob Marley's guitar that I got off the wall for you to hold and the guard that told us no one touches Bob's guitar and I slipped him a few bob?"

Noye was being playful now.

He loved Maria – but just between all the other women. She surely hasn't forgotten or forgiven him. "You didn't answer my question, Maria?" he said, teasing her.

"What's that Ken?"

"Do you still love me?"

"Always, Kenny," she said.

In between Noye's broken Spanish and her broken English, the two chatted and laughed about old times for about an hour.

She had the same effervescent personality that drew them together those decades ago on the run. Of course, back then, Maria had no idea about her companion's past – why the police really wanted him, or why he had become a household name for all the wrong reasons in the English-speaking world?

For nearly two years, the pair lived as if without a care in the world and yet, it was a chapter in their lives which was spawned by tragic events.

It was an intense and fiery relationship, but both profess that it was a passionate love affair unencumbered by the normal troubles of the world.

How could something so profound and special have been built while Noye was calculating his battle with international police forces? He was always capable of compartmentalising those parts of his life with hardly any blurred lines. There was business and then there was pleasure. For Noye, it was a game of cops n' robbers. A battle of wits. Maria was suitably shocked and devastated by the lurid revelations about her boyfriend's past.

It was Bonnie and Clyde except Bonnie had no idea about Clyde's activities. She was shocked that her 'Alan Green' (Noye's alias) was wanted for murder. She, more than anyone, knew that history – like love, loss and life – travels at breakneck speed around Noye. After his arrest, the Spanish police briefed journalists suggesting that Maria Hernandez was a police informer and the person who blew the whistle on Noye. Of course, Nick Biddiss and Kenny Noye knew better. That discussion was settled with the revelation of the statement given by the husband of the couple who spotted Ken at the equestrian event in Cadiz in May 1998. This has been a secret for 25 years. The real names and details of the couple whose tip-off finally brought one-of the biggest manhunts in UK history to a timely end are known to the authors and are being withheld.

It wasn't true about Maria then – and her desire to see Noye in prison every week while he was awaiting extradition was proof enough for most observers.

They haven't seen each other since Noye was spirited out of Spain and into protected airspace.

But now, a generation on, 25 years, they are back in contact. Each leading their own lives and in separate countries. Their relationship had its time but the extraordinary memories they shared will linger between the pair.

Others caught up in his world are left with conflicting emotions. Noye is a compellingly affable character, a sharp businessman and a self-confessed villain. Henry Milner – defence lawyer to the underworld, writer and solicitor, calls him an enigma who was entirely pleasant and professional during all their time working on cases and "he always paid his bills on time".

Many of those who hold him in high regard, compartmentalise the positive attributes and draw the shutters down on those events that they can't comprehend; the truth of which has already been contested in courts over the decades. More than anything, he has served his time – even five years more than the 16 years tariff he was sentenced to.

Maria has kept the postcards and photographs of their travels safe and secret, the destinations of which were a complete mystery to Nick Biddiss.

For Noye, his motivation for talking now is simply a matter of humanising a caricature that had refused to contemplate any measure of nuance, complexity or even contested evidence.

He says: "I am more than my mugshot. I am more than a tired headline or quote from the usual suspects. Whatever I've done or not done, I am close to 75 and spent nearly half my life in jail and I've paid the price for my sins, and I can live with that."

Nick Biddiss, his pursuer, wants to remind the reader that in the midst of a decades-long battle against corrupt police officers there are still those who doggedly pursue their calling. "We did our job and brought Ken back to justice," he says. "The rest was up to the jury. I am proud of the job we did as a team in Kent Police on behalf of the family."

With both Toni and Ken Cameron now dead, Nick often contemplates the Friday evenings he shared in Swanley at the family home with the pair and Danielle Cable as he tried to catch Noye. He never promised he would catch him, only that he would do his best. He is content that he and his team did both.

He had his own mementos of the investigation. He said: "When it was over, I got a note from Ken and Toni Cameron (Stephen's parents). It read: 'Thanks for all the good work. Please keep in touch – as a friend' – that meant a lot to me."

The Cameron family, who did not wish to contribute to this book, nonetheless are happy to put on the record that they are immensely grateful for all the work of Nick Biddiss and his team at Kent Police in investigating the case. The family contributed to the probation and parole hearings that resulted in the release of Kenneth Noye in 2019. In tandem with Nick Biddiss and most police officers, they wish that in respect of Noye, life should mean life.

Four members of the investigation team received commendations from Kent Police for their work on the case. Inexplicably, the one officer who had delivered on the manhunt was excluded from any award consideration. Twenty-five years after Nick Biddiss brought Noye back home to face a jury of his peers, no one would begrudge a commendation if it ever was to come to pass for the remarkable detective.

And what is there to learn from the death of Stephen Cameron, Noye's life on the run, his love affair and the background whiff of police corruption that has shadowed this case and Kenny Noye for nearly half a century?

One cannot blame Noye for corrupting the police. It has been a very public dirty secret which is just being fully acknowledged now, 50 years too late. That surely is a matter of police culture and the moral compass of officers, which is clearly outside the purview of Kenny Noye.

He just bribes them – they take the money.

***

Beyond that, the story of Noye's time on the run is marked by pain, trauma, love, loss and exuberance. The bloodbath predicted by some in the media and in the police following Kenneth Noye's release in 2019 never happened. There have been no gangland executions, grudges or old scores violently settled as many a headline had promised. The reported threats to Noye's life from underworld quarters have also proved to be without substance.

His life from his probation officer's perspective, is boring and dull in stark contrast to his time on the run. In the distance are the casualties, reflections and those private family moments with all its triumphs and tragedies over a turbulent half century.

Noye served 21 years in prison without a single recorded blemish on his prison record. He remains at liberty on Life Licence which means that if he re-offends, he can be recalled to prison at any time for a probation transgression.

For the moment though, he cannot travel abroad. Kenny Noye more than anything would love to hit the road again – this time as a tourist and not a fugitive.

EPILOGUE: COPS & ROBBERS!

PART 1

Where the past and the present collide, there is sometimes a prospect of a bright new dawn – but not on this journey. There have been too many casualties, victims, and too much collateral damage for a fresh start. But at the end of the road, is there room for any reconciliation and contrition? Is there a space where the quantum details of these events can be poured over by adversaries when they are their own jury – and where the only and final judgements will be left to their gods, as time relentlessly sends the players in this drama to their maker.

At 6.40am on November 26th 1983, amidst the banal surroundings of Heathrow International Trading Estate – the crime of the century was in progress. Six robbers stole £26 million in gold, diamonds and cash from a secure Brink's-Mat warehouse. None of the proceeds have been recovered. Two principals, John Palmer and Noye, believed to be central to the disposal of the gold were tried for laundering its proceeds.

The men were tried separately. Palmer was acquitted. In 1986, on more or less the same evidence, Noye was convicted. He received a 14-year jail sentence and reached a confidential settlement with Brink's-Mat insurers for his involvement with an alleged payment of over £3 million, although the terms are confidential to the parties.

Forty years on and the full truth of the Brink's-Mat case – and other crimes linked to Noye – are as elusive as ever. There are versions of the truth. Ones that are varnished, and others tarnished. There are the verdicts; apparently safe and secure. And then there is all that happened between the cracks in the pavement of the case. Police officers and villains know these grey areas and the uncomfortable realities all too well, but very few of these truths ever get an airing in public.

What fell between those cracks are known to two men synonymous with the case – Kenny Noye and the officer who broke the case – Flying Squad officer Detective Superintendent Ian Brown.

These two men have long nailed their colours to the mast. They understandably hold little affection for each other.

What combustible truths and fireworks would erupt at the coming together of these two prime voices? These two men, who lived and made history; what would happen if they were to meet and set the record straight on events that have captivated generations?

Does the incendiary truth involve the secrets of jury tampering or police corruption – two highly emotive strands of the games played during the years when both men were at the height of their respective careers.

Ian Brown was the Flying Squad detective who cracked the Brink's-Mat case. It was he who took the tip-off from a seasoned colleague that linked Noye with the principals in the robbery. "He is the best middleman in the business," Brown was told. "You should look at him. He is the go-to man for this kind of booty," he said of Noye.

EPILOGUE: COPS & ROBBERS!

The rest is underworld history and the spit and sawdust of dozens of TV dramas and documentaries. Ian Brown took all this on board and within weeks he had tracked gold being moved around London and the southwest including to Noye's luxurious homestead in Kent. It was his break-through and extraordinary good luck that would precipitate an upgraded Brink's-Mat inquiry team, and an ultimately successful one.

Brown was listening to the on-person radio communications as the SAS specialist surveillance officer, DC John Fordham was caught in full camouflage in the woods of West Kingsdown, Noye's home, on January 26th 1985. Brown listened as support officers raced to the scene and paramedics tried to revive the mortally wounded 45-year-old officer, stabbed to death by Kenny Noye.

Today he would meet the man who killed his colleague.

Like most police officers, for over 40 years he held a special place of disdain for Noye, who was acquitted on the grounds of self-defence for the death of DC Fordham. It was Brown's intervention in the case which placed Fordham on the ground as a specialist surveillance officer, along with a colleague. He always felt some responsibility, regret and a lot of sorrow at the events. Noye has long been labelled as the man who got away with murder; and as compelling a tabloid narrative that was, the facts of the case as outlined to the jury were persuasive and evidenced.

The case for self-defence was notably made by the state pathologist, who said that DC Fordham had attacked Noye first. Nonetheless, the mythology around this case and the distress at the loss of a serving policeman's life would leave Noye a marked man for life.

Today Noye would meet the man who set in progress the events which would make him tabloid fodder for the next four decades.

He would meet the man whose colleague he killed. He would meet the man who has made a second career out of putting him in jail for laundering the Brink's-Mat gold, lecturing on cruises with great flair and writing an autobiography in which Noye is featured prominently.

It was a blistering day. The dusty car park of the River Wey studio near Guildford in Surrey awaited the arrival of the two men. They were due to arrive separately. There would be no green room pre-greetings as would be normal in such constructed confrontations. Today they would meet when they would meet. The encounter would be recorded. They would meet on camera with every emotion caught in full digital resolution. No furrow or raised eyebrow would have a hiding place. No measure of disdain or disgust would be camouflaged. Two adversaries with a chequered history littered with notoriety, death, betrayal, corruption, and jail time would now come face to face and mano et mano to duel out their differences after 40 years apart.

Would they shake hands? What would Noye do if Brown refused the standard pleasantries and went onto an adversarial war footing? Would they have a last minute change of heart? Would 40 years of hurt provide a last-minute hitch?

Noye arrived first. Lean and muscled and mildly apprehensive. He was kept in an ante room overlooking the Wey. Barge pilots and their passengers glanced in his direction, unaware of his notoriety, and the events to come later that day. It wasn't Frost/Nixon clearly, but for both these men, it had that feel. Ian Brown made his own way and sat down for a drink and a snack while the stage was readied. He wrestled with giving Noye the time of day. Noye was a double killer, as the tabloids would baldly put it, and moreover, how could he shake the hand of the man who stabbed his colleague to death with 10 frenzied knife wounds to the chest? Brown understands the defence and the acquittal but nothing of those events or the explanations for them can bring John Fordham back.

Brown, though, believes in the rule of law. He agreed to the meet because he wanted to set the record straight about Brink's-Mat and the investigation into Noye as the 40th anniversary approached and "before all those who knew what happened passed on – including myself".

He wanted to see acceptance, contrition, and accountability in his adversary: "The last time I saw him face to face was in Lambeth Police station when he was being formally charged with the murder of DC Fordham in 1986. It's something I never thought would happen."

He was a Detective Inspector at Scotland Yard's C11 unit – the investigative intelligence division at the Metropolitan Police: "I'm quite looking forward to it actually. I've got my version of events. He has his. Let history decide."

As diminutive as the 5ft 9in Noye is, Brown, even at 80, is a hulk of a specimen. Still capable of a close to par round of golf, he looks every part the domineering ex-copper. Dignified and proud, he steadfastly made his way to meet Noye who was already standing between two chairs against a backdrop of an infinity white studio wall, lights, stands and cameras. Brown was concerned that any meeting would validate Noye, and he was minded not to engage in any pleasantries. He was a copper to his core. And Noye a villain to his. Normally, never the twain should meet....

The pair's eyes met. Brown stooped to address the dapper, yet casually dressed Noye.

Noye offered his hand. The greeting was reciprocated. No inch was given but the token pleasantries were exchanged and now the talking would begin.

What truths would these two men reveal? What secrets uncovered? The state files from the Crown Prosecution and Cabinet papers on Brink's-Mat and Noye are stored at the National Archives[77] and are restricted for up to 88 years with release dates for access ranging from 2066-2074. We'll be a long time waiting for the full story so let's savour the next best thing from the last two principals alive, willing to tell their story and go head-to-head in the process.

The jousting started immediately. Noye had a plan. He needed to right some wrongs. Brown has his strategy too. He would corner his nemesis and hold him to account for Brink's-Mat, for the death of DC Fordham and felt that he had little work to do to hold him to account for the death of Stephen Cameron. The jury and the court of public opinion had already done that. Noye, silent for more than 50 years on his criminality, his life and his businesses save for appearances in the dock, had some scores to settle and facts to recalibrate.

---

77   1645/85 State Files, National Archives, Kew.

COPS & ROBBERS

PART 2

Brown says: "I never thought this day would come."

"No, definitely not," Noye said.

"Can you remember where we last met?" Brown asks.

"In Lambeth Magistrates Court weren't it?" Noye recalled.

"Underneath, and a guy came down to talk to you [while in custody] at the time, a Chief Superintendent."

Noye was quick with an explosive response and fresh revelation.

"Ray Adams," he replies.

This senior officer, now retired (in 1993), was one of the most decorated Metropolitan Police officers – and one of the most controversial. Commander Adams has been mired in scandal and allegations of corruption for decades and chiefly for claims that Noye had him in his pocket. Adams would claim that it was the other way round and that Noye was in fact a police informant – his snitch. He was the subject of two major corruption allegations and 11 complaints. In 1990 the CPS announced that there was insufficient evidence to warrant charges against him.

"You've known him for years, years and years," Brown said.

Brown claimed that Noye was offering a deal through Adams; the return of the Brink's-Mat gold in return for a manslaughter charge. Noye claimed that he never offered that deal but that the deal was in fact offered by the police.

He said: "I was offered it, I was offered manslaughter. They went: 'Plead guilty to manslaughter and give us half the gold back. Give us half the gold back and we'll accept manslaughter.' And I went: 'No.' And my mum and dad come and see me in Brixton and they went: 'Ken please plead guilty to manslaughter, at least we know you're going to come home.'"

The then Detective Inspector Ian Brown was presiding over what must have been a highly charged and distressing atmosphere in the bowels of the Lambeth court. The certainties are that Adams, a long-time associate or contact of Noye was called in. Was he called in to offer a deal on behalf of Noye? Or was Adams brought in to offer Noye a deal on behalf of the police?

Brown says: "We could never agree to a manslaughter charge on the death of a policeman and so that was never really considered by the top brass." Noye was charged with the murder of DC Fordham that morning in Lambeth Magistrates Court.

Adams has consistently denied allegations of corruption and has never been charged for any such offence. Adams features in a highly confidential report noted earlier in the text and revealed by C4's *Despatches* 2022, 'Operation Russell', an investigation into police corruption where it confirms that Adams told a judge in 1977 that Noye was a registered confidential informant at the time, which was false.

By doing so, Adams persuaded the judge not to jail Noye for bribing a policeman. The suggestion in the media was that had Noye been jailed for the bribery charge, his card may have been marked and the subsequent killings would not have occurred. These sliding doors 'what if?' discussions won't bring Stephen Cameron or John Fordham back but it confirms that the matter of police corruption is still an issue of grave public interest. Noye has never discussed his relationship with Ray Adams publicly but was visited three times by police while in prison seeking information on Adams. However, investigators never were able to implicate the senior police officer in any wrongdoing.

Brown: "You were the very first person in British history to go to the Old Bailey charged with killing a police officer and getting off with it. You're the only one."[78]

Noye: "But not many police officers are dressed in masks."

Brown: "I didn't say murder and I said killing." The detective bats back, emphatically, mindful of the fact that Noye was found innocent of the murder of Fordham. The stakes could not be higher as they immediately tackled the death of Brown's colleague.

Brown: "Well, once John Fordham went, you're never going to get help from any police officer. Were you? That was the trouble! I mean, …the moment it happened; you were automatically guilty. And that isn't justice."[79]

Noye: "Ian, I'd like to say, I am very upset, obviously, especially with the death of John Fordham, right. I've never been a violent person."

Brown: "That I totally accept. I mean, you were Ken, what should we say – essentially a wheeler dealer career criminal."

---

78   Transcript day 1, interview Noye & Brown, Wey Studio 2022.
79   *Ibid.*

Noye: "Who sent him in to my house anyway… all masked up with the eye holes cut out and the mouthpiece, right."

Brown: "You're looking at him."

Noye: "Well, you shouldn't have sent him into my garden, trespassing without a search warrant. Your officers were acting a bit 'gung-ho' for quite a long time."

Brown brought it back to the Brink's-Mat gold which precipitated Fordham's covert visit to Noye's home.

Brown: "You say you were defending your family and that's absolutely fine. But the top and bottom of it, from a public point of view, is that there was still 11 bars of gold there."

Noye: "You know, I mean I hope you do, that I would never kill a policeman. It's not in [my] character… But if they were police officers, all they had to do was take their masks off and say they were police officers. And that would be that. but I've got a big place as you know and [they] masked up with the eye holes cut out, and I thought I was [a] dead [man]."

Noye grabbed a knife which he had used to scrape the battery of one of his cars earlier that day. The battery had gone flat because a tracker placed on the car by the police was powered by it and drained it empty.

Brown: "John Fordham and Murphy went into the garden to see where you went to get the gold, that was the object of the exercise… there was no intent to go to your house."

Noye: "All he had to do was pull that mask off and say we're in the army and that man would still be alive today. But in those days the only people that wore those masks were the IRA and armed robbers… I feel sorry for Murphy and John, obviously. But through that it's ruined his family's life, his relations lives, my family's life, my life. Because of that, you know, it was unnecessary. All they had to do was pull off the mask. And do you know something?"

"When he was laying there dying, the poor man. I said, 'Who sent you?' Because I thought his attire, you know, and I said, 'Who sent you?' And he said, 'We're IRA. Sorry, not IRA. SAS on manoeuvres.' What would you do if someone came around to your house?"

Brown: "Still, 10 times [in the chest] Ken?" Brown raised an eyebrow, challenging the self-defence argument that got Noye acquitted.

Noye: "It was only a three-inch knife, not the long blade they alleged. And no one can dispute that because the pathologist confirmed it. I never ever imagined it was 10 times but when you think you're going to die? You just don't realise it. When they said to me it's 10 times, I just couldn't believe it. I could not believe it because it happened so quickly. We were rolling around the ground fighting and then that happened I just couldn't believe it. I'm shouting out help…"

Brown: "Only two people know exactly what happened?"

Brown was in a contemplative mood and not conceding any ground. It was as if he was back in the control room on that fateful night listening on a live transmission to the events as they unfolded. Brown heard the panicked calls for help, including all the emergency sirens and the ambulance transmissions, as despatches slowly confirmed that the experienced covert operative, DC John Fordham was dead. There was no disguising his discomfort recalling these distressing events and hearing his nemesis do the same.

Noye: "So anyway, my barrister, my lawyer, Henry [Milner] went, 'Never in a million years are they going to believe you that he told you he was in the SAS, on manoeuvres and got lost.' I went, 'I'm not changing it, that's what he said.' No one believed me until Murphy [Fordham's specialist partner] got in the box. And he went: 'Have you ever been compromised in other people's land before?'

'Yes.'

'And what do you say?'

He said 'We usually bluff our way off out of it'.'

'You know you're trespassing, don't you?'

And he said 'We usually say we're SAS, we're on manoeuvres and we got lost.' Exactly what John said."

Brown: "Well, Noye you still have to come back to the fact that you had gold! So let's have a think right on the gold bullion. So, I've come to talk to this old copper and he asks, 'Who was on the job?' So I gave him a name. The copper said if they were on the job then I'd have a look at Kenneth Noye because that's his best mate. So I said, 'Where's Noye?' So he said, 'West Kingsdown.' So we go down to West Kingsdown and I go into Swanley police station but I'm warned before I go in there that you're well in there in more than one way. Because Ken, you used to wander in and out."

It was all about the gold. Brink's-Mat had taken a life. All that glitters attracted Brown's team to Noye's house. That was the magnet for law enforcement and ultimately the reason why Fordham lost his life.

Noye, indeed, had gold at his house. But his argument at his money laundering trial was that it wasn't Brink's-Mat gold which was the defence John Palmer used. It worked for Palmer at his trial but didn't work for Noye. Palmer blew kisses at the detectives upon his acquittal. Noye cursed the jury. He believed because of the death of Fordham he didn't stand a chance with the police or the jury.

Brown: "We were on the trail of the Brink's-Mat gold and followed a stolen car from your house and saw it park up and exchange gold. Two and two sometimes does make four, Ken. We raid your house, and we find gold. What are the odds?"

Noye: "I don't dispute anything you say, Ian, but it wasn't Brink's-Mat gold. I was charged with laundering Brink's-Mat but the gold I had wasn't from the raid. I had gold there most days but not Brink's-Mat gold, Ian."

Brown: "Well, I've got a video of the woman at the assay office saying she received the gold direct from Palmer… your partner in crime. It was a piece about that size [indicating a bar]. And it was pure gold. if it walks like a dog, barks like a dog and wags its tail it's a dog. It was Brink's-Mat gold, Ken."

Noye: "He [Palmer] would never have taken it there. They wouldn't say it's Brink's-Mat gold. They couldn't because it wasn't. That gold came from Brazil, and I proved it in the dock with the nine bars, right… they [the police] forensically tested and knew this ain't Brink's-Mat's gold so we better keep our mouths shut. When the judge ordered them to do it again [at trial] they came back and said this never ever could have been Brink's-Mat gold but I still went down for it, you know why? Because poor John Fordham, no question about it!"

Brown: "Are you saying you never dealt with Brink's-Mat gold?"

Noye: "Yeah."

Brown: "You never did?"

Noye: "No, I know where the gold went, and I know that I was asked to sell it. But I said this will interfere with my own gold business in Brazil that I was doing. And that's why to this day they've never found one gram of Brink's-Mat gold, that's the truth."

Brown: "Well, there we can agree to disagree, Ken."

The discussion turned to the matter of corruption, an area where they were more in step than expected.

Brown: "Back in our day, which is the 80s and onwards, I wouldn't say corruption was rife. But corruption was – half the time – it was you scratch my back and I'll scratch yours. And coppers and villains…got together, you give me this, I'll give you that. And I'll let you do this providing I get that. And there was an awful lot of that, that went on, which wasn't necessarily about cash. It was a 'help each other out' type thing. But that, of course, by today's standard it's corruption."

Noye: "I call [out] two types of corruption, corruption. One is that, say an armed robber does a robbery. He's got £500,000, police officers come along and nick 50 grand… So he gets probably less sentence… You can understand why he wants a few quid – the wages are not that great. So that's one type of corruption. The other type, which is worse, in my view, is when you get a villain, and you can't necessarily get the evidence to convict him, so you fit him up, which used to be rife in the 70s and the 80s."[80]

Noye, like most villains, is happy to play the system, likely

---

80   *Ibid.*

to bribe, cheat and corrupt it to escape culpability, consequences, and jail. He accepts that he plays dishonestly. That's what villains do. But when cops do it he rails against it. "If you're going to convict me – convict me honestly," he said.

Brown says it's more nuanced than that.

Brown: "Yeah, it does happen Ken… And the other side of the coin is of course a villain who's done seven armed robberies or four or three, and then he gets fitted up. [He] never thinks … Pardon me, I got away with three. In all my years I have never fitted up anyone. I don't believe in it. If I don't prove it, I'm not doing my job."

The pair are now in a comfortable rhythm. Noye estimates that about 10 percent of Metropolitan Police officers are bent. He should know better than most.

Brown does not disagree.

Brown: "The police force has cleaned up in an awful lot of ways. But the biggest problem is that by cleaning it up completely, no copper can go and talk to a villain and get anything out of him at all. You know in the olden days you used to be able to go, I used to be able to meet you in the pub and have a chat. And you could have said to me: 'I don't like Joe Smith, he's touching up little girls.' Which you would have done.

"You wouldn't have told me if he was dealing in nicked motorbikes. But you'd have told me if he was touching up little girls. And you might have mentioned it to me if he was dealing drugs to kids. But you can't do that anymore."

Noye: "Do you reckon that everyone has a price in the police force?"

Leaning forward in his seat, Noye puts the commercial proposition out there for discussion.

Brown concedes that he has been offered swathes of cash in the course of his duties as a police officer but doesn't answer the question directly.

Brown: "I mean, I've been offered a suitcase that size. It's drug money. Yeah, I know what you're saying, Ken, I do."

While operating in the Caribbean, Brown was dealing with millions of pounds in drugs, laundered money cases and contraband seizures. He admits he was not immune to temptation but like most officers he didn't cross the line.

Brown: "The big trouble with drugs is that there's too much money in it. I hate drugs with a vengeance and I ran a drug squad in the Caribbean. I've seen 500 kilos of coke worth and all the potential for corruption that goes with it."

If he had been corrupt Brown would have been a very wealthy man now. He led investigations and developed evidence that led to the seizure by the USA's Drug Enforcement Agency of a cocaine haul with a street value of a quarter of a billion dollars and was awarded a Queen's commendation for bravery. Today, he plays regular rounds of golf and lives a very low-key life in Kent, not too far away from Noye's old manor.

Before, signing off Brown brings up Noye's public reputation.

Brown: "Ken, it's amazing the murders you've been connected with. I suppose some of them were acquaintances. But I know its rubbish."

Noye: "Well, what can you do about it? If I complain, you

get a little apology about two inches by one if you're lucky. They've called me all the names that the only thing that I haven't been called is a rapist."

"Well, you know, there's always good news," Brown said, offering muted consolation.

At one stage Noye was connected to the murder of *BBC Crimewatch* presenter Jill Dando. Other suggestions claimed that at least 11 of his associates died in suspicious circumstances with Noye linked to those deaths without any evidence.

Brown: "There's quite a few dodgy people around but how they ever connected you to certain crimes? I mean, there was that one out in the Mediterranean (Corfu), was it?"

Noye: "He died on a boat. Keith Headley, a good friend of mine."

Brown: "Yeah, so you got blamed for that?"

Noye: "Yeah, but the Albanians tried to steal his speedboat, which is attached to his big boat, and he got upstairs and was shot by the robbers and that was the end of it. I was blamed for everything. Once I got convicted of Stephen Cameron's death then it was open season on me. It still is."

Noye was also named in the press as a prime suspect in the murder of his old-time accomplice, John Palmer. Notwithstanding the fact that he was in prison at the time, his name is always mentioned in connection with Goldfinger's demise at the hands of what police believe was a professional execution.

Each man took time out to distil the events as they unfolded.

"I never imagined that Ian would be as truthful about

police corruption as he was," Noye said. But that wasn't his only take away from the meeting. Kenny Noye added: "He said to me: 'You're not an inherently violent person. There is nothing in all the years in and out of prison to say that you are.' He wrote in his book that I was but [face to face] he said not, and this is very important to me."

Noye considers himself a businessman and everything he does can be distilled into a business decision. Sometimes those decisions have unintended consequences and occasionally, as history has proved, there is everlasting collateral damage.

Murder is bad for business. Noye says that he wouldn't involve himself wittingly with that and yet, there are undeniably two bodies in his wake. One case has been designated a murder and the other an innocent killing in the name of self-defence. This is the conundrum. The convenient monstrosity that is built around his crimes and events and his criminal enterprises does not quite match the picture that his police adversary paints in person, eyeball to eyeball. Only Noye knows the sincerity of his sadness at the death of two men – a decade apart at his hands – but it is some consolation to him now that Brown's personal verdict speaks more to the nature of his true character than the newspaper headlines and true crime hyperbole of the last quarter of a century.

For Brown, the stakes are clear. He said: "He has to take responsibility for the things he has done if he is to get credit for those he didn't do but has been blamed for. He can't have it two ways."

There was a hint of 'l'esprit de l'escalier' about the

meeting. Those things he wished he could or should have said to the man who killed his partner in justice. Brown is an old-style cop. Much more Columbo than *Miami Vice*'s Sonny Crockett. He is used to talking straight to criminals. And for the time being, feels he's said enough to hold his own against someone who he thought he would never meet again. Maybe who he hoped would never darken his path again. Time when it comes to death heals nothing. And yet…

Brown: "I thought I would feel an awful lot more animosity. What he did in my opinion was awful, dreadful, terrible, and I came in with that intention, and I'm not changing that at all. But I believe he's paid his price. And I believe he's paid a heavy price. And he's entitled to his day in the sun. There is much more to come from this story. But for now, I think we managed to set some things straight. I think he is guilty of laundering the Brink's-Mat gold but he still denies it. Do I think he has genuine remorse for John Fordham? Only he knows. We are both old men now with a decade or so left on this earth and clearly there are some secrets we'll both take to the grave."

The recording over, the pair took a breather before going their separate ways. They walked on Merrow Downs, a peaceful wooded area in the Surrey Hills far away from the turbulence of Brown's career as a Flying Squad detective in London and a drug gang buster in the Caribbean. And a world away from the inside of a prison cell, which Noye inhabited for more than three decades. An Entente Cordiale of sorts was reached. Brown was a man at peace with himself, but Noye was fighting to retrieve some sort of reputation outside of the caricature that he felt the media had created.

He said: "I'm not all the man I've been made out to be. They've nailed me for murders I never did or could have done. You've got to acknowledge that, Ian?"

The big man with the big personality paused for thought. "You're not any angel," Brown said. "But you're clearly a convenient answer to many unsolved murders that I know for a fact you had nothing to do with. That's the world we live in. Don't believe everything you read or see on TV."

Noye suggested continuing the conversation outside of the glare of the cameras. Numbers were exchanged. Plans were made. Brown would steer the coffee mornings away from his home golf course in Kent. Noye would keep Brown away from his private gym. The pair would trade their punches and re-run their trials and stories in future encounters.

It was left at that.

For the future, with some questions answered and many not, the landscape was laid bare. Brown would always be a copper and Noye a man forever on the run from a reputation that will haunt him until the day he dies, and beyond.

To him, his actual days on the run were truly his golden years.

He said: "Then I was what people saw before them. There was no history or legend or headlines. There was just me. The person I look at in the mirror every day. The person my children and grandchildren see. More than anytime, even my release from prison after 21 years, my days on the run were the closest to freedom I've ever known."

POSTSCRIPT

In late 2022, Noye bumped into the son of an old friend at an Italian restaurant in Kent. "My father would love to see you," Noye was told. "He's not been too well but he would love to catch up."

His father and his mother were the pair who saw Noye at an equestrian event near Cadiz in Spain and provided the information to the police that led to his capture.

It was the secret tip-off that Biddiss would not speak of. Doubtless, the middle-aged man did not know exactly the circumstances of his parents' last meeting with Noye. For 25 years Noye has known the full details of the disclosure. The couple perhaps suspected he did – but could not know for sure.

He held no animus towards them. It may have mattered then but not now. After the reach-out, Noye and his old friend chatted over the phone. They spoke of friends who passed away and of health and holidays. "Remember when we last met," he told Noye, raising the subject which Kenny Noye was happy to avoid. "Yep," was all he said.

The older man, who has been seriously ill for many years, said "Doesn't time fly." The small talk continued warmly, and the pair wished one another festive greetings and the best for each other's family. "Pop around anytime," he told Noye.

You got the feeling that the past was very much the past but there is one legacy issue that Noye is keen to address.

Danielle Cable is now a mother and remains in witness protection: "She is at no risk from me. I would be happy to assure her of that. I am devastated at Stephen's death and the circumstances around it. It should never have happened. As I walk free, so should she."

The Parole Board would not have released him if its members thought there was any risk to Danielle Cable.

"She gave honest evidence at the trial," Noye continues. "I have no issue with her. I am truly sorry for her loss, and I am glad she has moved on with her life. She may not believe me, but I do want to say this. I am not a danger to her in any respect. I was never a danger to her and there was never a million-pound price on her head, as the police suggested. She should be able to fully enjoy her family and friends because there are no threats to her from me – there never was!"

Detective Inspector Biddiss agrees: "I think the threat against Danielle is minimal now. She is safe. I am sure of that. Wouldn't it be wonderful if she could now have the same freedoms that Noye now enjoys?"

Kenneth Noye has now served his time and completed his sentence.

It would be timely if Danielle Cable could now end hers.

The simple gravestone at St Paul's Church in Swanley in Kent, marked *'Steve' (9.6.74 – 19.5.1996) Our truly beloved son'* carries with it the reminder that tragedy truly begets tragedy. The grave now contains the ashes of his mother Toni

(2016) and his father Ken (2022) who took his own life after a long battle with depression following the passing of his wife and son. Flowers, a can of beer and a small bottle of spirits crowd the base of the still-tended resting place. As the gravestone testifies, Stephen was a much-adored brother, godfather, fiancé, and friend to many.

With each passing day, week, month and decade, one cannot but imagine the life he could have lived; and the trauma that could have been averted, if the events of that terrible day in May 1996 had never happened.

KENNETH NOYE, TODAY

BIBLIOGRAPHY

Brown, Ian (2017): *From the Krays to the Drug Busts in the Caribbean*

Campbell, Duncan (2019): *Underworld: The Definitive History of Britain's Organised Crime*

Clarkson, Wensley (2006): *Noye: Public Enemy Number 1*

Gillard, Michael, Flynn, Laurie (2012): *Untouchables: Dirty cops, bent justice and racism in Scotland Yard*

Hall, Steve, Winlow, Simon (2015): *Revitalizing Criminological Theory: Towards a New Ultra Realism*

Holmes, Leslie (2020): *Police Corruption*

Johnson, Graham (2013): *Hack, Sex, Drugs and Scandal from Inside the Tabloid Jungle*

Lashmar, Paul (2014): *How to humiliate and shame: a reporter's guide to the power of the mugshot*

Lashmar, Paul, Hobbs, Dick (2018): *Diamonds, gold and crime displacement: Hatton Garden, and the evolution of organised crime in the UK*

Malcolm, Janet (1990): *The Journalist and the Murderer*

Milner, Henry (2020): *No Lawyers in Heaven, A Life Defending Serious Crime*

Pearson, Will (2006): *Death Warrant: Kenneth Noye, the Brink's-Mat Robbery and the Gold*

Roach, Jason, Pease, Ken (2016: *Are Serious Criminals Really Offence Versatile?*

Smith, Robert (2007): *Listening to voices from the margins of entrepreneurship: introduction*

Yardley, E, Wilson, D, Kelly, E (2018): *The Heist, Consumer Capitalism and the 'Criminal Undertaker'*

ABOUT THE AUTHORS

Donal MacIntyre is an Irish criminologist, award winning documentary maker, and investigative reporter.

Karl Howman is an experienced actor, producer, and director. Most recently, he co-directed and produced the 'Secret Spitfires' documentary and co-authored the book of the same name.